T0065390

THEOLOGY
FOR THE THIRD
MILLENNIUM

HANS KÜNG

THEOLOGY FOR THE THIRD MILLENNIUM

An Ecumenical View

Translated by Peter Heinegg

ANCHOR BOOKS
DOUBLEDAY
NEW YORK   LONDON   TORONTO   SYDNEY   AUCKLAND

AN ANCHOR BOOK
PUBLISHED BY DOUBLEDAY

a division of Bantam Doubleday Dell Publishing Group, Inc.
666 Fifth Avenue, New York, New York 10103

ANCHOR BOOKS, DOUBLEDAY, and the portrayal of an anchor
are trademarks of Doubleday, a division of Bantam Doubleday
Dell Publishing Group, Inc.

Theology for the Third Millennium was originally published in
hardcover by Doubleday in 1988. The Anchor Books edition is
published by arrangement with Doubleday, a division of
Bantam Doubleday Dell Publishing Group, Inc.

Library of Congress Cataloging-in-Publication Data
Küng, Hans, 1928—
    [Theologie im Aufbruch. English]
    Theology for the third millennium: an ecumenical
view / by Hans Küng; translated by Peter Heinegg.
        p. cm.
    Translation of: Theologie im Aufbruch.
    Includes indexes.
        1. Theology, Doctrinal.   2. Ecumenical movement.
3. Christianity and other religions.   4. Theology—
Methodology.   I. Title.
BT78.K8613   1988   87-29621
230—dc19   CIP
ISBN 9780385411257

English translation copyright © 1988 by William Collins Sons & Co., Ltd.,
and Doubleday, a division of Bantam Doubleday Dell Publishing Group, Inc.
This book was originally published in German in 1987 under the title
Theologie im Aufbruch (Copyright © 1987 by Piper Verlag).

146742244

To Cambridge University,
the University of Michigan,
and the University of Toronto
as a sign of gratitude for
their honorary doctorates

Contents

Foreword

This book is a document of a theologian's intellectual career. It discloses the standards and guidelines I have followed as I do theology and as I intend to go on doing it. This path led in a period of around three decades through confrontation with various Christian traditions to a truly ecumenical theology: *"ad intra"* (inwards, focused on the Christian churches) and *"ad extra"* (outwards, oriented to the world religions). I could never have taken this path without continual reflection on the principles of understanding, the "hermeneutics," of Christian theology. Needless to say, reflecting in a "faith-free" environment, far removed from the contents of the Christian faith, has never appealed to me. I found myself directly challenged by the task of rethinking my way through the Christian message—against the constantly changing experiential horizon of our time. In other words, I have never felt compelled as a theologian, first to write a learned methodological and epistemological theory (hermeneutics) before proceeding to deal with the substance of theology. "My" hermeneutics—in the final analysis, despite all the controversies, it has always been seeking internal Catholic and ecumenical consensus—was rather woven into the process of theological work, and it always had to prove itself, theologically and practically, in the "stuff" of theology.

To be sure, this book gives an account of a personal path in theology. Nonetheless the reader will be able to see in it a *theological hermeneutics* as a whole. It is marked throughout by the labors I have done since the first ecumenical papers I wrote around the end of the fifties. It obviously cannot address all the questions of theological hermeneutics (for example those rooted in history or the philosophy of language), but it stands as a *coherent systematic whole*. What appears at first to be a series of hermeneutical arguments on the margin of larger publications proves, when seen together, to be a structure built up of integrated components for the *foundation of an ecumenical theology.*

The point is: After the paradigm changes of the Reformation in the sixteenth century and of modernity in the seventeenth and eighteenth century, we experience, as I believe, at the end of the twentieth century, a new paradigm change to a "New Age" that we tentatively call "postmodern." This book tries to overcome the hermeneutical problems of Christian theology left over by the Reformation and the Enlightenment and to find the way into the third millennium. Problems of history, present and past, are intertwined.

Chapter One in Part A on Erasmus (A.I.), written in memory of that great Catholic theologian of reform on the 450th anniversary of his death (1986), takes us into the heart of the problems—as contested today as they were then—of theology and the magisterium, reform and the Reformation. It is followed by a treatment of basic theological such issues as scripture and tradition (A.II.), scripture and the church (A.III.), scriptural exegesis and dogma (A.IV.). Taken as a whole, these are *classical conflicts,* and no foundation for an ecumenical theology can be laid unless they are cleared up.

Indeed, without clarifying the "classical conflicts," there can also be no "future perspectives," no "departure" for new shores, which for Christian theology—in the framework of postmodernity—are the world religions. Part B contains four essays on the *principles and paradigms of Christian theology.* They are the result of an analysis of some modern theoretical approaches to science and philosophy (T. S. Kuhn), which have been extraordinarily helpful to me in understanding the current "tangled" situation in theology and the Church.

In *Christianity and the World Religions* (German edition, 1984), together with other colleagues I presented the idea that Christian theology today can be carried on adequately only against the *horizon of the world religions.* Part C takes this for granted. Paradigm analysis is particularly helpful for understanding other religions (variables and constants, the upheavals and continuity, are present in Christianity as they are, for instance, in Buddhism) and provides the necessary depth of focus that is ultimately needed in theology for *the* question: the question of the one true religion among many religions: the question of truth.

Therefore the introductory chapter with the title "Direction: On the Way to 'Postmodernity' " will describe the horizon in which everything that follows has to be seen. The book—despite the present revival of Protestant fundamentalism and Roman-Catholic tradition-alism—wants to lay an ecumenical foundation for the third millen-nium—in a time of transition from modernity to *"postmodernity"*—which, as we shall see, did not begin in our days. The aim of the book is to help religion to perform a new critical and liberating function of both the individual and society.

I believe I owe it to the reader to reproduce here the texts that have already been published, without making any crucial alterations. Shortening and minor editorial changes were made only when there was overlapping or sections that were not directly relevant to the hermeneutical problems. To make for greater clarity all around, the section headings were adjusted to fit the themes of the book, and the individual articles were placed, by period and subject, in introductory passages to the chapters in question.

In conclusion, a word of thanks to the persons who were impor-tant to me on my way to a hermeneutics of Christian theology, and who have also proved their good will and loyalty to me in hard times: *Wilhelm Klein,* for seven critical years my mentor in the Collegium Germanicum-Hungaricum in Rome, who set an example for me of evangelical Catholicity. *Yves Congar,* who pointed the way for me in questions of understanding and reforming the Church; *Karl Barth,* without whom I would hardly have taken up ecumenical theology as my task in life; *Ernst Käsemann* and *Herbert Haag,* who—represent-ing many exegetes—challenged me to do dogmatic theology in a historico-critically responsible fashion. And I should mention all my students and colleagues in the Tübingen Institute for Ecumenical Research—first of all *Hermann Häring* and *Karl-Joseph Kuschel*—who continually provided me with criticism and stimulation.

But if I wanted to list still more names, I should have to mention many people in Tübingen and all over the world, from whom I was fortunate to learn and who helped me to find my way in the ecumene of the churches and the religions. I am especially grateful to my colleagues, men and women, in Basel, New York, Chicago, Ann Arbor, and Toronto, where I was able to teach as a visiting professor. After threatening confrontations with Rome that at bottom were caused by the Vatican's attachment to a different hermeneutics, a different para-digm, and a different definition of the relations between exegesis and dogmatic theology, in 1984 and 1985 I took it as a sign of encourage-ment when I was awarded honorary doctorates by Cambridge Uni-versity, the University of Michigan, and the University of Toronto. For that reason this book is dedicated to these universities and to my colleagues there as a sign of my gratitude.

Tübingen, January 1988

Hans Küng

THEOLOGY
FOR THE THIRD
MILLENNIUM

Direction: On the Way to "Postmodernity"

Theological revolution: We are looking for a new direction, we are developing a program for a theology that is

— nowadays, more than ever, exposed to manifold tensions, changing currents, and divergent systems; and finds itself, as far as its grand tradition goes, in a crisis of credibility and plausibility;

— but that can make its way out of this crisis neither through an unenlightened, backward orientation to traditional forms of belief nor through glibly opportunistic strategies of adaptation to stylistic changes in science and scholarship;

— and that can win for itself a new credibility and social relevance only through an intellectually responsible account of Christian faith which meets the demands both of the Gospel and of facing the third millennium. We need this account for the journey into a period of world history that, whether or not we are quite ready to believe in a "New Age," has rightly been characterized by many analysts as no longer modern, but postmodern.

1. Postmodern—a Heuristic Concept

Mies van der Rohe, together with Frank Lloyd Wright, Walter Gropius, and Le Corbusier, was one of the four evangelists of modern architecture. In 1969, shortly before his death, he was asked what he would have most liked to have built, but never could. Van der Rohe, who had been born a hundred years before (1886) in Aachen, answered: a cathedral![1] This architect of regular patterns and rationality, of objectivity and practicality, of clarity and this-worldliness, was in fact anything but "postmodern" in architecture. And it was in the world of architecture that the word *postmodern* (a familiar term in literary criticism since the 1950s) first became all the rage.

Yet who knows—this last wish of the great director of the Bauhaus, builder of countless modern high-rises in North America, may have been, after all, something like a postmodern *wish?* Did he want to build something that was more than the expression of humanity emancipated from God, something that gave artistic form to another dimension? Had Mies van der Rohe been given his youth back, he would undoubtedly not have succumbed to romantic nostalgia and put a neo-Gothic cathedral or baroque church (expressions of a premodern spirit) alongside the skyscrapers of New York. No, master of modern materials and construction methods that he was, he probably would have built a modern cathedral. But, like Le Corbusier's church in Ronchamp or Henri Matisse's chapel in Venice, its use of structure, color, and ornament would have created a sense of something more than simply the modern, the rational, the practical, the objective. It would have suggested something "totally other," something transcendentally religious.

There is no ignoring the fact that the word "postmodern" can be used and misused by all parties: Neoconservatives, who want everything to return to the way it was, can bedeck themselves with it just as well as radical critics, who want everything not yet in existence to fall, at long last, into place; as can utopians in search of a different lifestyle and different contemporaries, as well as cynics, who can see through all movements and countermovements, and who consider all styles exhausted and all new mores allowed.

For myself, *postmodernity* is neither a magic word that explains everything nor a polemical catch phrase, but a heuristic term. It characterizes an epoch that upon closer inspection proves to have set in decades ago (in the face of all the resistance to it on the Right and on the Left) and is now making broad inroads into the consciousness of the masses.

The word *"modern"* is an old one. It derives from late antiquity, though admittedly it was not until the early Enlightenment, in seventeenth century France, that it was used as a positive label for a new sense of time: as an expression of protest against the Renaissance image of history, which was cyclical and oriented toward antiquity. For all the distance it now began to place between itself and the ancient Christian past of the dark "Middle Ages," the Renaissance did *not* use "modern" to designate an epoch; it was much too "backwards-looking" in its relation to antiquity for that. Only in the seventeenth century did there arise a new feeling of superiority, based on the successes of "modern" science and philosophy, beginning with Copernicus and Descartes. This feeling was voiced in a controversy, the *"Querelle des Anciens et des Modernes"* that lasted around twenty years and can be traced back to a famous session of the Académie Française in 1687.[2] Today the same word, "modern," is often used for an era that is basically over and done with, while "postmodern" serves as a code word for an epoch that has only just begun in this century, a period whose intrinsic value we acknowledge but cannot yet quite comprehend.

One symptomatic item here (which indirectly confirms our periodization) is the fact that the secular *idea of progress,* so characteristic of modernity (and, once again, contrary to the backwards-oriented Renaissance) was likewise first framed in the seventeenth century and then extended in the eighteenth century to every domain of life as a temporal model for all history.[3] And so only then was the new word "progress" coined, appearing at the same time as "history." Finally in the nineteenth century, at the apex of scientific-technological-industrial development, faith in progress became quite simply a modern, secular substitute religion for both liberals and socialists, at once a banner and a driving force of a political movement. But as early as the turn of the century—after critical precursors such as Kierkegaard, Baudelaire, and Nietzsche—the quasi-religious certainty about progress underwent a crisis: one that, after the First World War at the latest, spread to great masses of people in the West.

This much should make it clear that I am in no way concerned here with defending the term "postmodern," frequently overrated as it is. Nor do I wish to speak of postmodern in the sense of a rather shortlived artistic *style.* What is at stake here is our own *age;* someday, I presume, we can exchange this word for another, once we have gotten a clearer notion of the peculiar features of that age (in any case terms like "post-Enlightenment" or *"posthistoire"* are no better). If it were up to me, I would prefer calling this emerging epoch of ours "ecumenical," in the sense of a new global understanding of the various denominations, religions, and regions; that is, if the religious and theological origins of this term were not all too clear, and if this *oikoumenē*, this inhabited earth, had not become, to so great an extent, uninhabitable—a state that, of course, is essentially connected with "modern" developments. We have reached a crisis that some today would understand apocalyptically as an "end time," while others, unwilling to abandon all hope, would see as a time of transition.

A look at the recently published collection of articles entitled *Postmodernity: Signs of a Cultural Transformation* reveals not only the bewildering multiplicity of meanings ascribed to "postmodernity," but also the *time gaps in the use* of the term from one realm of experience to another.[4] In art and literature, "modernity" is applied as a rule to the period around the turn of the century. But if we view this time from the perspective of our culture as a whole, we can clearly recognize, after the turning point of the First World War, the dawn of postmodernity. Again, "postmodernity" was first used to refer to the sixties and seventies, but the social and cultural phenomena to which those years were reacting have deeper roots and were preceded by long decades of preparation.

More profound reflection on the crisis of modernity and the beginnings of "postmodernity" kept dating it earlier and earlier—understandably enough—and gradually pushed it back to the *political-cultural collapse and upheaval* of World War I. This is the point of departure for the "report" or, rather, essay "Postmodern Knowledge," by the French philosopher Jean-François Lyotard, who draws upon American sociologists and critics, and expends an exorbitant amount of complicated abstraction from systems theory, communications theory, and social theory. For some readers Lyotard's work is a key text for the discussion of postmodernity. In any event he too characterizes as postmodern "the state of culture after the transformations that have affected the rules of the game in science, literature, and the arts since the end of the 19th century."[5] In this context people often overlook the fact that art, which is more dependent than, say, philosophy, natural science, or political theory upon its patrons in government and the Church, made a belated entrance into modernity—not until the end of the ancien régime, around 1800. Nevertheless, once the breakthrough occurred, with Impressionism, art reached its modern apogee ("classical modernity") with uncanny speed, in painting, sculpture, architecture, and music. But in the end it too was swept up into the crisis of modernity and is nowadays groping to find postmodern paths. Do threshold experiences point to the thresholds of new epochs? In the course of this book we shall explore the problem of historical (value-free) periodization in general and that of postmodernity in particular. For now let a few preliminary indications serve to announce the general direction of the argument:

2. Crisis and the Departure Toward the New

In establishing an ecumenical theology I am positively concerned with analyzing the long term, complex *sociocultural upheaval* that, as many contemporary interpreters see it, has a double significance:

(1) Modernity was prepared for in the Renaissance but also checked by its backwards orientation to antiquity as the normative model, and not until the seventeenth century did it break through in the form of a new confidence in reason. This modernity based on rationality and the Enlightenment, on science and technology, nationalism and imperialism, on humanity's dominion over itself and the world, and the consequent loss of nature and God, now faces a *crisis*. In modern architecture (to take only an *example* and only *one* example), this critical situation is everywhere characterized by terms like residential boxes, container architecture, the concrete wilderness, coldness, alienation, environmental devastation, exploitation.

(2) In the midst of our farewell to modernity we are already *in transition to something new*. We cannot yet precisely grasp and comprehend it, or get an overview and a name for it. But we can catch a glimmering of something when, in "postmodern" architecture, terms like these appear: brick instead of concrete, slate instead of asbestos cement, bright colors instead of gray on gray, or, on the same note, warmth instead of sobriety, variety instead of monotony, harmony instead of soullessness.

Needless to say, just as in architecture and other arts a short-lived pop modernity does not yet constitute an epochal postmodernity, so in politics and society not every intellectual fashion or every ideological trend in politics constitutes a new age. Thus anyone who has read philosopher-sociologist Jürgen Habermas's "Philosophical Discourse on Modernity" and taken note of his detecting a "new obscurity," along with his polemic against the word "postmodern," may relax in

the knowledge that in this book "postmodern" assuredly does not
mean, in the sense Habermas is worried about, *a farewell to modernity as a return to the premodern.*[6] Hence it does not mean opposition
to modernity and flight from it. Readers looking for *that* may consult
Cardinal Ratzinger's *Report on the Faith,* which gives decided prefer-
ence to the spirituality of the Patristic Age and of the Middle Ages, as
opposed to our decadent modern period and the Reformation that led
up to it.[7] Here "postmodern" means an immanent critique of modernity, means an enlightenment on the Enlightenment, means—instead of the curial crabwalk (under the motto, "Forward, we have to
go back")—sober, upright movement forward to the future. But how
can this be possible?

3. The Function of Religion in Postmodernity

In the face of the "new obscurity" blocking both oversight and
insight, it seems to me that it can only help if we do *not*—like so many
pioneering thinkers from Heidegger through Popper to the New Left
—*bracket* the question of religion. (It is of course quite "modern" to
do so, though religion *has* played a role in modernity too, even while
being repressed.[8]) *Rather,* we must *consider it along with everything
else, in postmodern fashion.* Needless to say, by religion I do not mean
some great *un*historical, eternal force, but the expression of a *trans*-
historical, trans-social reality in a state of self-transforming historical
and social realization. Tolerance through ignorance is not enough!
Just like everything else, from architecture to politics, religion needs
serious analysis if we wish to have any understanding of "the intellectual situation of the time" (as Karl Jaspers entitled his famous work
from the year 1931). In doing such an analysis I am working from the
assumption that (1) the *intellectual crisis* of our time, which has been
visible since World War One and has been diagnosed by Jaspers and
many others, is decisively *co-determined* by the *religious* crisis, and
that (2) without diagnosing and solving the religious crisis, no diagno-
sis and solution of the intellectual situation of our age can be successful and no clear views of it will be possible.

Still, are we not simply being neoconservative and reactionary if
we speak up for religion today? On this issue the principle must be
enunciated: We must unhesitatingly resist the global *antimodernism,*
the programmatic Counter-Enlightenment that one sees people to-

day—and not only in the Church—seeking again to promote with every means at their disposal. The theologian will be careful not to take belated revenge for the watchword "the death of God" (now gone out of fashion) with the watchword, "the death of modernity." Thus the "project of modernity" must be respected.

But, conversely, an apologetic *modernism*, a carbon-copy Enlightenment, the "perspective of a radicalized Enlightenment" will likewise fail to resolve the crisis of modernity.[9] Reason just will not be sublated through reason, the basic deficiencies of science and the great damage done by technology cannot be eliminated simply by applying yet more science and technology, as the movers and shakers in economics and politics, in a remarkable coalition with the "unyielding Enlightenment spirits," think they can. Limited in this way, we can make no sense not only of the new religious movements in Christianity, Judaism, Islam, in the Indian and Far Eastern religions, but also of the peace and ecology movements, the manifold attempts at self-discovery and self-realization, the protests against meaninglessness and the demands for a new ethic; we cannot sound the depths of all this if we shut out the specifically religious problems.

Why don't people openly admit the fact—on the critical Left as well as on the positivistic Right?: After all the diagnoses and prognoses of Feuerbach, Marx, and Nietzsche, the *death of religion expected in late modernity has not taken place,* however much the unenlightened childhood faith of countless individuals has (rightly) been called into question. Not religion, but its dying off, was the grand illusion.[10] Religion is present once more in Western societies and in public too (contrary to all the functionalist theories of the privatization of religion). East and West, North and South, in cultures and subcultures, in scholarly discussions and in the media, in small groups (of young people and intellectuals, base communities, etc.) and in great religious-political movements both conservative and progressive, from Poland to the U.S.A., from Israel to South Africa, from Iran to the Philippines. The scientific world picture and the religious orientation to reality, political commitment, and religious faith are, at least in the advanced societies of the West, no longer perceived as incompatible.

After the short-lived trends of the fifties, sixties, and seventies, many people have come to see clearly that "in a trying time" what is at issue is not just "forgetfulness of being" (Martin Heidegger) but forgetfulness of God, "the eclipse of God" (Martin Buber). "One-dimensional man" cannot procure for himself the dimension of transcendence, and a "transcending without transcendence" (Ernst Bloch), a "principle of hope" must remain empty without a final ground and meaning. And "strategic" planning of the future with no help except from mathematical formulas, curves, and equations is recognized nowadays even by thoughtful economists as merely a rational superstition. Planners are now required to have a flair for patterns of societal behavior. It gives one pause to observe that even a coolly analytical systems theorist like Niklas Luhmann looks upon domains of life that have now become autonomous through the secularization process as "without religious content" and hence with structures that are "inherently paradoxical . . . unless they can be reformulated in religious terms."[11] It is similarly notable that an American sociologist like Daniel Bell believes that in the face of the "cultural contradictions of capitalism" the moral foundations of secularized society can be restored only by a renewal of religious consciousness: "the great renewal: religion and culture in the post-industrial age."[12] Waiting for *God* or vain, meaningless waiting for *Godot*— that is the alternative today.

To spell out my own position in thesis form: Postmodernity cannot be simply reduced to a Counter-Enlightenment and identified with neoconservatism. It is a matter neither of rapturous apologetics for modernity nor of self-confident condemnation of it. As I see it,

— modernity is neither, as for the neoconservatives, a "finished program" (modernity's house was not, after all, completed),

— nor is it, as for Habermas, an "unfinished project" (modernity's house has been, with the two World Wars, at least in the case of fascism and Stalinism, burned down to the foundation walls);

— rather, modernity finds itself in transition, as a *paradigm that has grown old* and that must be built up anew, "sublated," in the threefold Hegelian sense. That means:

(1) It is imperative to *preserve* the *critical power* of the Enlightenment as opposed to social exploitation and intellectual obscurantism of every sort;

(2) We must *deny*, however, the *reductionism* of modernity, with respect to the deeper spiritual and religious levels of reality. We must also deny modernity's superstitious faith in reason, science, and progress, along with all the self-destructive forces that this faith has un-

leashed (including nationalism, colonialism, and imperialism) in the course of history;

(3) Finally we must *transcend* and move beyond modernity, we must *sublate* it into a paradigm of postmodernity, in which repressed and stunted dimensions, not least of all those of religion, aim to produce a new, liberating, enriching effect.

It seems regrettable, therefore, that on this issue Jürgen Habermas, the last eminent representative of the critical theory espoused by the Frankfurt School, did not address, analyze, and develop further the crucial insights and impulses of his teachers in Frankfurt. One thinks in particular of the work of *Max Horkheimer*, who in the face of the conundrums of modernity did not, like his friend Theodor Adorno, retreat into the aesthetic experiences of modern art for an independent source of insight, but resolutely faced the religious problem, at once overwhelmed and disappointed by Schopenhauer and Nietzsche. To be sure, Max Horkheimer, who like Adorno had been born and raised a Jew, could not, in the face of the Holocaust, return to the ancient faith of his fathers. Linking together by a tour de force the Old Testament prohibition against images, Kant's critique of knowledge, and modern agnosticism, Horkheimer could not and would not positively say what the Absolute is.[13] Still he was convinced till the day he died

— that without "the totally Other," without "theology," without faith in God, there is no meaning in life that transcends pure self-preservation;

— that without religion no valid distinction can be found between true and false, love and hate, readiness to help and lust for profit, morality and immorality;

— that without "the totally Other" the longing for perfect justice must remain unfulfilled, and in the end the murderer must finally triumph over the innocent victim;

— that without a last of all-first of all, supremely real reality, which we call God, our "need for consolation" (to borrow a phrase from Habermas) remains unsatisfied—for time and eternity. Doesn't philosophy—to speak only of philosophy—continue to have to look to religion here? The French philosopher Emmanuel Lévinas, a believing Jew, seems to have been right: "Religion knows much better.

Religion believes it knows much better. I do not believe that philosophy can console. To console is a wholly different function; it is a religious function."[14]

No doubt about it, much that is half-baked and contradictory marks every period of transition to a new "total constellation," a new macroparadigm. Especially contradictory are phenomena and movements that signal a "return of religion" or a "new piety," a comeback for lost religion or new individual and collective religious experiences.[15] Yet, unless all the indications are misleading, religion, which has in the modern period (for thoroughly understandable reasons) been ignored, tolerated, repressed, and persecuted, should once again play an important, though more diffuse, role in the postmodern paradigm. After all, the new religious sensibility has to a large extent set off on its own, outside the bounds of the institutional religions and churches, or at least against the grain of their official teaching. And after every epochal paradigm change the same religion turns into a different one.

Consider the Catholic Church. Until the Second Vatican Council it sought to preserve its medieval-Counter-Reformation paradigm with authoritarian regulations, disciplinary sanctions, and political strategies. In the face of the threat in the nineteenth century from modernity, particularly from liberalism and socialism, it took refuge in the (typically modern) process of centralization and bureaucratization. Now this same Church will have to think over the following question if it will spiritually survive in the third millennium and cope with its challenges: Is an authoritarian-inquisitorial imposition by the Curia (even after Vatican II) of the hierarchical-bureaucratic organizational structure that was raised at Vatican I (1870) to the de facto status of an object of faith through sacral legitimization, is the reconsecration we see once again today of these essentially premodern, feudal church structures (stressing their "mysterious" nature), is *this* the right answer to the new postmodern religious situation, in which the closed cultural milieu of Catholicism has to a great extent dissolved?[16] Public-opinion polls show only too clearly how much the largely anonymous church bureaucracy (financially very powerful, but not greatly loved), a bureaucracy which as late as the nineteenth century could still rely on both a closed Catholic milieu and a strong popular foundation, has now alienated itself from believers, especially those in the younger generation. (Though it customarily ascribes this alienation not to itself, but to the "spirit of the age" and to the fault of believers).

There are, of course—impelled by the influence of the Second Vatican Council—strong countermovements: conciliar factors, synodal organs, basal church structures. And yet in the long run the current Janus-faced condition of the "wintertime Church" (Karl Rahner) must give way to one unequivocal state. It will be decided whether the Catholic Church, on the local as well as the universal plane, wishes to be hierarchical-bureaucratic in the spirit of Vatican I or close to its foundations in the spirit of Vatican II, whether it will face the future centralistically or pluralistically, with dogma or dialogue, naively self-confident or, for all faith's doubts, truly certain.[17]

Theology—whether Catholic, Protestant, or Orthodox—sees itself in this sort of situation face to face with mighty tasks. And, given the arguments over liberation theology in Latin America, Africa, and Asia, along with those over moral theology and sexual ethics in the United States, and over dogmatic questions of faith (infallibility, the structure of functions in the Church, Christology), even the public at large has realized that discussions about the interpretation of the Bible and of Christian tradition in the context of contemporary social reality are no innocuous intellectual sandbox game, but theoretical reflections with supremely relevant practical consequences. I am convinced that only when theology has resolved the "classical conflicts" (Part A) that have been backed up since the Reformation, will it be theoretically and practically capable of working out "Future Perspectives" (Part B), and to dare to make a "new departure toward a theology of the world religions" (Part C) in terms of the Christian ecumene. Only in such a way will theology be prepared for the coming of the third millennium.

A.

CLASSICAL CONFLICTS

I

Ecumenical Theology
Caught in the Cross Fire

Consequences of the Dispute
Between Rome, Luther, and Erasmus

In December 1549—three years after Luther's death—they were giving 9-1 odds on who would be the successor of Paul III, the Farnese pope. Who would succeed a pope who, with his four children and three grandchildren (already made cardinals between the ages of fourteen and sixteen), had personally remained a man of the Renaissance, but had later prompted the turn toward reform in the Church by naming capable, irreproachable cardinals (one of whom was the lay diplomat Contarini), by supporting Ignatius Loyola, and by calling the Council of Trent? Who would it be? None other—so the thinking went in Rome—than the charming, pious Englishman with the extraordinary humanistic education, Cardinal *Reginald Pole*, a nephew of Henry VIII. And Pole, who had been born in London in 1500, was an "Erasmian." He came from Erasmus of Rotterdam's circle of English friends, which included such important humanists as the Lord Chancellor Thomas More, the learned dean of St. Paul's, John Colet, the Hellenist Thomas Linacre, and others. Pole seemed to be the right successor of such a pope in such trying times.

1. Chances for a Third Force?

What a perspective: three years after Luther's death an *Erasmian reformer* of this sort *in the chair of St. Peter.* Finally. No more papacies under the sign of Venus, as with Alexander VI, Rodrigo Borgia; under the sign of Mars, as with Julius II, Giuliano della Rovere; under the sign of Apollo, as with Leo X, Giovanni de' Medici; or under the sign of compromise between paganism and Christianity, as with Paul III, Alessandro Farnese. But also, conversely, no more papacies under the sign of the grimly ascetical, backwards-oriented Zelanti, the Zealots, who had become increasingly numerous in the "holy city" after the devastating sack of Rome in 1527. Could there be, at long, long last, a forward-looking pope, moved by the spirit of evangelical humanism, under the sign of Jesus himself?

The depth of the curia's fears of the reforms it might expect from Pole could be measured by the outpouring of *calumnies* aimed at him before and during the conclave: "Lutheran," "heretic," "father of an illegitimate son." . . . Nevertheless on the first ballot, held December 3, 1549, Pole received twenty-one votes and on the following day as many as twenty-four. But because twenty-eight votes were needed, and it was impossible to round up that many against the opposition of the cardinals who were partisans of France, his friends in the imperial party did their utmost to elect Pole on the following night *"per modum adorationis,"* by "adoration" or acclamation, which would have enabled his opponents to agree to electing him without giving a formal yes. But then came the great surprise: Asked whether he would accept the election—in the middle of the night, *per adorationem*—Pole fell silent and went back to his cell "dumb as an ox" (as he himself said later). On the next day, however, the one vote that had been promised him failed to come through. We may wonder: Was Pole perhaps also an Erasmian in the sense that in a crucial hour he proved to be an undecided *"cunctator"* (delayer, hesitater), and let slip the moment for action? It could be. He was an Erasmian at least in that, instead of accepting the election and personally and practically taking reform into his own hands, he sat in his cell during the conclave that had now dragged on for two whole months and—wrote a *book*. A book about . . . the power and responsibility of the pope!

And, as Kurt Vonnegut said, so it goes: The lost opportunity could not be recovered, although on the seventy-first day of the conclave Pole still had the same high vote count as in the beginning. The man who had probably done the most to prevent his election and had publicly accused the young foreigner (Pole was only forty-nine) of heresy, especially on the subject of justification and Trent, was himself a candidate (of the French): the overbearing, high-handed founder of the strict Theatine Order, *Gian Pietro Carafa*. Spokesman for the conservative-restoration group and founder of the central Roman Inquisition *("Sacrum Officium Sanctissimae Inquisitionis,"* 1542) that he was, Carafa finally did win the favor of the College of Cardinals six years later, when he was eighty years old. He came to the papacy after Julius III, who resisted reform, and Marcellus II, who welcomed it but died after only twenty days. This was in 1555, the year of the Peace of Augsburg *("Cuius regio, eius religio")* and the beginning of the denominational age. Carafa was crowned as *Paul IV*—and soon feared.[1]

2. The Restoration of the Counter-Reformation

Under this powerful papal reactionary—who despite all his promises of reform treated himself to a splendid princely household peopled with good-for-nothing nephews, two of whom were executed as criminals under Carafa's successor, and then plunged into a deluded, fruitless war against Spain and the emperor—the battle against the Reformation turned in a different direction. Rome now lashed out against the reformers in its own camp. The nearer to the Holy See, the more dangerous the enemy. Then as now, Protestants were more dangerous than Turks, critical Catholics more dangerous than Protestants. The Inquisition became the favorite agency of Paul IV: Countless innocent people were placed under suspicion, and humanistic, reform-minded cardinals like Pole and Morone faced charges. Morone was locked up for two long years in the Castel Sant'Angelo and not released till after the death of this pope.

"Even if my own father were a heretic, I would gather the wood to burn him with": that was the calling card of the former grand inquisitor, now pope. Paul IV also had the first *Index of Forbidden Books* drawn up. No wonder, either, that in the "first class," among all the arch-heretics whose writings were to be obliterated, one and all, he put Erasmus of Rotterdam. Erasmus was unique in receiving the additional stricture, "with all his commentaries, annotations, scholia, dialogues, letters, censures, translations, books and writings, even if they contain nothing at all against or about religion."[2] In his doctoral dissertation at the University of Basel, "Erasmus in the Judgment of Posterity," Andreas Flitner, now Professor of Education at Tübingen, has given us a comprehensive account of this whole conflict.[3] One could find Erasmus on the Index as late as 1890. Not until 1900 did his name suddenly disappear.

There can be no doubt that with Paul IV's anti-Erasmian pontificate (the most unfortunate since the days of St. Peter, in the words of the dying pope himself) Rome had taken a definitive stand: not only against the Protestant Reformation of the Reformers, but also against open-minded internal Catholic reform in the spirit of Erasmus. Rome was now committed to a *medieval-Counter-Reformation restoration.* This meant, to be sure, doing away with blatant abuses, and in that sense "internal Catholic" (or rather "system-immanent") reform; in other words, reform not as a means of ecumenical understanding and reconciliation but as a Counter-Reformation battle plan and weapon. Unconditional, uncritical conformity to Rome; rejection of the Reformers' concerns with reform; keeping doctrine pure by inquisitorial methods, secular denominational politics, and, if need be, "wars of religion": all presuppose the primacy not of Scripture, of the Gospel, but of the popes. In any event the goal of all this was the renewal of the medieval "Roman Catholic" status quo.

3. Erasmus the Unloved

But might not Erasmus's *reform program*—had it been accepted at the opportune moment by Pope Leo X and the bishops—have prevented *the schism in the Church* after all? Both Catholic and Protestant church historians have their doubts here. But dare we always put such complete trust in their historical objectivity, given the way their denominational resentment often makes its presence felt?

Astonishingly enough, even such excellent scholars of the late Middle Ages as the former Tübingen Reformation historian, *Heiko A. Oberman,* underestimated the explosive power, for example, of Erasmus's *Enchiridion militis Christiani* (the "manual of the Christian soldier," written in 1503 at the request of the wife of a military man at the Burgundian court) and labeled it "the most boring book in the history of piety."[4] That sort of judgment has an obvious connection with the prejudice of many Protestant historians, for whom Erasmus —as the undecided, anxious, cowardly, ambiguous theologian, diplomat, and traitor—provides a welcome dark background to make the hero of faith, Dr. Martin Luther, shine forth all the more brightly.

The only striking thing here is that Erasmus has a bad press even with orthodox Catholic church historians, who gladly underplay his significance or slap negative labels on him. One need only read the article on Erasmus in the Catholic *Lexicon of Theology and the Church* by the Reformation historian from Münster, Erwin Iserloh.[5] As late as 1984/85 Iserloh thought it important to present to the public a whole collection of second-rate anti-Lutheran controversial theologians under the title, *Catholic Theologians of the Reformation* —naturally without including Erasmus, who was at the zenith of his fame immediately before the Reformation.[6] (He was called *"Doctor universalis,"* "prince of learning," and "defender of genuine theology," and had not one equal among "Catholic theologians.") Iserloh's treatment of Erasmus (thoroughly in accord with his teacher, Joseph Lortz) is typical of sectarian-minded Roman Catholic Church historiography: Erasmus's obscure origin (which in the final analysis must be attributed to the rule of compulsory celibacy) is given a psychologizing and moralizing interpretation. Iserloh exploits the fact that Erasmus was an illegitimate child, his birthdate uncertain, the result of a liaison between the priest Roger Gerard and the daughter of a physician, that by the time he was about fourteen he had lost both parents and was placed in a monastery by his guardians: "The stain of his birth, which he never got over, and the lack of a family and home largely explain the unrest in Erasmus, his suspicious avoidance of people, his fear of committing himself, his sensitivity, and craving for recognition." So be careful with this man! The historian's final dogmatic verdict—not worth quoting here—is thus already being readied in the cradle. But in the end Erasmus, the teacher of teachers, did get his just deserts from Catholic theologians (Franz Xaver Funk, later Alfons Auer and Rudolf Padberg, among others).

Let us not be discouraged then as ecumenists to think of poor Erasmus caught between the cross fire. Ordained to the priesthood, but freed from his monastic vows, named to the Imperial Council and still in financial straits, he trod his difficult path through life with astonishing consistency and not a little courage. He launched out on a widely admired, complex intellectual career: a university professor and, still more, a cosmopolitan independent scholar who, apart from longish stays in Paris and Italy, felt at home above all in England and in Basel (less so in Louvain and Freiburg). He was, said Stephan Zweig, "the first conscious European, the first militant friend of peace, the most eloquent advocate of a humanistic ideal warmly disposed toward the world and mind."[7] But he was also—a point that gets decidedly short shrift in Zweig's otherwise brilliant essay, "The Triumph and Tragedy of Erasmus of Rotterdam"—a Christian profoundly moved by the Gospel.

And so, once again, we undauntedly ask the question: Mightn't the reform program of Erasmus of Rotterdam—had it won a timely acceptance—have prevented the schism in the Church? Following in the footsteps of the early, congenial biography of Erasmus by *Johan Huizinga* (1923), the man who is perhaps the leading Erasmus specialist today, another Dutchman, *Cornelis Augustijn,* has gathered up the threads of the often sharply contrasting research in German, French, and English (Erasmus, the irresolute Anti-Luther, the rationalistic early Enlightenment figure, the classical humanist) in his biography of Erasmus.[8] This is a book on which the reader can confidently rely for its account of the most important historical facts and circumstances. For Augustijn the central theme of his great countryman, one which emerges very early on, is this: "How can one in all honesty be at once a man of culture and a Christian?"[9] In linking, then, education and piety, culture and religion, antiquity and Christianity, Erasmus proposed that one could be authentically human by being a Christian, and be a Christian by being human.

4. A Reformer Before the Reformers

Works like the famous *Enchiridion* (1503), in which the humanist, under the influence of his English friends, made a clear shift toward biblical piety, and which, according to Erasmus's American biographer, Roland H. Bainton, "contributed the most of all his works toward making him the spokesman for the liberal Catholic reform movement, the advisor of popes, and the mentor of Europe."[10] This book, according to Augustijn, must be read "through the eyes of his contemporaries." If we did so, we would notice that, "It was not 'boredom' they experienced, but dismay." At what? "At the disdain, if not downright rejection of a large part of the external structure of religion, of ritual, of church regulations and customs, of the privileged position of priests and monks, and all this in favor of inner substance, on which all stress is now laid."[11] In fact, in the controversies of his time Erasmus thought of himself "as a defender of the true freedom that Christ brought and guarded against attacks by the Pharisees, that Paul defended against the Judaizers, who wanted to lead the first century Church back to Judaism."[12] "Judaism" is surely understood here—not without danger—as referring not to a people or religious community, but to an attitude of alienated religiosity. Erasmus was deeply convinced that here he had reached the core of the Bible's message (so many of these thoughts could also be found in the authors of antiquity). The *goal* of his work now became the *the renewal of the Church, theology, and popular piety,* founded on the Bible. This was not the abstract, bourgeois ideal of education enshrined in the nineteenth- and twentieth-century *Gymnasium,* but a thoroughly Christianized vision of antiquity and a simplified, ennobled Christianity: "Christian humanism" or "biblical humanism" (J. Lindeboom) as it is called.[13]

The note that was first sounded in the *Enchiridion*—and that, as he himself observes, often grated on the ears of the authorities—was powerfully orchestrated in *The Praise of Folly* in the form of critical satire. Erasmus, a writer who perfectly mastered many literary genres, clarified that note

— in the new edition of the *Adagia* (1515), the extremely popular *collection of classical proverbs,* with his own brilliant commentary. In these essays Erasmus not only champions classical studies *(bonae litterae),* but attacks with great severity the tyranny of princes and the evils of war, while strongly advocating changes in the Church and society. Two years later in his moving antiwar piece, *"Querela pacis"* (the complaint of peace, which is persecuted in all lands) he proposes (in vain) a European peace treaty between the German Empire, Spain, France, and England;

— then in the *Institutio principis Christiani* (1516), an anti-Machiavellian "mirror for princes," dedicated to the future emperor, Charles V, Erasmus demands that the prince be both a friend of philosophy, so that he may be freed from all popular, but false, opinions and evil passions, and a philosopher and Christian in one, capable of ruling, on the model of the eternal deity, over men, all of whom were created free. Characteristically, though, there is no mention of the right of resistance;

— finally, in the same year, 1516—all things considered, an enormous body of work by this delicate, apparently weak, sensitive man, forever concerned about his health and hygiene—came a bold book, dedicated, not without reason, to Leo X: the *Instrumentum Novi Testamenti,* the *first printed Greek edition and a new Latin edition of the New Testament,* together with introductory articles. It improved the Latin Vulgate, which had been used for centuries. It was greeted with protest from traditionalists who invoked the infallibility of the Church, but Luther immediately took it as the basis of his German translation of the Bible.

These key publications, which made the scholar from Basel the most celebrated intellectual of this decade before the Reformation (he was called the "light of the world") and the center of a network of Christian humanists that spanned all of Europe ("prince of the humanists" was another of his titles), make clear at once the *reform program* of this Christian humanism:

(1) Erasmus was interested in a *different kind of biblical scholarship.* Granted, as someone who had been schooled above all in the methods of Origen, he had nothing in principle against an allegorical, spiritual interpretation of the New Testament, at least so long as this—especially among preachers—did not degenerate into arbitrariness and abstruseness. But in a new age one could not go on repeating medieval exegesis (above all the *Glossa Ordinaria* from the twelfth century) and swearing by the Vulgate. No, the Bible is a literary work; and the basis for interpreting it must be—as it was, by the way, for Origen and Jerome, even back then—philosophy, the striving not primarily for as profound a figurative, spiritual meaning as possible, but for the *literal meaning of Scripture.* Knowledge of the ancient languages was indispensable for this, but so too—never mind centuries-old habits in theology and the liturgy—was a new, more exact Bible translation, first into Latin, then into the vernacular languages as well: "If only the farmer with his hand on the plow would sing something of it to himself, if the weaver would hum something of it to the rhythm of his shuttle, if the traveler would shorten his journey with stories of this sort!"[14]

(2) Erasmus was interested in a *different kind of systematic theology:* For all the banter he also directed at philosophers, poets, rhetoricians, and merchants in the *Moriae encomium, The Praise of Folly,* dedicated to his friend Thomas More, author of the *Utopia,* which criticized the society of his day, Erasmus could never pour enough mockery over the merely learned theologians, that conceited, irritable breed of men (similar to the teachers). They thought they could

fathom God's unfathomable mysteries, and in the process they ran up against the most impossible questions (could God also have entered the form of a woman, a devil, a donkey, a pumpkin, a pebble?) Furthermore, the Apostles knew nothing about transubstantiation in the Eucharist, Mary's immaculate conception, and other *quaestiones disputatae*. Despite all his respect for Peter Lombard and Thomas Aquinas, the language of scholasticism (what barbarous Latin, in some places!) was as little suited for modern times as the often arbitrarily reductive scholastic method. *Back to the sources* was the motto. Christianity and antiquity, *sacrae litterae* and *bonae litterae*, were not mutually exclusive. The new age required a theology that, like the very oldest theology, recognized the Holy Scriptures as its sole guideline, that in its understanding of Scripture looked to the Fathers of the Church instead of to scholasticism, and so translated the original Christian message, making it understandable to present-day readers. Questions that had nothing to do with the Bible and were absurd did not belong in theology. The prerequisite for the study of theology had to be the study of Scripture, together—in good Catholic fashion—with the study of the Fathers, which Erasmus tirelessly endeavored to promote and make possible through critical editions of the most important church Fathers. In this sort of theology *exegesis* becomes *the basic theological discipline*. Church dogma, canon law, and ecclesiastical practice are subjected to criticism from the standpoint of the biblical text. The whole focus is not on metaphysical speculation, but on Christ's saving deeds and humanity's way to salvation.

(3) At the same time Erasmus was interested in a *different sort of popular piety:* Whether the target be the reeling off of prayers or the invocation of the fourteen "auxiliary saints" (Apollonia for toothache, Anthony for lost objects, etc.), the chalking up of more and more masses and pilgrimages or lucrative miracle stories, the misuse of the confessional, or costly indulgences, Erasmus spares no abuse and no superstition with his irony, satire, and biblically based criticism. That was not the least reason why many people, clerics and monks especially, felt his critique to be subversive, indeed destructive. Blending courage with cunning, he often speaks with scorn and scoffing through allegorical figures such as "Folly" or "Peace." But there was one point that could not, because of the nature of the subject, be elaborated on in *The Praise of Folly*, and that in the *Colloquia familiaria*, the "familiar conversations," those splendid genre scenes

from sixteenth-century Europe, was hidden beneath the jibes and mockery. Still, Erasmus's other writings make it unmistakably clear that the piety of the people should take its positive bearings from the biblical message, more precisely from the Jesus of the gospels as he went on his way, a pattern for us, past false scribes and hypocritical priests. The man from Rotterdam's popular *Paraphrases* were aimed above all at smoothing the path toward *understanding the true Jesus* for *educated lay people.*

(4) Erasmus was interested in a *different kind of clergy:* "As if there were no Christianity outside a cowl . . . !" Thus Erasmus writes at the end of the *Enchiridion.* There was nothing he criticized so relentlessly as monasticism—his own personal experience keeps echoing through here. The impudent monks: No others stood out so dramatically for their ignorance, superstition, ridiculous pathos, and antics in the pulpit. For them the belly, money, or honor was more important than following Christ. The rules of their order were more significant than the Gospel, their name in religion more meaningful than baptism, their habit worth more than everything else. Truly, this "boring" *Enchiridion* radically questions no more and no less than the whole *previous ideal of piety.* Invoking the one same baptism that all have received, Erasmus abolishes the essential distinction between clergy and laity. He relativizes all traditional external observances and spirit-less ceremonies, pleading for a sober, up-to-date, everyday piety, valid for everyone and focused on Jesus Christ. While he does not totally reject celibacy, he does label it as undesirable under prevailing circumstances, and in contrast he praises marriage highly in *The Praise of Folly* (1518)—to the enormous vexation of the clerical professors at Louvain and many preachers.

(5) Erasmus was also interested in a *different kind of hierarchy.* He was inexorable in showing up the discrepancy between the lofty claims of the "successors of the Apostles" and the reality of their so very unapostolic life. For members of the hierarchy everything seemed to revolve primarily around their own honor, power, glory, and the Church's rules, pomp, and splendor. What a bureaucracy, with its countless functionaries! Instead of communion, excommunication; instead of preaching, the Gospel anathemas and interdicts. And with all of them—both higher and lower clergy—money, income, and expenses held the center stage. Very well, "but if the popes, the deputies of Christ, would only try to live as he did, namely

to imitate his poverty, his work, his teaching, his cross, his readiness to die . . . whose heart would be more afflicted than theirs?"[15] When the anonymous dialogue, *"Julius exclusus e coelis,"* appeared, about the godforsaken, warlike pope Julius II, who stuck the wrong keys (the ones to his treasure vault) into the gates of heaven, and who was then turned away by Peter, the first pope, it was immediately ascribed to Erasmus. It was understood by all of educated Europe not only as a timely satire (because of the confrontation between the pope and the Gospel), but also as sharp theological criticism. What, they wondered, would come next?

It had become increasingly clear to Erasmus in those decisive days how vast a gulf was yawning between the "successors of the Apostles" and the Apostles themselves, between the triumphalist Church of the present and the simple Church of the earliest days, in short between Christianity today and Christ Jesus back then. Church and pope were a hindrance, not a help, on the way to God. And he realized with increasing clarity what true Christianity meant in the here and now: It meant committing oneself not to church law, church dogma, and the Church's system, but to Holy Scripture and its living Christ; committing oneself, not to a lofty Christology, to which the lofty hierarchy could then quite easily appeal, but to the human, humiliated Jesus of the Gospels, who makes common cause in meekness and gentleness, with the lowly and despised, who has overcome the world not with syllogisms, money, and war, but with his willingness to serve and love. This practical Christianity, based on humility, meekness, tolerance, peacefulness, and love, was what Erasmus—no doubt rely less on Plutarch and Cicero (A. Renaudet) and more on the Greek Fathers of the Church (L. Bouyer) called the "philosophy of Christ" or "Christian philosophy."[16] How could the future not belong to this sort of Bible-oriented program of reform, presented so many years before Luther, Zwingli, and the other Reformers—if it had been accepted in due time?

A superfluous question, some will say. For no one could deny that Erasmus's plan for reform—which I have presented here, in any case, more compactly than he himself ever formulated it—was never accepted by the people who made the political decisions. In a very short time, as often happens on sultry summer days, heavy storm clouds gathered, and the horizon went almost completely dark. And then the storm broke loose, such as no one in Christendom had known in human memory. Soon nobody was talking any more about a Golden Age, as they had in the beginning of the pontificate of Leo X. Now people saw apocalyptic times on the way.

5. *The Emergency: Wittenberg Versus Rome*

In *Rome* the Medici pope, a great lord of high birth and position, never dreamt of taking seriously the demands for reform issued by the admired, learned Erasmus or, in general, the *"gravamina nationis Germanicae"* (the grievances of the German nation). Give up all the Renaissance splendor? Renounce the enjoyment of the papacy, when God himself had given it? Turn the Roman curia upside down, rearrange the system of finance and governance, and set off soberly in the footsteps of the Lord and Master? What an affront to him, the Holy Father and Lord of Christendom! And if some unknown little monk in the Teutonic fogs of the north thought he had to sound the trumpet for radical conversion, then in the old manner, tried a thousand times over—with the help of excommunication and the strong secular arm, which likewise had no use for unrest—he would be quickly done away with.

In *Germany,* however, the unknown little monk, an unruly battler by instinct and intellect, likewise never dreamt of swerving from his knowledge of the true Gospel, which had dawned on him only after long agonies of conscience. This knowledge linked him with the great Erasmus on the deciding issues, and Luther had no intention of backing down on his theological, religious, and political demands. What an affront to him, the Man of Conscience! True, just a hundred years before, the Bohemian Reformer Jan Hus had been burnt at the stake at the Council of Constance, despite a safe-conduct from the emperor. But if those Romans were once again threatening excommunication, without a legal hearing and due process, if they were immediately proceeding after the election of Emperor Charles V to his, Martin Luther's, excommunication, to burning books, and demanding that the emperor carry out the imperial ban, then people would see who it was, when all was said and done, that had the final say in the Holy Roman Empire of the German nation. They would see whether the newly discovered Gospel of Jesus Christ might not prevail in this end-time, when the pope, by refusing reform and denying the Gospel, was every day more clearly unmasking himself as the Antichrist . . .

As if overnight, the learned conversation of the humanists and the pointless discussion of the theologians had turned into an *emergency,* where, like it or not, everyone was in a life-and-death situation, where one could no longer be content with Erasmian admonitions to patience and warnings about being sure not to irritate the pope and the princes, where one had to decide, pro or con. And *deciding* was precisely what *Erasmus in no way* wanted to do. His slogan, *"nulli concedo"* (I give way to nobody), could, if necessary, also be understood by Erasmus, the anxious and over-careful, the man who shied away from conflict and needed harmony, to mean "I opt for nobody." This was not just out of weakness, or even cowardice, as some people supposed at the time and often later on, but in the final analysis out of the firm conviction and will to preserve his intellectual independence, the foundation of his existence, for which he had suffered, written, and fought his share all his life long—for scholarship and finally, too, for the sake of the Church. Erasmus the critic of the Church and biblical theologian was viewed by the public as a kindred spirit, indeed as the spiritual foster father, of Luther, as the one who laid the egg that Luther hatched; and he wanted to remain above the warring parties. As a free spirit, he wanted to remain free, even in the struggle. As a centrist and averse to all extremes, he wanted to hear both sides and mediate between them. He wanted the *"Et-et,"* the "on the one hand, on the other hand."

On the one hand: no condemnation of Luther without a thorough investigation. On the substance of the case the man from Rotterdam could largely agree with the man from Wittenberg. Should one wish to suppress all of Luther's teaching, one would have to suppress a good part of the Gospel. He was not prepared to call Luther a heretic, and he stubbornly refused all the urgings, from Rome and elsewhere in the Church, to write against Luther. He also doggedly ignored all the pressing invitations—even those of the successor to the Medici pope, Hadrian VI, Charles V's tutor and the first Dutch pope, who, of course, from the first viewed Luther's works as highly damaging—to come to Rome to take on a post. No, Erasmus the great Independent was not born to be a curial court theologian and cardinal.

On the other hand, however: no identification with Luther. Erasmus saw Luther as like one of the German lansquenets, a hulking muscle man laying about him on all sides, a man who was overthrowing much that should have been left standing. He was terrified by German consistency. If Erasmus approved of Luther at first, this did not mean that he had to approve of everything that Luther had written since. In no way could he, or would he, the highly educated, reserved, sensitive, and ultimately unaggressive intellectual type, identify himself with that intemperate religious fanatic. Where Luther was right, he agreed with him; but where Luther was wrong, one could not expect agreement from him. Thus in the end Erasmus preferred to stick to the pope and the emperor.

With this sort of highly ambivalent politics and diplomacy one gets caught *in the cross fire.* But wasn't Erasmus of Rotterdam possibly the only one who was right: precisely because he found right and wrong on both sides, and stood up like no one else for peace through moderation, discernment, and amiability?

6. Between Rome and Wittenberg: Neutrality Instead of Commitment

There can be no denying that Erasmus, the scholar forever reflecting and making distinctions, the complex, often contradictory character whom Huizinga has analyzed so tellingly, made *strategic and tactical mistakes* that inevitably had catastrophic consequences for him. Consider a few well known facts:

— As early as December 11, 1516 (a year before Luther's theses on indulgences) Spalatin, secretary to the Elector of Saxony, had reported that in the city of Wittenberg there was a young (unnamed) Augustinian monk, a great admirer of Erasmus, but with different ideas on divine justice and original sin: We do not become just because we act justly, as Aristotle thought. Only if we are just—transformed in our person—can we also act justly. Shouldn't Erasmus, busy as he was, have taken this account seriously as a *first warning signal?*

— In March, 1518, when Erasmus sent his "Theses on Indulgences," along with two other pieces, to his friend, the Lord Chancellor, Thomas More (though he did not sign his name to them), didn't Erasmus have to suspect what people, at least in Rome, noticed at once: that this was no ordinary controversy, but a *broad assault on the Roman system?* Should he have let himself be content to remark to John Colet: "The curia in Rome has abandoned all shame. For what is more shameless than perpetual indulgences?"[17]

— Erasmus had considered Luther's first writings to be legitimate, if provocative, but he feared the affair might lead to an uproar.

Didn't he then have to tolerate the publication of an almost 500-page collection of Lutheran writings by his Basel publisher and friend, Hieronymus Froben (the book became a giant success) and (despite his opponents' accusation that he was a Lutheran, indeed Luther's mentor) lay his cards on the table? Didn't he have to take a univocal, though nuanced, *position against traditional theology and piety,* to stand up against all the indescribable conditions and abuses, on behalf of radical reform and renewal of the Church in head and members?

— In 1519 Luther wrote him for the first time, with the words, "So acknowledge, then, my revered Erasmus, lovable one, if you will, this little brother *[fraterculum]* in Christ as well."[18] Should Erasmus, now already fifty years old, despite the danger he was in at the University of Louvain (along with Cologne the center of the campaign against Luther), *have rejected the hand of the younger man,* by invoking his wish to be neutral and his service to scholarship?

— Didn't Erasmus have an obligation *to go public,* at the very latest in the year 1520, when the papal bull of excommunication (which he clearly recognized as both foolish and tragic) arrived in the Netherlands, and Luther's books were openly burned for the first time in Louvain? Neither his letter to the pope (distancing himself from Luther), nor his personal plea before the German princes in Cologne, had any effect. Ought he not to have given seriously, and in public, the ironic answer that he privately gave the Elector of Saxony to the question of what errors Luther had committed: "Luther sinned in two ways: He laid a hand on the pope's throne and the monks' bellies"?[19]

In the *year of decision,* 1520—the year of Luther's three great programmatic writings, "To the Christian Nobility," *"De captivitate babylonica ecclesiae"* ("On the Babylonian Captivity of the Church"), and "On the Freedom of a Christian Man"—no one could be in the dark any longer about the fact that what was happening now had ceased to be an argument among theologians or even just a church controversy. It was now a *world-historical test of strength.* Was Europe to stay with the old medieval Roman system, its power structures, its institutions and sacraments—for Luther a "Babylonian captivity"—or not? How could Erasmus wish to remain neutral between Rome and Luther, merely rebuking the pope's misuse of power and bad morals, and criticizing Luther's arrogance and violence? The roar of battle grew louder, and the gentle voice of the peace-loving Erasmus, urging moderation, tolerance, and reconciliation, was heeded less and less. His recommendation of a general amnesty, of limited freedom of the press, and various reforms was illusory. His distinction between *"fundamenta"* (essential dogmas) and *"adiaphora"* (nonessential dogmas) would not bear fruit until later . . .

For many people Erasmus, the initiator of the reform movement, now took a back seat far behind Luther, its executor, the reformer behind the leader of the Reformation. Did the sower of the wind seem to be afraid of the whirlwind? Erasmus had not gone to Rome, but neither had he gone to the imperial Diet of Worms in 1521—contrary to his original intention. Always concerned anyway over the plague, syphilis, and colds, he had withdrawn to neutral Basel, and there in 1523 he refused, diplomatically but not wisely, to speak to the banned and proscribed imperial knight, Ulrich von Hutten, who was now bitterly poor, deathly ill, and begging him for a hearing. The upshot was that the disappointed Hutten, a partisan first of Reuchlin, then of Luther, and finally of von Sickingen, put Erasmus down before the entire German public in a widely read *expostulatio* as a weak and cowardly opportunist, who always ran at the right moment from the vanquished to the powerful. Deeply hurt, Erasmus responded. But unfortunately his answer was made public a few days after Hutten had died, under Zwingli's protection, on the Ufenau in Lake Zurich; and it harmed Erasmus more than it helped him. He never afterwards shook off the reputation for halfheartedness, double-dealing, and opportunism.

After refusing for years to write against him Erasmus finally did let himself be stung by Luther and in the fall of 1524 he published, not very eagerly, a piece against him, the high-minded, objective *Diatribe de libero arbitrio* (Disquisition on Free Will). For Luther, predestination and freedom of the will were no mere topics for academic debate, but a question of his personal existence and theological foundations, and he answered with a passionate rejoinder defending predestination, *De servo arbitrio* (December 1525). But by then Erasmus had definitively lost most of the Lutherans; and the Catholics, who suspected him of harboring Lutheran views, had not been won over either. The basic attitudes of Luther and Erasmus were too different, and which of the two had the better arguments, theologically speaking, strikes me as an open question to this day.

Erasmus was first beloved and admired, then wooed and desired by both sides, but finally mistrusted, suspected, calumniated, and scorned. What was imposing about him was, and still is, that even though he became more pessimistic, and more conservative too, having lost a few of his illusions, he stuck to his moderate, centrist course till the end. In tranquil resignation, not shrinking from loneliness, he remained in every situation the mediator and reconciler. "He does not sail unhappily, who holds a middle course *[medium cursum tenet]* between two opposite evils," he had replied to Luther.[20] He chose a *via media*, not really between God and Belial (he would have looked on that as impious), but between Scylla and Charybdis, between Rome and Wittenberg. He was bound to both, sold to none.

In his public answer to Hutten, *Spongia* (meaning a sponge to wipe away Hutten's reproaches—1523) Erasmus once again presents his point of view with precise care. He always disapproved of the tyranny and vices of the Church and Rome's arrogance, but also always rejected turmoil and division. He would die for the Gospel of Christ—if that had to be and he had the strength—but not for Luther's paradoxes. No martyrdom for Martin Luther, and no martyrdom for Rome either, if the only thing at stake were the objects of scholastic disputes and not actual articles of faith supported by the *consensus Ecclesiae*, the believing testimony of the whole church community. And so much of what was taught in the Roman Church was just matters that one should discuss but not die for: whether the primacy of the bishop of Rome was instituted by Christ, whether the cardinalate was necessary in the Church, whether confession was ordained by Christ, whether the bishops can oblige the faithful under pain of mortal sin with their rules, whether free will contributes to redemption, whether any human deed can be called good, whether the mass can be described as a sacrifice, whether faith alone effects redemption . . . "What will the end be," he writes in the conclusion of his *Apology*, "if the one party has nothing but tumults, disputes, and bickering, while the other has nothing but censures, bulls, dogmas, and burnings at the stake. What kind of great feat is it, then, to throw a little human being, who will die anyway, into the fire? To convert and convince—that is a great feat."[21]

Though Martin Luther found his audience dwindling among the Lutherans in the north (apart from Melanchthon), he was still listened to by the reformers in the south. They were, for the most part, his students, and they appealed to him: in Zurich Huldrych Zwingli, in Basel Johannes Oecolampadius, in Strassburg Martin Bucer. Violently persecuted by his Catholic colleagues at Louvain, condemned several times by the Sorbonne (1525–31), Erasmus was also supported in Spain—where his influence was surprisingly strong—against the Franciscans and the Dominicans by the grand inquisitor, primate, and king. A conference at Valladolid, called in 1527 to scrutinize his thought—interestingly enough, this same conference had taken up the critical questions of trinitarian doctrine and Christology—was adjourned after several weeks because of the threat of plague, and never reconvened.

After 1525 the dispute between Catholics and Lutherans was increasingly matched by the *dispute between Lutherans and Lutherans.* The great controversy over the Lord's Supper, culminating in 1529 in the Marburg Colloquium between Luther and Zwingli, divided the Lutherans and the Swiss (later the "Reformed") once and for all. And when in the same year the Reformation was introduced into Basel amidst iconoclasm, overthrowing of the city council, and abolition of the mass, Erasmus, now sixty years old, emigrated. Given a solemn farewell nevertheless, he left Basel and moved to Catholic Freiburg—where, to be sure, he never felt at home. He was in any case glad that after six years, in May 1535, though sick, more mistrustful than ever, and no longer quite intellectually capable, he was able to return to his beloved Basel. By now the sun had set for him: Many of his enemies in the Church and the world had been promoted; many of his friends had died; his translator and student Berquin had been condemned to the stake in Paris; Zwingli had been defeated in the first "war of religion," then quartered and burnt; Oecolampadius, shattered by the news, had died shortly afterwards; Chancellor Thomas More and Cardinal John Fisher had been executed, at around this same time, by order of Henry VIII . . .

Still, Erasmus went on working and publishing for *consensus,* for *concordia.* In 1533 his last writing on peace appeared—not, it is true, the last thing he did, but nonetheless something like his swan song—with the title, "On Restoring the Unity of the Church," and set afoot concrete efforts at reunion. The nearly seventy-year-old man, now in Basel, still had one full year to live. And again and again, self-critical and self-absorbed as he was, he wondered: Had he been on the right track? Wasn't there a great deal that he should have not written or written differently? But then again he had done everything, patiently, too patiently, to defuse conflicts through understanding, to maintain endangered contacts through his correspondence, to send everywhere sensible (and often apparently contradictory) answers to different questions and situations, and thereby convince irreconcilable elements and individuals through the Bible and reason. And as far as Luther was concerned . . .

7. Martin Luther's Share of the Guilt

As far as Luther was concerned, Erasmus was convinced that he had, at least in principle, done the right thing, that—for all his standing up for reform and renewal, against abuses and grievances, in the spirit of the Gospel, long before Luther—he had refused Luther his allegiance. No question, *Rome* bore the *main burden of guilt.* And *conformity* with Rome (including court theology and the cardinalate) was never his position. But who could fail to see that *part of the guilt* also belonged to the vehemently wrathful *Luther,* the *"simul iustus et peccator"* (at once just and a sinner) in person?

— Hadn't Luther, the immoderate, presented his justified demands all lumped together, generalizing and in needlessly shrill tones? Had he not been *aggressive* and sometimes a *demagogue* to boot? Was it necessary to take the papal bull threatening excommunication, along with the decretals, and publicly burn them in Wittenberg? How was it that in every opponent (and *not* just the pope) he literally saw the devil?

— When the fanatical *enthusiasts,* Karlstadt and Thomas Münzer at their head, invoked their personal interpretation of Scripture, as opposed to Luther's, and the Holy Spirit, hadn't Luther vigorously denied them "the freedom of a Christian man" he had claimed for himself?

— Didn't Luther have a share of the guilt for the *Peasants' Revolt,* which swept through the German Empire, together with its catastrophic consequences? When the peasants rose up in revolution in southwestern Germany, at first demanding only the rights that the nearby Swiss had long enjoyed, hadn't Luther left them in the lurch? Indeed, hadn't he driven them into death and misery, when he hotheadedly incited the princes "Against the Murderous and Thieving Hordes of the Peasants" (1525), goad them to pitiless, blood measures? Luther was now unpopular among Protestants too as he grew into the (increasingly more conservative) role of "servant of the princes." With his help, these sovereigns built and expanded a na-

tional church system, one in which the sovereign—each one now a
little pope—could even determine the religion of his people—a new
"Babylonian captivity"?

— And finally hadn't the man from Wittenberg also *fallen like a
wild beast* on him, on Erasmus, who had argued patiently and calmly
—in academic style—with Luther? Although Erasmus's arguments
for human freedom and responsibility were really well grounded in
Scripture, hadn't Luther reviled him as a dolt, a freethinker, and a
skeptic, as a new pagan, a despiser of Scripture, an enemy of Christianity, and a destroyer of religion?

— All in all, was the Reformation, with all the blood, sweat, and
tears it cost, with all the radical disruption and manifold devastation
of common life it brought—was it really worth it? Had people now
become so much more pious and the churches so much more Christian? Perhaps there were also objective historical reasons for the fits of
depression the older Luther is reported to have suffered from.

— And now, on top of everything, there was the threat of the
most terrible evil that can come upon humanity: *war.* The great war
in Germany between the Protestant Schmalkaldic League (1531) and
the Catholics loyal to the emperor was only temporarily delayed by
the Nuremberg Armistice (which in fact would last only until Luther's
death in 1546).

Thus wasn't Erasmus right? The cautious scholar, who found all
display of his inner feelings distasteful, constantly stood up for objectivity, for the broadest sort of tolerance, if need be for acknowledging
differences within unity, at all events for understanding and peace
against emotionalism, hatred, fanaticism, and tumult. By contrast,
Luther, the unpredictable man of action, who all too often seemed to
replace arguments with fervor and rage, laid a burden on his Church
and every individual in it, with immense consequences for the state
and for society. For that reason alone total identification with him was
out of the question. In a phrase, *reform yes, revolution no:* that was
Erasmus's position.

Poor Europe, how much trouble it would have been spared if
people had listened more to Erasmus, instead of to Luther; if the *third
force,* which he embodied, the force of understanding, had gotten a
chance, first of all in Rome, but finally in the Reformation camp too,
where he had so many friends. But history, following Luther, Rome

(and Machiavelli) seemed to bypass Erasmus, the loser. Only in a later period, when after all the wars of religion, the horrible Thirty Years War and the Age of Sectarianism, a new paradigm change—from the Reformation to modernity, to the Enlightenment—had ripened, did many of Erasmus's ideas finally win the day. Hugo Grotius, for example, the anti-Machiavellian promoter of international law, was moved by the Erasmian spirit, as was the Lutheran theologian Georg Calixtus, who was a tireless supporter of religious unity and also inspired Leibniz. Erasmus was widely read once more in the eighteenth century Enlightenment. For Nietzsche, who criticized the Reformation as a reaction against the early "Enlightenment of the Renaissance," the "banner of the Enlightenment," which he himself wished to carry on, bore "three names: Petrarch, Erasmus, Voltaire."[22]

The Austrian historian Friedrich Heer, who made the "third force" the subject of a book as wide-ranging as it is personally committed—he could not yet anticipate, back in 1959, the upheaval soon to rack the Catholic Church with the accession of John XXIII and the announcement of the Council—has drawn up the following sad balance sheet for the individual countries of Europe after the collapse of the "third force": *"The defeat of the third force meant:* for Germany the century-long civil war, which culminated in the Thirty Years War; for France the 150-year-long civil war, now hot, now cold, between the 'royal Catholic religion' and the Huguenots, which ended with the destruction or exile of a flourishing segment of the French nobility, French bourgeoisie, and French intelligentsia; for Spain internal separation from Europe through the destruction or exile of its Erasmian humanists, its Jews, Marranos, and Protestants; for Italy the expulsion of the religious nonconformists, the constriction into the ghetto-states of the sixteenth to the nineteenth centuries, which with their state police and inquisitions stifled the inner life or at least desperately repressed it; for England the definitive distancing from Europe as an *alter orbis,* as another 'continent'; for Europe as a whole the final (until the twentieth century) fixing in place as the 'West,' as western Europe, sharply set off against the East, Russia, the Eastern Church, against its own masses, the lowly people, against the underground of the person."[23]

In the face of this monstrous story of guilt, I ask, doesn't Erasmus of Rotterdam stand justified before history? In the year of Erasmus's death—and here at the end of the historical arc, before we cast a glance into the present, we come back once again to the beginning—

Reginald Pole and Pietro Carafa were named cardinals. Paul III, who had toyed with the idea of a Council and had invited Erasmus to collaborate on it, finally convened the famous nine-member commission, whose most prominent members, along with the lay cardinal Contarini, turned out to be those two very different cardinals, Pole and Carafa, and whose surprisingly candid "Report on Church Reform" *(Consilium de emendanda Ecclesia)* was generally viewed as a shift in the Vatican toward church renewal. For Erasmus all these initiatives came too late. He died on the night of the eleventh to the twelfth of July, 1536, fully conscious, with verses from the Psalms on his lips. His last words were in Dutch, the language of his childhood: *"Lieve God"* ("dear God"). A Catholic theologian to the end, he was solemnly buried in the Protestant cathedral of Basel by the city's Protestant pastor, in the presence of the Protestant mayor and town council, and the professors and students of the university. I wonder, was this high-strung man, compared with the not very tender-minded heroes of his day—Luther, Zwingli, Calvin, Ignatius Loyola—perhaps the one sovereign ecumenist? And yet I hesitate:

8. On the Responsibility of Theology at the Moment of Truth

To put it bluntly, Erasmus of Rotterdam was always in conflict with himself. *In conflict* not so much, to quote Cornelis Augustijn (from whose interpretation I have been able to learn so much), on account of the (indisputable) "interiorization and spiritualization" that are the "most important qualities" of Erasmus's ideas.[24] In the final analysis that in no way prevented him from engaging in a highly realistic critique of the Church, in church reform, and church politics. He strikes me as in conflict with himself—for all our sympathy with his individual situation, for all our knowledge of the catastrophes he rightly warned about—for one reason: There is, after all, an *inescapable, unpostponable, nontransferable responsibility* that the Christian faces at the *moment of truth.* It cannot be rationalized away with any argument, any tactics or maneuvering. And this moment of truth arrived for the Catholic theologian with the appearance of the Augustinian monk Martin Luther. It is not the bias of hindsight, an insistence on being right, or hasty condemnation, if we miss the protest Erasmus failed to register in the name of the Gospel against the tyranny of Rome at this moment of truth, if we miss it and complain about its absence. We look for *unambiguous, public protest* against the unchristian spirit of the Roman curia and the Roman system, but a protest that at the same time points to the onesidedness and shortsightedness of Martin Luther's person and theology.

In *private letters* (the relevant ones were not included in any of his published collections of letters) Erasmus could *speak quite clearly:* "I see in the 'monarchy of the Roman high priest' (these words are in Greek for security reasons) the plague of Christianity. The Dominicans shamelessly flatter him in all things." But, he immediately adds, "I don't know whether it's good to touch on this sore openly. That was a task for the princes. Still, I fear they will collaborate with the pope and divide the booty. I don't know what got into Eck's head that he attacks Luther so."[25] To be sure, Werner Kaegi was right to maintain in his memorial address in Basel on July 17, 1969, "Erasmus was not at home in fatherlands and states, but in the Church. He criticized her so bitterly because he loved her."[26] But, one wonders, why at the critical moment didn't he raise his voice out of love and act with the greatest personal energy, as Luther did? Why, instead of forever vacillating between yes and no, didn't he come forth boldly and take a position?

Or was church reform a priori impossible without a schism in the Church? History, admittedly, is not made simply by individuals, but by the structures that determine these individuals. I would nonetheless like to disagree with the inscription that stands in the German National Church in Rome above the grave of the Dutchman Hadrian VI, the last non-Italian pope (until the present day): *"Proh dolor, quantum refert in quae tempora vel optimi cuiusque virtus incidat"* (Alas, how much depends on the sort of age in which the activity of even the best of men takes place.) All too easily the failure of historical personalities is excused here by "bad times," in this case Hadrian's. During the year and a half of his pontificate Hadrian was totally isolated and politically clumsy. The former Louvain professor, both tutor and councilor of Charles V, did not even speak Italian and made no attempt to contact the Italian reform party.

For many thoroughly realistic people of his time (in both camps), Erasmus was the only man who might perhaps have prevented the schism, by speaking with authority to both sides. Hence it is in no way unrealistic to ponder the following:

— What would have happened had Erasmus, using all his personal authority, succeeded in converting to his views of reform just the young *Charles V,* whose "councilor" he was? Charles was a barely twenty-year-old-man (born, like Reginald Pole, in 1500) who, raised a strict Catholic by Hadrian VI, had not the slightest inner sympathy for the Lutheran cause and instead tried everywhere to save the "old faith," which was de facto the medieval Church.

— What might have happened, or been prevented from happening, if at the right moment Erasmus had come forward with *clear suggestions for practical solutions,* in public, then and there? Suppose he had launched such an initiative at the famous meeting of the three monarchs (Henry VIII, Francis I, and Charles V, in whose entourage he was traveling) in Calais in the summer of 1520. Or if the next year he had done so at the imperial Diet of Worms, where as the adviser of the emperor, the boyhood friend of the papal legate Aleander, and a person sympathetic to the Protestants, Erasmus occupied a unique mediating position.

— What would have happened if, under the spell of a dramatic public intervention by Erasmus—who between 1515 and 1525 enjoyed an incomparable prestige all over Europe, who had disciples and supporters in all countries—it had proved possible *to concede to the Protestants* no more than the *vernacular, the chalice for the laity, and marriage for priests?* In that case could the doctrine of justification still have developed the strength to split the Church?

— Erasmus did not attend the *Imperial Diet at Augsburg* in 1530, to which he had received an urgent invitation from the emperor, and at which the Lutherans were under the leadership not of Luther, but of Melanchthon, whose thinking was in many ways Erasmian. Thus didn't Erasmus miss the last, truly historical chance to function as a personally present mediator to reconcile both the humiliated papal adherents (daunted by the Sack of Rome in 1527 and the spread of the Reformation in Holland, Scandinavia, and England) and the disillusioned Lutherans (sobered by the Peasants War and the counter-churches of Zwingli, the fanatical Enthusiasts, and the Anabaptists), to reconcile them in the Erasmian spirit, with the help of the moderate Augsburg Confession?

— Didn't *England* subsequently show that the Pauline-Lutheran understanding of justification could be taken seriously, that the vernacular, the chalice for the laity, and priestly marriage could be introduced while still keeping (as Luther originally wished) the

presbyterial-episcopal structure and the continuity of the now reformed Church with the medieval Church?

— What was wanted then was *no new Church* (associated with a
person's name, "Lutheran" or "Erasmian), *but the old Church renewed: "Ecclesia catholica reformata—Ecclesia catholica semper
reformanda"!*

I ask: At such a *moment of truth* didn't the professor have to
become the confessor—*opportune, importune,* in season or out of
season—whether it was convenient or inconvenient, with whatever
success or failure? Anyway, man is always justified by faith—not by
success. The fact that Erasmus wrote in Latin and dealt with an elite,
that he had neither a pulpit nor a university chair (all points rightly
stressed by Augustijn) can hardly serve as an explanation why Erasmus didn't put his cards on the table. To wish to be a detached
observer, a neutral onlooker here was an illusion. His influential supporters everywhere in Europe properly expected that instead of writing letters in all directions, Erasmus would go public with a major,
explicit statement, as Luther had: united with Luther in a clear protest against the Roman system, while at the same time correcting
Luther's onesidedness, and thus bearing witness to the grand Catholic
continuity and universality.

There is at the moment of truth a *status confessionis* that can no
longer be the *casus disputationis.* But Erasmus did *not* feel that he
had been born to this role of confessor, much less to that of a prophet.
Neither his character nor his theology, as far as he could see, had
predestined him in that direction. "Yet," said Ulrich Zasius, the renowned jurist from Freiburg, "if Erasmus had had the determination
to write as fearlessly and comment as sharply as Luther did; and, in
addition, if Luther had acquired the eloquence, the literary style, the
modesty and cleverness of Erasmus: What more perfect human being
could the gods have created? I am devoted to both, I prefer Erasmus."[27] So, did Erasmus have too little of what Luther had too much?
Too little potential for prophetic protest against usurped priestly authority? Too little power of resistance and willingness to take risks,
drawing upon the freedom of a Christian man, against unchristian
despotism? Too little of Paul's "speaking out before them all" to Peter
and "opposing him to his face," because he and his people "acted

insincerely" and "were not straightforward about the truth of the gospel" (Gal 2:11–14)?

9. Ecumenical Theology Between Aggression and Flight

As was obvious, in the case of Erasmus we could not engage in antiquarian historiography: The drama of those days throbs too powerfully down to our own time. The aftershocks from the basic conflicts between theology and the Church are still too strongly felt. The theological issues that had to be contested are too much like those of today. As far as establishing an ecumenical theology is concerned, we are dealing here with an exemplary fundamental conflict.

In the face of the church establishment and its theology (the Roman, German, or Roman-German court theologies), all of which demanded *conformity*, Luther and Erasmus embodied two patterns of dealing with conflict in the Church at the moment of truth: *aggressiveness* or *neutrality, attacking* or *fleeing*. Behavioral research calls our attention to the fact that aggression or flight in the presence of the threat of danger must be described in the same analytical context. "Aggressiveness" means to remove the threatening event, person, or institution, while "flight" means to remove oneself from the threatening event, person, or institution. But both modes of behavior, highly emotionally conditioned as they are, are ultimately panic reactions.

Is there a middle ground between hostile assault and sidling avoidance, between attacking and fleeing? Although, like most theologians north of the Alps, Erasmus did not believe in papal infallibility, neither did he mention in his *Mirror for Princes* (for all his strictures against Machiavellianism), nor did he ever practice, what someone like Thomas Aquinas—faced with tyrants—was thoroughly familiar with, and what, along with many others, the Thomist cardinal Cajetan de Vio (whom Martin Luther would have to deal with in the first hearing at Augsburg in 1518) had clearly affirmed in his treatise on the authority of popes and councils (1511): *ius resistendi,* the right to resist. The doctrine of active resistance argued that every Christian has the duty to resist even the pope to his face, if the pontiff was publicly harming the Church. This follows for all of Catholic tradition from the phrase already quoted in connection with Paul's conduct toward Peter in Antioch: "before them all" (Luther correctly translates, "before them all, in public"), "speaking out," *"opposed* him to his face." Thus we see neither attacking nor avoiding but resisting, or as Horst Eberhard Richter phrased the alternative to flight, *"Hold your ground!"* Holding one's ground, in loyalty to the Christian cause, incorruptible, and without fear of reprisals.

For that reason Erasmus and Luther could serve ecumenically minded theologians today—given the new wave of reaction and restoration from Rome—as historical models for the weal and woe, the victories and defeats, in short for the "triumph and tragedy" (Stephan Zweig) of reform theology. Here theologians can engage in a bit of self-analysis and grief work—as well as self-appraisal and strategy— for a contemporary theology of eminent political-practical and theological-spiritual significance. In the face of structural (religious-secular) violence in the Church both Luther and Erasmus embody, each in his own way, the fate of reform theology, which now as ever can— when an emergency arises—get caught up in a tug of war between schismatic protest and the contrary forces of adjustment. In this tug of war we find:

— *Luther's aggression*, which when unrestrainedly indulged in and quickly escalated leads to revolution and finally to division;

— and *Erasmus's flight*, which with him and others leads to resignation, and with many once again to conformism.

— Over against both responses we must set *Pauline resistance* and *steadfastness*, which can lead in the end, after a phase of temporary loyal opposition, to church renewal from within without causing any break. The Second Vatican Council remains for me a model for fundamental reform *"sine tumultu,"* without uproar, without violence, division, and war, prepared and then carried out by those who in hard times, and finally under Pius XII, held their ground despite all the dirty tricks by Rome.

I should like to emphasize that this resistance and steadfastness in the domain of the Church should by no means be understood only in the social-psychological sense, but spiritually as well. Paul's words in Romans about "suffering" apply both to the time of the Reformation and to the present, and correspond exactly to the experience of many ecumenically committed men and women in our churches: "We rejoice in our sufferings, knowing that suffering produces endurance, and endurance produces character, and character produces hope, and hope does not disappoint us" (Rom 5:3–5).

We are now ready to conclude by wrapping up the thoughts expressed here and—instructed by both Erasmus and Luther—by drawing consequences for the future. I summarize:

(1) For one whole decade, from 1510 to 1520, Erasmus was the controversial but incontestable exponent of Catholic reform theology in all its ecumenical breadth. He lived in a Church that had become increasingly less Catholic and more Roman. He was the outstanding leader of a *different* (not "Roman") kind of *Catholicity,* a living synthesis of human universality and evangelical Christianity, a great representative of the loyal, evangelically minded opposition in his Church, working on the strength of his own authority and personal worth. Erasmus and his friends embodied at that time the *second force,* counteracting the curial-Roman Church: an annoyance to be sure, criticized and suspect, but within the spectrum of Catholic reform opposition, and so both tolerable and tolerated.

(2) With the *appearance of Luther,* however, everything suddenly changed. Quickly, too quickly and arbitrarily, through the enormous power of Rome and against the will of Erasmus, Luther was excommunicated. Then in the 1520s Luther, along with his followers, became the *second force,* a true counterforce directed against the papal Church. His excommunication by the pope was the cause of Luther's aggression. Even before the discussion with Luther could be carried out within the framework of the Church—something for which Erasmus, who never looked on him as a heretic constantly pleaded—Luther was branded as uncatholic. The controversial but unequivocal and respected second force of Erasmus now developed into an ipso facto divided, ambiguous *third force caught in the cross fire,* forced to distance itself equally from Rome and Wittenberg.

(3) The fact that the discussion with Luther, thanks to Rome's overhasty, irresponsible, and unchristian intervention, could no longer be carried out within the Church necessarily plunged Catholic reform theologians into the greatest difficulties. Rome forced upon them an option that they had precisely wished to avoid: to identify themselves with Rome in an act of full conformity, to speak out as a united front for supposed "Catholic" teaching, and at the same time

to discredit the concerns for reform as expressed in the Reformation. In the confrontation between the pope and Luther the Catholic reform theologians were thus forced up against an *insane alternative:* Rome *or* Wittenberg, a Roman Church or a German Church. But those who, like Erasmus, could and would identify totally with neither Rome nor Wittenberg, with neither a Roman nor a German church, at the moment of truth had to "flee." And in this flight the third force finally lost everything it had: its power. The Erasmian reform movement went under, however much Erasmus's ideas of reform may have survived underground and celebrated their return in the Enlightenment—though for the Catholic Church, because of the usual time lag, this would not come until Vatican II, which now finally granted the use of vernacular in the liturgy, the chalice for the laity, and much else, four hundred fifty years too late.

(4) An *emergency* has now arisen, however, especially for Catholic theology *today:* So long as theology stays strictly within the system, so long as its thinking is pastoral instead of programmatic and engages in subjective examination of conscience instead of objective exploration of foundations, so long as it asks questions but doesn't press them, interprets and adapts instead of analyzing and confronting, so long as it reconciles contradictions dialectically instead of decisively getting rid of them, so long as it engages in cosmetic surgery instead of radical criticism, so long as it pleads for innocuous reforms that don't endanger the structure of authority and power, so long as in doing "political theology" it diverts the potential for internal church reform toward the outside, onto society—so long as theologians do all this, they will be admitted by the members of the hierarchy, tolerated, occasionally caressed and invited to commissions, conferences, Catholic congresses, and even to Rome. Then they are allowed to function for popes and bishops as "Holy Ghost writers," allowed to draw up momentous papers for delivery at inconsequential synods, to make brave presentations about which the not very courageous bishops and curia pass judgment. Finally they may even compose catechisms, all of which naturally have to be in conformity with the system. An emergency? No, all this isn't an emergency, it is at best the way Catholic theology plays the game.

A state of emergency occurs when a Catholic theologian dares to bell the cat, to demand the truth be truthfully told, to alter the foundations by exploring them, to test the system and its claims, in good Pauline style to "resist, publicly, face to face," and to demand a "change in keeping with the truth of the Gospel"—even if he is officially punished for it by being excluded from the community of Catholic theologians. Then suddenly it is a life-and-death issue not only for him but for all Catholic theologians. Then the crucial question arises, whose side is one on, given the dilemma of official churchly arrogance versus the autonomous rights of theology. Then we face the basic questions: Speak or be silent? Stand fast or flee? Who determines what a Catholic theologian is? Who sets down what is legitimate or illegitimate within the Catholic Church? Who has the right to censure, to excommunicate? And what is meant by the *ius resistendi*, the right to dissent? History shows that Rome—after phases of allowing a liberal limited identification—has always gone back to pressuring Catholic theologians with that insane alternative (either conform to Rome in everything, or you're not Catholic) and to forcing total identification upon them. But history also shows that, after winning many battles Rome still lost the war. And, from Luther and Galileo all the way to Vatican II, when all was said and done, Rome has continually had to be corrected by history. *"Historia docet"* (history teaches), but will people ever learn from history? Today the Roman curia is trying to revise the heresy trials of the sixteenth (Luther) and seventeenth (Galileo) century without an all too clear loss of face, but it continues the heresy trials of the twentieth century with methods not much improved over the old ones.

(5) In the theological landscape of the present the fronts have long ceased to be identical with Rome, Wittenberg, and Basel. The situation has become more nuanced, fronts and camps now overlap one another. On the one hand, the bureaucratization of the Church, the simultaneous centralization and sacralization that have occurred since the nineteenth century, make criticism and reform rather more difficult than before. On the other hand, the solid foundation of the Church as a popular institution, the closed cultural milieu of Catholicism—the presupposition for a successful restoration of the centralized-bureaucratic system today—has largely disintegrated. The *basic attitude of ecumenical theology, whether Catholic or Protestant*, which has recognized the interdependence between liberation in the world and liberation in the Church, between human rights and Christian rights, may be sketched out as follows:

— With *Erasmus and Luther* ecumenical theology shares a *distance* from the Roman system, its legalism, triumphalism, conformism, integralism, and infallibilism. This system is currently being restored again everywhere in the world. An effort is being made to counter movements among the rank and file by nominating conservative bishops, to use Vatican City law (in Germany) to discipline insubordinate kindergarten teachers and instructors of religion, nurses and doctors, chaplains and pastors, Ph.D. candidates and professors, and thereby establish a clerical state within the state. Integralistic secret organizations from the era of dictator Francisco Franco, such as the *Opus Dei,* enjoy the highest honor and support. Curial financial scandals, which far exceed those of yore (involving the German bishops and the Fuggers) cannot be met with official denial. If Desiderius Erasmus came back today, he would hardly recognize in the current Pontiff from Poland an Erasmian (to say nothing of the successor of Grand Inquisitor Carafa from Bavaria).

— With *Luther,* however, unlike Erasmus, ecumenical theology argues the necessity of a *basic theological explanation:* an account of those typically "Roman Catholic" claims, of the dogmatism, papalism, and Marianism that are at home neither in the New Testament nor in the ancient Church, but in the Middle Ages, Counter-Reformation, or nineteenth century.

— With *Erasmus,* however, unlike Luther, a *schism in the Church* is no longer an option for ecumenical theology. We have had enough schisms and schisms of schisms. In our day when a schism threatened in Holland, it was averted, to the advantage of all concerned—although, of course, the Dutch themselves had to make great sacrifices. And, as for contemporary Protestantism, the attractiveness of many "leading" successors of Martin Luther, especially in Germany, is hardly likely to tempt Catholic reform theologians to convert. The bourgeois heirs of the Reformer are scarcely a "second force" vis-à-vis Rome. The leadership of the Protestant churches has left all protest to the Catholics: Unprotesting Protestantism likes to pose with the Pontiff for . . . photo opportunities. There is a highly dubious pseudo-ecumenical power cartel with Roman Catholics in power, always in agreement when common interests (church taxes) and demands of state and society are at issue (money and morality), never in agreement, when—after 500 years—the issue is the lightening of churchly burdens on the shoulders of men and women: mixed marriages, divorced persons, and celibate priests, the removal of hindrances and the lifting of excommunication between the local churches, or finally restoring Protestant-Catholic communion (allowing common celebrations of the Lord's Supper or the Eucharist, and hence as well ecumenical meetings and church congresses like the one at Augsburg on Pentecost, 1971). A holy—no, an unholy—alliance. Tough, determined work is called for to resist the renewed narrowness and intimidation that is placing people under legal disabilities and brainwashing them.[28]

What we need today more than ever is a theology and a Church that bring to life the best of Luther *and* Erasmus: Martin Luther's prophetic power, but without fanaticism and aggressiveness, and at the same time Erasmus's universal openness and peace-loving tolerance, but without neutral indecision and flight from commitment and risk.

What is needed is a basic ecumenical approach, in other words, that no longer sees in every other theology and church an opponent, but a partner; an ecumenical theology intent on understanding instead of separation. This means understanding in two directions: *inwards* (which was Luther's perspective as a reformer) in the area of the inter-churchly, and internal, Christian ecumene; but also *outwards* (something to which Erasmus as a humanist was especially attuned), outside the Church and Christianity, into the area of the world ecumene with all its different cultures, kinds of knowledge, and religions. And absolutely all of this is designed to serve the *mission* of the Church in this society, for there can be no ecumenical church without an ecumenical theology. So long, in the meantime, as this kind of long-term goal has not been reached, we may find comfort in a sentence that Erasmus wrote a year before his death in his reply to Luther: *"Fero igitur hanc Ecclesiam donec videro meliorem: et eadem me ferre cogitur, donec upse fiam melior":* "Thus I put up with this Church, until I see a better one; and she is forced to put up with me, until I myself become better."[29]

II

The Bible and
Church Tradition

*Unfinished Business Between
Catholicism, Protestantism and Orthodoxy*

My purpose here is to shed some new light on the familiar arrangements in the museum of the theological mind. The world-historical struggle over the *reformation of the Church* was fundamentally a struggle over the primacy of Sacred Scripture as opposed to church tradition. Luther and Erasmus made that clear. One and a half millenia of church history had left the Western Church—still more than the Eastern Church, which persisted in the Hellenistic paradigm, keeping to the ancient Christian-Byzantine total constellation of values—with a tremendous mass of more or less obligatory traditions in church doctrine, liturgy, and discipline: from indulgences and the invocation of innumerable "saints" to the assertion that Jesus Christ himself had instituted confession, the sacrament of marriage, the ordination of priests, and Rome's primacy of jurisdiction.

This "oral tradition" had found expression in countless confessions of faith, conciliar, episcopal, and papal documents, in theological Bible commentaries and manuals, liturgical formularies and saints' legends. All sorts of conditions, some of them deplorable, all sorts of usages and abuses, regulated the entire life of both the community and individuals from the cradle to the grave and from morning to evening. According to Luther this was the "Babylonian captivity of the Church," from which there can be only one liberation: the return to Christian origins, to the Gospel of Jesus Christ himself, as it was fortunately given shape in writing once and for all in the documents of the New Testament. *"Sola Scriptura,"* "Scripture alone," was to be the *supreme norm* for church dogma and ethics, for the liturgy, canon law, and popular piety. In the face of the mighty church structure built in the Middle Ages *Luther's demand for the primacy of Scripture*—once the pope, as master of the house, refused in advance to pay Luther any heed—started a de facto revolution. Thanks to Rome's unwillingness to reform, but also to Luther's excesses and fanaticism, that demand led to the second great church schism that even someone like Erasmus could not prevent. Now, in addition to the split between the Eastern Church and the Western Church, there was a split (to oversimplify) between the Protestant North and the Catholic South, running straight through Germany, through Europe, and then through the New World as well.

1. Scripture "and" Tradition: The Catholic Answer to Luther

Out of Spain and Italy came the *Counter-Reformation,* which—after initially displaying conciliatory tendencies in the style of Erasmus—increasingly turned into a reactionary movement whose primary goal was to restore the medieval status *quo ante.* At the Council of Trent (in what is today the southern Tyrol) it was codified into church history and church law. In thoroughly logical fashion the council laid down, with the authority of the magisterium, in the very first decree of 1546 (the year Luther died) the *equal importance of Scripture and Tradition.* This is what Karl Barth in our century has called the "damned Catholic And": "The holy church Council knows that this truth and order is preserved in the written books *and ("et")* the unwritten traditions. . . ." It follows from this that "the traditions that concern faith and morals are to be acknowledged and revered with the same feeling of piety and respect" *(pari pietatis affectu et reverentiae)* as the books of the Old and New Testament."[1]

But ancient and medieval exegesis still took it for granted that all the Church's truth of faith and morals are contained in the Bible, at least implicitly. This is Scripture as the life and source of divine tradition *(divinae traditionis caput et origo).* But after the Council of Trent influential theologians such as Peter Canisius and Robert Bellarmine spread the notion, as coming from the council, that divine revelation is contained "partly" in Scripture, "partly" in Tradition. This was just the teaching that the Roman curia and its court theologians intended to have defined as exactly as possible at the Second Vatican Council. But what in fact is the case with that comfortable "partly in Scripture, partly in Tradition" doctrine, by which all Roman uses and abuses can easily be justified?

Well before the Second Vatican Council Catholic theologians—first the Spaniard E. Ortigues and then in particular the Tübingen professor J. R. Geiselmann—showed that the "partly-partly" idea represents an outright misunderstanding of the Tridentine decree. Conciliar documents make it clear that the partly-partly formulation was stricken from the record and replaced by an "and" *(et),* when objections were raised by council fathers who were convinced that the whole gospel truth, and not just a part of it, was laid down in the Bible. This means that the Council of Trent in no way approved the idea that the contents of Holy Scripture are incomplete. That idea—if we except Melchior Cano as an isolated pre-Tridentine theologian—represents an extremist development in Roman controversial theology. On the contrary, we have every right to take the view that the various church documents and monuments of tradition—papal, conciliar, and episcopal decisions, works by the Fathers of the Church and theologians, creeds, catechisms, the liturgy, church piety and art—are all to be understood as instruments for interpreting the original biblical message. No more and no less.

2. Scripture "or" Tradition: A Weak Compromise by Vatican II

It is a problem of great practical importance that Vatican II—400 years after Trent!—still could not manage to provide a clear, careful definition, not even in its constitution on revelation, *Dei Verbum* (1965), for the relationship between Scripture and Tradition, which theologians have thoroughly investigated in this century. The curial preparatory commission for the council, spellbound by that unhistorical, Counter-Reformation notion and transparently playing church politics, had defended the *two-source-theory* of Scripture *and* Tradition. At the council itself, unfortunately, nothing better than a compromise was possible. For, under pressure from the curial minority, which controlled the conciliar mechanism, the council ultimately left open the definition of the relationship between Scripture and Tradition: Revelation has been laid down, the text now reads, "in Scripture or *[vel]* Tradition."

People hailed as "progress" what was hardly an advance: Scripture and Tradition, instead of being separated, are now brought as close together as possible and made to flow into one—something like the way hot and cold water mingle as they pour out of a modern faucet. This allows a mixing that may be quite practical in everyday life but is harmful to theology and the Church: What Scripture does not provide, Tradition must produce. For both, however, the Church's magisterium, which is de facto uncontrolled, functions as the concretely *(proxime)* determining voice. It proclaims arbitrarily what is obligatory in Tradition and how Scripture is to be understood —down to the latest dogmas concerning Mary and the pope. In the constitution on revelation this unresolved theological problem is pretty much disguised with a *quasi-trinitarian formula.* While praise is lavished upon a self-fabricated harmony (which sounds even more melodious in Latin than in English), the *norma normans* (Scripture in its function of setting the standard for everything) is, in fact, covered up with an invocation of God's wise decree: "Thus it becomes apparent that sacred Tradition, the Holy Scriptures, and the Church's magisterium, in keeping with God's wise decree, are so intertwined and joined to one another that none exists without the others, and all together, each in its way, effectively serve the salvation of souls through the work of the Holy Spirit" (article 10).

And so, from its first day to its last, Vatican II suffered from the fact that the *question of what the supreme criterion is for the magisterium,* the final and highest norm for the renewal of the Church, remained *undecided.* The statement that "the magisterium [is] not over the Word of God, but serves it" continues to be ambiguous, insofar as the "Word of God" means here not just Scripture, but Scripture *and* Tradition (which thus includes papal pronouncements), so that the vicious circle is not broken.

Indeed all of Catholic theology and praxis continues to suffer from it to this day. The ones to profit from the conciliar compromise were once again the members of the power complex that sought, for understandable reasons, to prevent a decision in favor of the New Testament: the Roman curia, their professors and canon lawyers. It must have seemed an empty ritual to the conciliar theologians, who had the daily experience of seeing how at every session of the council a large, precious Gospel was borne in solemn candle-lit procession all the way through St. Peter's and set up on the altar. The one consolation was that in the last chapter of the constitution on revelation neither Tradition nor the magisterium, finally, but *Scripture alone* was characterized as *"the soul of theology."* One cannot quote this phrase often enough.

3. Scripture—Taken Literally: The Protestant Version of Infallibility

Anyone who has openly criticized this sort of Roman Catholic compromise is hardly in danger of moving over to the Protestant camp and absolutizing Protestant standards and models of thought. For the replacement of the Roman magisterium with the "teaching authority" of the Bible, which occurred in the course of Protestant theology and church history, compels us to ask equally critical and pressing questions. In many cases did not the infallibility of the bishop of Rome or ecumenical council give way to the infallibility of a "paper pope"?

While Catholicism stresses tradition and the infallibility of certain propositions defined by the Church, Protestantism early on countered this with belief in the infallibility of the propositions in the Bible. But, because of anti-Catholic polemics, here too the formulation of the problem went awry. In their battle against the traditions handed down by the Church, the Reformers had advanced the cause of Scripture but not its infallibility. Calvin had practiced philological and historical criticism, on occasion (above all with the Epistle of James and Revelation) Luther had not shied away from direct criticism of the text. But in the seventeenth century Lutheran and Reformed orthodoxy systematically expanded the notion of inspiration that had indeed been shared by both the Reformers and the Council of Trent (but that was not forced) into one of literal or verbal inspiration of Scripture.

In consequence, revelation was now identified with the unique, past result of the scriptural word, which comes into being in the biblical author through the working of the Holy Spirit. This makes the authors of the books of the Bible into unhistorical, schematic creatures, through whom the Holy Spirit immediately dictates everything. Thus every word of Scripture has a share in the perfection and inerrancy of God himself. This means that human imperfection and proneness to error have been wholly eliminated. For then the Spirit of

God, who can neither deceive nor be deceived, would have to be charged with imperfection and error. This is how inspiration and the inerrancy derived from it is extended in rigorous, systematic fashion to all the individual statements in the Bible: *verbal inspiration demands verbal inerrancy.* This doctrine is still defended today—but is it still valid?

As we know, the theory of verbal inspiration and verbal inerrancy was profoundly shaken by the Enlightenment. The historicocritical question, now directed at the books at the Bible, brought their genuine humanity and historicity to light. In the process, furthermore, the biblical authors' capacity for error became more than clear. Nonetheless, one can always build up walls and hide behind them to avoid this indisputable view. The idea of literal inspiration has survived not only in numerous sects, but also in many Protestant churches, particularly in modern American fundamentalism and in some European pietistic movements: Among those who believe in the Bible instead of in Christ, *biblicism has remained a continuous danger for Protestant theology.* Where it takes hold, the actual foundation of belief is no longer the Christian message, nor Christ himself as proclaimed to the world, but the infallible word of the Bible as such. As some Catholics believed less in God and his Christ than in "their" Church and in "their" pope, so many Protestants believe in "their" Bible. The apotheosis of the Church is matched by the apotheosis of Scripture.

But what is to be said nowadays about the doctrine of inspiration from the critical standpoint of ecumenism? First of all, there is no overlooking the fact that the teaching has an old tradition behind it and that, under the influence of Hellenistic theories of inspiration, it was developed in the ancient Church. The biblical authors were thought of as something like secretaries taking dictation from the Holy Spirit, as "inspired" in that sense. At times they were even compared to a flute, totally passive in the hands of the flutist. It was above all Augustine, who saw man only as a tool of the Holy Spirit, and claimed that the Spirit alone determined the form and content of the Scriptures. That was why the Bible had to be free from contradictions, defects, and errors. And if necessary, it had to be kept free from every sort of contradiction through harmonization, allegorism, or mystification. Augustine's influence remained crucial through the Middle Ages all the way into the modern period. Thus Trent also declared that the books of the Bible and the Apocrypha had been "dictated either orally by Christ or by the Holy Spirit."[2]

4. Does Inspired Mean Unerring?
Vatican II and the Bible

Naturally at Trent there was no talk of the Bible's inerrancy as a result of inspiration. For verbal inspiration was asserted and thought through with systematic consistency only in Protestantism. Not until the end of the nineteenth century did the Roman popes take advantage of this doctrine, in order to make their own policy on the Bible: just when they were feeling the pressure from "destructive" historico-critical exegesis. This was a remarkable time lag. Vatican I (1870), which speaks of Scripture as inspired ("written under the inspiration of the Holy Spirit, they have God as their author") makes a comment here that still sounds rather indirect and guarded: The Scriptures are said to "contain revelation[!] without error."[3] But beginning with Leo XIII, and especially as part of the campaign against modernism, the complete and absolute inerrancy of Scripture, even in historical and scientific matters, was continually, explicitly, and programmatically defended in papal pronouncements.

Anyone who took part in the Second Vatican Council as a *peritus* knows that the curial commission charged with preparing the schema on revelation also tried to force this notion on the council. In the original draft of this commission one could likewise read about the *"absolute inerrancy of the whole of Sacred Scripture."* This idea is extended to every domain, sacred and profane, and beyond that is characterized as an old and constant conviction of the Church. Fortunately in its first session (1962) the council rejected this theological construction by an overwhelming majority. In a personal intervention, John XXIII removed the schema on revelation from the agenda, but after the all too early death of this first great ecumenical pope his nervously maneuvering successor, Paul VI, to everyone's surprise put it back on the agenda of the third session.

It is worthwhile to trace in some detail the alterations this schema went through in the third session of the council. On the problem of *inspiration* this session undoubtedly marked a *turning point.* The original six long articles were now contracted into a single short article. The chapter heading went from apologetical ("Inerrancy") to constructive ("Inspiration"). The individual authors of the New Testament ("hagiographers") are no longer described as God's "instruments" but as "true authors." Theological observers and interpreters of the council are right, therefore, to note that Vatican II rejected the teaching that the human activity of the "hagiographers" was in any way eliminated, impeded, or replaced. It wanted to avoid a return to old theories of verbal inspiration and so too any kind of impersonal, mechanistic interpretation of the origin of Scripture.

On the question of the *inerrancy* of Scripture the speech by Cardinal Franz König of Vienna on concrete *errors* in the Bible was of fundamental importance. König frankly pointed out "that in Holy Scripture the historical and scientific accounts sometimes diverge from the truth" *(a veritate quandoque deficere)*. For example, according to Mark 2:26 David is supposed to have entered the house of God and to have eaten the showbread under the high priest Abiathar; in fact, of course, this happened—we are told in 1 Sam 21:1-2—not under Abiathar but under his father Ahimelech. Or in Matt 27:9 the fulfillment of a prophecy of "Jeremiah" is reported, which is in truth a prophecy of Zachariah (11:13), and so on. Cardinal König wanted the discussion of the issue of inerrancy to be "candid, unambiguous, unaffected, and fearless." For deviation from the truth on historical and scientific questions in no way endangered the authority of Scripture. Rather God accepted the human author with all his weaknesses and mistakes—and reached his goal nevertheless: to teach men and women the "truth" of revelation.

Under the influence of the theological commission, which was crowded with members of the curia, the council itself now agreed to a weak *compromise*. One clear solution would have been to take König's advice, *drop* the expression "without any error" *(sine ullo errore)*, and instead to phrase it positively that the books of the Bible "teach the truth integrally and unshakably" *(integre et inconcusse)*. The commission, however, took the two positive words that suited it *(firmiter et fideliter,* "firmly and faithfully"), and let stand the "without any error." Only rather than "without any error" *(sine ullo errore)* the commission now said only "without error" *(sine errore)*. Can we call such language "candid, unambiguous, unaffected, and fearless"? In article 11 of the constitution on revelation the text now reads: "Since, therefore, everything that the inspired authors or hagiographers say has to be considered as said by the Holy Spirit, we must confess of the books of Scripture that they *certainly, faithfully, and without error* teach the truth that God wished to have written down in the Bible for the sake of our salvation" (my italics). In other words, like the definition of the relationship between Scripture and Tradition, the problem of inspiration and inerrancy is likewise still waiting a constructive theological solution in the ecumenical spirit.

In any case, after the council solemnly affirmed in article 12 of the constitution on revelation the *necessity of a historico-critical reading of Scripture* and made it the duty of the exegete, it should have been more difficult to cling to the outmoded ideas of verbal inspiration and verbal inerrancy.

5. The Ecumenical Solution: Scripture as Testimony to Revelation

But how can we speak ecumenically about the relationship between Scripture and revelation? I am working from the assumption that there is unanimous agreement nowadays among informed Catholic and Protestant Christians on two basic conclusions:

(1) *There must be no historical-anthropological reduction of Scripture.* The old doctrine of inspiration was *concerned*, in a way we should take seriously, with helping to promote the realization that God himself acts through the human word of the Bible to the believer; he allows this human word in preaching to become the tool of his Spirit, and so moves people to believe.

(2) *The historical-anthropological relativity of Scripture must be taken seriously.* Every doctrine of inspiration is *limited* by the fact that the biblical Scriptures are at the same time wholly human texts by human authors. They have to be measured and relativized by their human authors' gifts and shortcomings, their possibilities for knowledge and error, so that mistakes of the most varied sort cannot be excluded in advance.

Can these two insights be at all reconciled? Only when we recognize that God writes straight even in crooked lines and can reach his goals *by way of our humanity and historicity* without doing any violence to human beings. It is only in and through all the human fragility and all the historical relativity and limitedness of the biblical authors, who often can speak only in stammering language and with inadequate conceptual means, that God's call, as it rang out in the people of Israel and finally in Jesus, is truly heard, believed, understood, and realized.

How then should we understand *inspiration* in a manner that suits both Scripture and our own time? Just as it would be false to pin down the working of God's Spirit in the Church (in the sense of *assistentia*) to any specific act of definition by a pope or council, it would likewise be false to limit it in Holy Scripture (in the sense of *inspiratio*) to any specific acts of writing by an Apostle or biblical writer. The *entire* course of the origin, collection, and transmission of the Word, the entire process of believing acceptance and proclaiming transmission of the biblical message is—for believers—under the leadership and dispensation of the Spirit. In other words, inspiration is rightly understood only when not only the history of the writing down of Scripture, but its entire history before and after this, is understood as "inspired" by the Spirit: not dictated by the Spirit, but *penetrated and filled with the Spirit.* We are not talking about a miracle, as in the Qur'an, say, which, according to the traditional view, was directly revealed to the Prophet from heaven (by angels) as a holy Book, free from error, whose every line is infallible: a book that therefore has to be taken literally and hence may not even be interpreted and commented on. We do not have to wash our hands before handling the Bible. The New Testament Scriptures nowhere claim to have fallen directly from heaven; rather they often quite unself-consciously stress their human origin (along with the Apostolic Letters, Luke 1:2 is especially informative on the subject of how the Gospels came into being). And if the witnesses feel they have been moved by the Holy Spirit, this is not an assertion to the hearers or readers of the New Testament that they must acknowledge something like an act of inspiration. It is simply presupposed that every reception and proclamation of the Gospel takes place a priori "in the Holy Spirit" (1 Pet 1:12, 1 Cor 7:40).

Thus the revelation of the Old and New Testament can under no circumstances be simply identified with Scripture: *Scripture is not revelation, it attests to revelation.* It is witness-to-revelation. God is at work here only in an indirect and hidden fashion. Only in *faith* is the *kerygma* experienced as truly God's own Word to humanity (cf. 1 Thess 2:13). But if the humanity, autonomy, and historicity of the biblical writers are preserved, *their* writings may be understood as testimony to the Word of *God.* The operation of the Spirit excludes neither defects nor mistakes, neither obscurity nor confusion, neither limitation nor error. The testimonies recorded in the New Testament have neither the same texture nor the same value. Some are brighter, some darker; some are more intelligible, some less; some are stronger, some weaker; some are more original, some derivative. There are testimonies that can diverge, contrast, and partially contradict one another. They are held together by the fundamental testimony that Jesus Christ has revealed the God who interacts with us.

6. Is the Orthodox Tradition in Keeping with Scripture?: The Problem of the Eastern Church

There is no ecumenically significant question facing the Catholic Church that doesn't contain its counter-question. Hitherto we have discussed the problem of Scripture and Tradition, and Scripture and revelation in the context of Catholic and Protestant theology. What is the situation, though, with the orthodox theology of the eastern churches? What authority does it invoke in establishing the truth, when Catholic theology relies on the authority of the Church and Protestant theology on the authority of Scripture?

Orthodox theology invokes neither the Church's magisterium nor Scripture alone, but *orthodox tradition,* as it has been embodied by the *Patres,* or patristics, the Greek Fathers of the Church. It is a "theology of the Fathers." This is altogether proper insofar as these theologians of Christian antiquity, who are in many ways closer to Christian origins than, say, medieval scholasticism is, attest to the biblical message and interpret it for their time. Of course, there is no mistaking the fact that this involves the overvaluation of individual Church Fathers or the Church Fathers as a whole: Their authority and teaching often actually play a larger role than the original biblical message. And their statements are often naively placed on the same level as those of the Bible, instead of being critically measured against them. In addition, the *ecumenical councils* are especially overvalued, their decrees treated as if they were divinely inspired and the infallibility of their teachings accepted de facto, if not actually asserted on principle.

Given such an overvaluation of the Fathers or of the councils, more careful attention should be paid to what even some orthodox theologians have argued; namely

— that not only the Fathers of the Church, but the ecumenical councils, often reciprocally disavow, explicitly reject, or in fact correct one another;

— that the ecumenical councils do not therefore a priori have the truth on their side; that the truth rather becomes manifest only when the conciliar statements have been "received" or acknowledged by the Church as a whole;

— that the councils themselves establish no new doctrines at all; they merely wished to state and confirm the agreement of a doctrine with the original apostolic testimony of faith.

Ecumenical councils *can* be an expression of the truth in the Church. But they do not necessarily express it, as if by virtue of the will of those convoked or of the participants, to whom the Spirit of God might be thought of as having given, at their wish and request, an a priori guarantee that all their statements would be true. Councils are rather expressions of the truth after the fact, *if* and *insofar* as they bear authentic witness to the truth of the Gospel. This is the classic orthodox Catholic notion of councils as formulated by the great theological representative of the first ecumenical council, Athanasius, as well as by many Greek Fathers, and finally by the leading theologian of the West, Augustine. For Athanasius the Council of Nicaea's claim to truth was not dependent on its ecumenicity but on the fact that Nicaea broaches the substance of the apostolic faith, the *kerygma* as fixed in writing. According to him, the Council of Nicaea says the truth not because an ecumenical council, thanks to the help of the Holy Spirit, could never be mistaken, but because it has the true Christian tradition behind it, because it hands down the original faith of the Apostles, because it "breathes Scripture"; that is, it shows off the Gospel in an authentic and credible light. To the extent that councils in this manner effect *paradosis*, "transmission,"—which is to say they in fact pass on the "traditional teaching,"—they have authority and validity. Hence councils cannot control the truth of Christ, but they can and may strive to reach it; for that reason the Spirit of Christ has been given to the bishops and the council participants, as it has to every Christian as well.

It may be historically understandable that people later tried to upgrade the councils theologically with their own authority and acceptance. With the aid of various *"theologoumena,"* Nicaea was later grandly stylized into a gathering of martyrs and confessors. Nicaea saw the affirmation of a *"sententia divina,"* the "inspiration" of the council or of Emperor Constantine, who had convened the council; the presence of Jesus at the council; finally, in particular, the application of the mystical (but not historical) number 381 to the Fathers of Nicaea . . .

Here we have to stay theologically sober. In view of these later mystical and juridical *Byzantine "upgrading of councils,"* and then especially in view of both the *specifically Roman* concepts that have clearly prevailed since the fifth-century popes and the *Roman-Catholic* dogmas promulgated at Vatican I, we must hold fast to the classic orthodox and Catholic notion of councils. And from this it follows that all statements by the Fathers of the Church and the councils always have to be measured critically against the original Christian message. Nowadays a historico-critical exegesis of Scripture demands a *historico-critical patrology.* The original biblical witness to Jesus, the New Testament, must remain the *norma normans* (normative norm) for all postbiblical traditions. These traditions—and especially their binding conciliar declarations—can certainly likewise acquire a normative character, but by their very nature only in a derivative way, as a norm that has itself been shaped *(norma normata)* by the Gospel.

7. Yes to the Bible, Tradition, and Authority; No to Biblicism, Traditionalism, and Authoritarianism

For the sake of providing an unambiguous foundation for my argument I shall once more define precisely the position of an ecumenical theology that attempts to integrate in a critical-constructive fashion the legacy of Protestantism, Orthodoxy, and Catholicism. Each confession should preserve what is good in its own tradition, but it should overcome its sectarian limitations and accept what is good in the other confessions:

a) With *Protestant theology* we must affirm the *Bible as the permanent and unshakable basis* for any ecumenical, truly Christian theology. The Bible has a lasting normative authority and importance as the written expression, acknowledged by the entire Church, of the original, foundational witness of Jesus Christ.

A Yes to the Bible, then, but—along with many Protestant theologians—an equally decisive No to the sort of biblicism that makes an idol of the literal text and rejects all criticism of the Bible as unevangelical, for the sake of a supposedly Protestant orthodoxy. The Protestant theologian too has not only the right but the duty to distinguish between testimonies that are clear and less clear, stronger and weaker, original and derivative, central and peripheral, lucid and obscure, testimonies that for all they have in common can diverge, contrast, and partially contradict one another.

Protestant theologians too—but others as well—thus have the right and the duty to do conscientious *biblical criticism:* textual and literary criticism, historical and theological criticism. This will not weaken the authority of the Bible, but make its light shine out anew.

b) With *orthodox theology* we must *respect biblical tradition:* Christian truth, as it lives on in the Church, as the Church in former times, often in great distress, tried to protect it with boundary posts and danger signs, confessions and definitions; the Christian truth that our fathers and mothers, brothers and sisters long studied and taught in theology, but that continues to live not only in the decisions of the councils and the writing of the theologians, but also in the everyday preaching of our pastors and lay people, in the liturgy, in the sacraments, and, especially, in the lived, practical witness of individual Christians and communities at the grass-roots level.

A Yes to tradition, then, but—along with many orthodox theologians—an equally decisive No to the *traditionalism* that idolizes tradition and rejects every criticism of it as unorthodox. The orthodox theologian, too, has the right and the duty to monitor, with as much precision as possible, tradition as taught and lived in preaching, theology, liturgy, and church discipline, with an eye not only to continuity but also to discontinuity, and to distinguish between clear and less clear, powerful and weak, good and bad interpretations of the Christian message: to distinguish between

— a development *in keeping with the Gospel* (*evolutio secundum evangelium*), which deserves to be encouraged (e.g., the formation of the episcopate, of synods),

— a development *outside the Gospel* (*evolutio praeter evangelium*), which can be tolerated (e.g., certain liturgical vestments, instruments, customs), and finally

— a development *contrary to the Gospel* (*evolutio contra evangelium*), which must be condemned (e.g., any sort of paternalism, clericalism, or triumphalism).

In this process the theologian will also take seriously the binding, broadly accepted prescription of outstanding historical importance by the ecumenical councils—especially the joint ecumenical councils of Nicaea and Chalcedon—and to give a critical account of them according to the norm of the New Testament message. Every "principle of tradition" must allow the "principle of Scripture" to take precedence over it and provide its justification.

Orthodox theologians—but surely others too—have the right and the duty to do a nuanced *critique of tradition:* criticism of dogmas, theology, church structures, and liturgy. This does not weaken the authority of tradition, but purifies it and shows it once more to good advantage.

c) With *Catholic theology* we must respect the *authority of the Church:* the pastoral authority of the Church's leadership on the local, regional, and world level; in particular the authority—to the extent that one is doing ecumenical theology as a Catholic theologian—of the bishops, including the bishop of Rome. Their "magisterium" too can have a meaningful function in the Church, if it understands its role as one of pastoral preaching, exercised according to the norm of the Gospel, and if it recognizes its own functional limits, especially with regard to theological scholarship.

A Yes, then, to authority, but—along with many Catholic theologians—an equally decisive No to the sort of *churchly authoritarianism* that makes an idol of authority and rejects and suppresses as uncatholic all criticism of authority, for the sake of a supposed Catholic orthodoxy. Instead of speaking concretely of the pope and the bishops, people then use the abstract, anonymous term "magisterium": a word that has no basis either in Scripture or in ancient tradition, that presupposes the fully unbiblical distinction between the teaching Church (*Ecclesia docens*) and the learning Church (*Ecclesia discens*), and that was introduced for the first time in the nineteenth century in connection with the doctrine of infallibility proclaimed by Vatican I.

Catholic theologians too have the right and duty to engage in *public criticism of the Church:* They have the duty candidly and clearly to announce their valid objections and, if need be, like Paul to "resist Peter to his face," if in official preaching, in textbooks and catechisms, encyclicals and pastoral letters, and, generally speaking, in the pastoral care and religious life of the community and of individuals the biblical accents are consciously or unconsciously displaced, the original proportions are distorted, and thus the peripheral things are pushed to the center and the central things to the periphery; if, in other words, Christian truth is covered up or forgotten by the church authorities themselves, and their own errors and half-truths are ignored, denied, or even widely disseminated. The theologian here will continually call attention everywhere and with every means available to the main point, the "hierarchy of truths," the "center of Scripture," and in this way will try to raise the subject of the message of Jesus Christ in a way that is both comprehensive and discriminating. This will not bury the authority of the Church, but present it in a new, credible form.

8. What Christians Believe In

What, then, do Christians actually believe in? What is the basis of Christian faith? Is it the Church, Tradition, or the Bible? Answer: It is neither the Church nor Tradition nor the Bible:

— Even the Protestant Christian does not believe in the Bible, but in the one to whom the Bible bears witness.

— Even the Orthodox Christian does not believe in Tradition, but in the one whom Tradition hands down.

— Even the Catholic Christian does not believe in the Church, but in the one whom the Church proclaims.

— The unconditionally reliable reality, to which men and women can hold fast for all time and eternity, is not the Bible texts and not the Fathers of the Church, nor the Church's magisterium, but *God himself, as he spoke for believers through Jesus Christ.* The texts of the Bible, the sayings of the Fathers and church authorities mean to be—with varying degrees of importance—no more and no less than an expression of this belief.

Thus Jesus as God's Christ remains Lord over the Church's authority, over Tradition, and the Scriptures. The Bible itself, however, insofar as it bears witness to Jesus Christ, is the source and measure of faith and theology in the Church: *norma normans non normata.* It is Jesus Christ himself who constitutes the spiritual power of Scripture, which can again and again win respect and recognition for itself: for all the limitations and liability to error of our exegesis, theology, and preaching, of decisions by the councils and pronouncements by the magisterium. Therefore Christians do not believe, so to speak, *first* in the authority of the Church, of Tradition, or of Scripture, and *then* in the truth of the Gospel, in Jesus Christ, and in God, his Father. Christians believe rather in the Jesus originally attested to in Scripture, in the Christ, in God himself. Anyone who experiences Scripture this way, as the Gospel in faith, becomes certain that the Bible is interpenetrated and filled with the Spirit, that it is truly "inspired." Jesus, the Christ of God, and through him God himself, is the basis of faith.

In this sense we can also speak of *the truth* in the Church. Ultimately truth in the Church means, above and beyond all true propositions, the truth as it is regarded in the Old and New Testament, where the term "truth" (Hebrew *emeth,* Greek *aletheia*) means *fidelity,* constancy, reliability. The fidelity, that is, of the God of the covenant to his word and to his promise. There is not a single passage in Scripture that says Scripture contains no errors. Nowhere is the Church's magisterium or a council guaranteed that it could be or remain without error. But on the strength of the witness of Scripture Christians can be sure of the fidelity of their God, who will never become a liar, who remains true to himself and his word and so to the human race as well, who in the end made his word definitively true by fulfilling all God's words in the one Word: in him who is "the Word" and "the truth" (John 1:1–2; 14:6).[4]

III

Schism Because
of the Bible?

---

*On the Problem of the Unity
of Scripture and the Church*

Thus far we have discussed two connected series of problems: Scripture, Tradition, and the Church on the one hand; Scripture and revelation on the other. I argued that we should take Scripture seriously as the *norma normans non normata,* in dialogue with Tradition but against all traditionalism; that we should understand Scripture as a witness to revelation, but against all fundamentalism and biblicism. In the following section we shall go one logical step further and ask: How is Scripture itself to be understood, how is it to be interpreted? And so the question of *understanding Scripture* arises. What role do we assign to the discipline of expounding Scripture—exegesis—in relation to the discipline that systematically ponders the contents of faith—dogmatics?

The question that we only hinted at in the previous chapter returns now in all earnestness: If the New Testament displays a high degree of variability and even contradictoriness, how can it claim to be the *norm of the Church,* how can it be the *basis of church unity?* The Tübingen professor of New Testament and student of Bultmann, *Ernst Käsemann,* dealt with this problem as early as the end of the 1950s in his famous essay, "Is the Unity of the Church Grounded in the New Testament Canon?" I responded to Käsemann as a Catholic theologian joining in reflection from the school of Karl Barth on the position of the Protestant dogmatic theologian from Tübingen, Hermann Diem.[1] It would make no sense to pick up the thread of that discussion about early Catholicism once more. That is why I have shortened the following remarks by dropping those passages. I am concentrating here on the problem—raised by the New Testament itself—of the variety and unity of the testimony of Scripture. This is an issue that confronts every exegete: not least of all with regard to the unity of the Church.

1. Is the Unity of the Church Grounded in the New Testament Canon?: Ernst Käsemann

Ernst Käsemann asked this question pointedly, and just as pointedly answered no.[2] Käsemann adduces three reasons that he documents with a great many examples, which I can only hint at:

a) *The variability of the New Testament* kerygma *itself:* According to Käsemann, the most obvious sign of this variability is the fact that the New Testament canon offers not one Gospel, but four, all of which "differ considerably in their order, selection, and presentation" and this not only because of the various peculiar features of the four evangelists, not only because of the various traditions used in each case, but in particular because of the "various theological-dogmatic attitudes of the evangelists."[3] Hence Jesus is seen differently from the point of view of the exalted *Kyrios,* who is the object of faith.[4] Likewise the common confession of Jesus' divine sonship is given different interpretations, depending on the theological bias of the source.[5] Given this state of affairs, the evangelists can also freely criticize one another.[6]

b) *The extraordinary abundance of theological positions (which spills over into the New Testament) in ancient Christianity:* The Scriptures of the New Testament canon pose "an immense abundance of unsolved and in part probably unsolvable historical and theological problems."[7] This is due, on the one hand, to the "fragmentary character" of our knowledge of the history and preaching of ancient Christendom.[8] For example, it is precisely on account of the great mass of different traditions that we find it extraordinarily difficult to trace the authentic tradition about Jesus in the New Testament.[9] That is due, on the other hand, to the "conversational character" of most of the statements in the New Testament: They don't make up any sort of summa of *"dicta probantia"* (sayings that establish some point); rather they aim to answer concrete questions, to admonish and comfort concrete persons, and to fend off concrete errors.[10] They assume definite premises and leave many sorts of conclusions open. The voices that make themselves heard in the New Testament canon form "a vanishing minority, as compared with the numerous voices that carried on the message but left behind no written record and thus no permanent memory. What entitles us to assume that these many others could say and did say nothing different from the New Testament writers?"[11] The New Testament canon reproduces for us "only snatches of the conversation that went on in ancient Christendom."[12]

c) *The partially manifest incompatibility of the theological positions in the New Testament:* The variability in the New Testament texts is so great "that we have to confirm the presence not just of considerable tensions but often too of irreconcilable theological contradictions."[13] This holds first for the Gospels and all the more for the rest of the New Testament writings.[14] As early as the Gospels we see not just a continuity but a separation between Jesus and his disciples: "Even the oldest community partly understands and partly misunderstands. It at once attests to and obscures the sublimity of its Lord. Its faith too was contained in the clay vessels of its humanity, and its orthodoxy was just as doubtful as orthodoxy always is."[15]

From these three circumstances Käsemann draws his unmistakable conclusion: "The New Testament canon as such does not establish the unity of the Church. As such, that is, as the historian now has access to it, it establishes, on the contrary, the multiplicity of confessions."[16]

All the various present-day churches appeal to the New Testament canon—rightly; for even back in ancient Christendom there was an abundance of different confessions alongside, together with, and opposed to one another.

Is Käsemann, then, proposing an Enlightenment sort of religious indifferentism? On the contrary, he argues for *the discernment of spirits.* "We shall have to bear in the mind the solidarity and difference between the letter and the spirit. What Paul brought out in 2 Cor 3 vis-à-vis the Old Testament should not be limited to the Old Testament. It holds every bit as much for the New Testament canon."[17] For in the New Testament canon too one doesn't have God in custody; taken in its mere facticity, as the letter that kills, the New Testament canon is no longer the word of God. It becomes and is this only when through the letter (which must be unraveled just as soberly) the Spirit manifests itself and leads the way to all truth in a way that is always new and contemporary. Only in the canon understood according to the Spirit does God address us and manifest himself in the present. This means, "that the canon is not simply identical to the Gospel, and is God's word only insofar as it is and becomes Gospel. Then and to that extent it also establishes the unity of the Church. For the one Church in all times and places is based on the Gospel alone."[18]

This, then, is what the discernment of spirits means: understanding Scripture from the standpoint of their objective center, from the perspective of the message that it expresses.[19] That is, critical understanding of the Scripture from the standpoint of the "Gospel," which must not be separated from Scripture nor simply identified with it. It is essential to make this center our point of departure, and to tread the centrist path of reform between fanatical enthusiasm on the Left (in which camp the Protestant Enlightenment must be reckoned), which seeks to take possession of the Gospel by stepping right over Scripture, and Catholic traditionalism on the Right (where Protestant orthodoxy by and large belongs), which imagines that the Gospel is simply present and available in Scripture, without continually measuring Scripture against the critical authority of the Gospel. Scripture and Gospel, canon and Gospel, stand in a dialectical tension, which for Protestant theology implies a lasting responsibility: constant fresh reflection on the Gospel in Scripture, which gives this Scripture (in itself only a venerable historical document) its authority for the believer.[20]

What is the "Gospel," as Käsemann sees it? He thinks that the historian alone cannot answer this question, but only the believer, to the extent that he is transported by the Spirit and listens to Scripture. The believer hears the Gospel that reveals itself to him, reaches him as *justification of the sinner.* The justification of the sinner is the center of Scripture: "The Bible is neither God's word in the objective sense, nor a dogmatic system, but the expression of the history and preaching of ancient Christendom. Nevertheless, the Church, which laid down its canon, asserts that in just this way she is the upholder of the Gospel. She asserts this because she sees the history that has been recorded and now reveals itself here as located under the aspect of the justification of the sinner, and can assert that only in this respect.

But since her assertion is testimony and confession, at the same time she calls upon us to place ourselves with our own history likewise under the process of the justification of the sinner. Thereby we are led to decide not only whether or not we wish to accept this last, but likewise whether such a confession rightly grasps the center of Scripture."[21]

So that is Käsemann's answer to the question, "Is the unity of the Church grounded in the New Testament canon?" It is an answer that attests to the deep seriousness and radical honesty of this exegete. It would be false and unfair to look upon the saliently destructive criticism here as Käsemann's real purpose, as certain inquisitorial brethren have done (the Protestants have their inquisition too). Opening himself to the power of the Gospel is the central concern of this theologian, who has proved the temper of his Protestant faith not only in long years of service as a pastor but in persecution as well. His experiences in the Confessing Church are likely the reason why Käsemann distinguished himself in the Bultmann school by his interest in ecclesiology.[22] There his theological interest lay not in the multiplicity of denominations but in the unity of the Church—the unity, of course, that rests on the Gospel and can never be found as such, but is present only to faith: "The unity of the Church, like the Gospel, is confessed not by the *beati possidentes* but by those attacked and unsecured in and despite the denominations, with and also contrary to the New Testament canon, insofar as they are the people who hear and believe the Gospel."[23]

But can we be satisfied with Käsemann's answer? Voices were raised in opposition among serious Protestant groups as well. In a book entitled *The Unity of Scripture*, Tübingen Protestant theologian Hermann Diem sought to fashion not just an important section of his dogmatic theology, but an argument against Käsemann.[24]

2. The Dispute over Unity: Hermann Diem

The systematic theologian Hermann Diem has sympathy for the question raised by his colleagues in New Testament studies. He also to a large extent affirms Käsemann's answer. Because this much is certain for Diem: The writings collected in the New Testament canon do not form any sort of "doctrinal unit."[25] It was not the Reformers, but only the Lutheran and Reformed denominational churches, that taught the doctrinal unity of Scripture, a doctrinal system of statements from Scripture; plucked, that is, from the whole Scripture, whether in a more biblicist or more dogmatic fashion. These same churches understood the Bible as a "principle" and "sum" of theology instead of as a text for preaching, and they logically asserted the literal inspiration and divinity of Scripture. They were the first ones who were not content with the actual givenness of the scriptural canon, but taught that it was, as a matter of principle, closed. Preaching and faith suffered as a result.[26]

Hence, Diem says, we should gladly welcome the fact that historico-critical scholarship has forced the Church and theology to scrutinize its teaching on Scripture. For the present stage of the discussion, "It is significant that the New Testament historians who have become especially active on this subject today cannot be viewed so easily as outside intruders in theology, as it may have been sensible to assume in the past. The reason is simply that New Testament scholarship today, on the basis of its research findings, generally stresses the *kerygmatic character* of the New Testament writings, and thereby stands by the Reformers and confirms their use of Scripture. In addition, their main objection against the prevailing use of Scripture *is the dogmatic patronizing of exegesis;* thus it starts off exactly at the point where we observed the falling off from the Reformation to old Protestant dogmatics. Hence it will be necessary in any case to examine whether the Reformers' use of Scripture has not been better preserved here than by the post-Reformation dogmatic theologians."[27]

But as resolutely as Diem defends the thesis "There is no integrated New Testament doctrinal system," Käsemann argues just as resolutely that *"there is no canon in the canon."* Here is where Diem's conflict with Käsemann breaks out into the open, or rather once again we can see the conflict that is immanent in the churches of the Reformation and can be observed in every phase of their history.

"Käsemann has trenchantly spelled out what many New Testament scholars opposed to the post-Reformation dogmatic theologians have thought of as the new solution to the problem of the canon: *Acquiring a canon within the canon with the help of justification as a hermeneutical standard.* This is basically no new contribution, just an appeal to *Luther,* who wanted Scripture to be measured by what in it "does Christ" *(Christum treibt),* by which he ultimately meant *sola gratia* and *sola fide* as well. The scholars who make this appeal think they have gotten back to the Reformers' use of Scripture before it was corrupted by old Protestant dogmatics? Are they right?"[28] According

to Diem they are not. The justification of the sinner, to be sure, is no
doctrine but a process, in which justification in Christ is awarded to
the hearer through the preaching of the Gospel. But if Käsemann
demands that we place ourselves with our own history under the
process of the justification of the sinner, then Diem asks "whether he
[Käsemann] actually faces and can face this kerygmatic history, or
whether he doesn't necessarily paralyze the obligatory nature of the
process that begins to affect him when the Scripture is proclaimed, by
the very fact that he makes it into a history that is not binding on him
until he has approved it after critical examination."[29]

Kerygmatic history has to be taken seriously as a binding process,
precisely because the effective limits of the canon, which the Church
recognizes, have been taken into account: "This process of kerygmatic history, which has binding power over us, consists in the fact
that the Church has heard the word of God exclusively in the proclamation of these testimonies, and we therefore are likewise to go on
proclaiming and hearing it exclusively through these testimonies.
*One can only acknowledge this fact, as a matter of principle one can
in no way justify it. The* only *theological justification that is* possible
here *consists in that one makes appropriate use of the scriptural
canon by preaching it while trusting in its self-evident character.* In
this actual *use* of Scripture also lies its only possible theological *demarcation from church* tradition. And with that we are back with the
Reformation."[30]

Only against this background, says Diem, can the unity of Scripture be rightly viewed. It lies not in an integrated body of teaching,
but in the self-evident character of the proclaimed Scripture, in
whose testimonies Jesus Christ proclaims himself and as such is heard
by the Church.[31] There are considerable differences, to be sure, between the individual witnesses within the unity of the New Testament *kerygma.* These differences result from the different *kerygmatic situation* of each one: The testimonies given in the New
Testament are those of specific persons in specific situations with
specific goals.[32] Reorganizing, extending, and recreating the message
would become imperative then, just as it becomes imperative today
to translate those testimonies afresh into the language of the contemporary kerygmatic situation. The concrete kerygmatic situation can
demand that, in a given situation, given witnesses will be preferred
and others set aside. In doing this, however, we have to heed the
limits of the canon, which make us acknowledge even the witnesses

that have been set aside as authentic witnesses of Christ's message: "The whole point here is that the evaluation *based on the situation* does not turn into one *based on principle*, in other words that the canon of Scripture is the *text* that at all events must remain intact, whereas all our attempts at explaining it are only *commentaries*, which, with all their constantly changing findings, cannot supersede the text."[33] Just because of this the canon has not only a prohibitive but also, and in the first instance, a positive meaning: It protects the interpreter from his own arbitrary whims.[34]

Thus Diem agrees with Käsemann that Scripture is not a unified doctrinal system, but disagrees with him in clinging to the unity of Scripture as proclaimed, so as to make that his vantage point for understanding—despite all the arbitrary thinking of individual interpreters—the unity of the Church. It must be acknowledged that all through his work Diem takes highly unusual pains for a systematic theologian to confront the problems posed by present-day exegesis. He does this not in a predominantly apologetic fashion but while making a thoroughly constructive evaluation of many of the results of that exegesis. One of his central concerns is to bridge the contemporary gap between exegesis and dogmatic theology.

But, unless I am mistaken, Diem's and Käsemann's basic theological principles stand in irreconcilable opposition. Just as for Käsemann Diem's "canon" will never become the "Gospel," so for Diem Käsemann's "Gospel" will never become the "canon." As their Catholic colleague I can scarcely do anything to reconcile them, though perhaps I can help to clarify their positions. I shall now try to do this— and only this—in a brief space.

3. Narrowing the Area
of Discussion: Agreements

a) Where can the Catholic theologian, if he does not simply side-step the results of modern exegesis, agree with *Ernst Käsemann?* He can assent in the following ways:

   (1) with respect to the fact that the New Testament canon is not unified;

   (2) with respect to the factors that determine this absence of unity: the variability of the New Testament *kerygma* itself, which is rooted not only in the peculiar features of the evan-

gelists and of the traditions they use, but in their different theological attitudes; the abundance of theological positions, which spill over into the New Testament, in ancient Christendom. Such abundance makes our knowledge on this subject (including the conversational character of most of the testimony in the New Testament) appear extremely fragmentary; the partially manifest differences, which cannot be simply harmonized away, between the various theological positions both in the Gospels and in the rest of the New Testament;

(3) with respect to listening in faith to the "Gospel" that justifies the sinner (understanding that Gospel according to the spirit, not the letter, with an eye on its center) within the non-unified New Testament canon.

b) Where can the Catholic theologian, taking into consideration the points we have just conceded to Käsemann, agree with *Hermann Diem?* He can assent in the following ways:

(1) with respect to rejection of a New Testament doctrinal system. Because the New Testament was never intended to be a *summa theologiae,* we must reject any harmonization of the texts that dissolves the differences in a violent manner. The *summa theologiae* sort of approach is as unsuitable to the New Testament as lecture-demonstrations of the *dicta probantia* instead of the transmission in preaching, as personal witness, of the testimony from the New Testament; that is why faith is not simply directed to a divine Scripture, but, on the basis of the Scripture that is proclaimed, to the Lord Jesus Christ and his God and Father, to whom it attests;

(2) with respect to the meaning of the kerygmatic situation. This in two senses: That the testimonies of the New Testament derive from different people in different situations with different theological-dogmatic purposes, and those testimonies must be readdressed to different people with different purposes in different situations, must be transmitted from the ancient kerygmatic situation into the new one; that a translation of the New Testament *kerygma* is possible in which from case to case different testimonies and aspects can stand in the foreground and others in the background;

(3) with respect to the facticity of the New Testament canon and of its unity: The unity of Scripture cannot be derived from some logical, systematic consistency; it is rather a de facto given. The Church has heard the word of God in the proclamation of precisely these testimonies—and no others; and she passes on these testimonies in her preaching, likewise exclusively, as the word of God.

Only when we dare, in theological controversy, to see the agreement with our interlocutor sympathetically and without fear, not denying that we do agree (with theologians, as with politicians, fear of consensus is often greater than fear of disagreement), will we be able to concentrate the discussion on the actual points of controversy. And these do not lie in the doctrine of justification, nor—as people artificially try to construe the issue—in Christology or pneumatology, but in ecclesiology. Questions concerning the Church are the only ones— for the time being, at least—where the disputants are fighting tooth and nail. And so it is precisely here that ecumenically minded theology has the responsibility to seek for new, constructive solutions— even if the first step in this direction is pointed confrontation.

4. The Reason for the Multiplicity of Confessions: Selection

The New Testament canon forms the prerequisite for the multiplicity of confessions and denominations. Käsemann has to be granted that much; because (1) there is a variety of Christian confessions, (2) the different Christian confessions appeal to the New Testament canon and trace back their roots to that canon, (3) these different appeals to the New Testament canon have a *fundamentum in re,* that is, a basis in the number, complexity, and contradictoriness of the theological positions in the New Testament canon itself. To that extent, then, the New Testament canon forms the prerequisite for the multiplicity of confessions.

But, assuming the non-integrated state of the canon, how does the multiplicity of confessions come into being? This question is not answered simply by pointing to the disunity of the canon. Because, for all its disunity, the New Testament canon is nevertheless *one* and has been evidently received as *one* by the Church—in a history that was, to be sure, extraordinarily checkered. In the course of it the different testimonies have been understood not only as, say, an instructive, negative study in contrasts with the Gospel, but as a positively appropriate expression and reflection of the Gospel. The question, therefore, is How, with this New Testament canon that is, despite all its disunity, *one,* did the multiplicity of confessions come about? There is no getting around the answer: through *choice.* That is, Christians did not take seriously the *one* New Testament canon (one despite all its disunity) and strive for a *comprehensive* understanding of it—for all the difficulties standing in the way. Rather they used the disunity of the one canon to make a selection from it. In this way one can achieve under certain circumstances an imposing concentration of the *kerygma,* but at the same time a reduction of this *kerygma,* which takes place at the expense of the New Testament and the unity of the Church standing behind this canon.

What is the meaning of this fundamental renunciation of a comprehensive understanding and a serious consideration of the *whole* New Testament in favor of a concentrated *selection?* It comes down to a fundamental renunciation of "Catholicity" in understanding Scripture in favor of "heresy" (from *hairein,* to take or choose). Strictly speaking, one must say, therefore, that the New Testament canon is in its disunity certainly a *prerequisite,* an *occasion* of the multiplicity of confessions, but not in the precise sense the *grounds* or *cause.* The inflammable material, the wooden framework that supports a house, can indeed be the prerequisite and occasion for the burning of the house; but the cause of the fire is the arsonist who sets the match to the wood. The actual cause of the multiplicity of confessions is not the New Testament canon, which, when understood in the Catholic manner (*kath'olou,* according to the whole) in its unity, is the prerequisite for the unity of the *ekklesia,* but *hairesis* (choosing), which dissolves the unity of the Church.[35] Choice in interpreting the New Testament is possible in two ways: in principle (Käsemann) or in fact (Diem).

The choice of applying to New Testament interpretation a formal hermeneutical standard that at the same time proves to be a material standard of selection is one made *in principle.* This sort of choice is the kind Ernst Käsemann himself makes. Needless to say, Käsemann doesn't want simply to eliminate certain texts or books from the New Testament canon. Instead they are to remain in the canon and to be taken seriously in their own way. In that sense Käsemann does not propose making a choice. But he does wish to "discern" the spirits of the New Testament. He applies the Pauline "discernment of spirits" —which Paul himself never applied to the (Old Testament) canon—to the (New Testament) canon, to discriminate not between the different good spirits or good witnesses (those recognized by the Church through the canon), but between good and *evil* spirits even in the New Testament—with anecdotical references to the uncertainty and questionableness of everything human. Käsemann will not listen to the "Gospel" from the New Testament spirits that have been declared evil. He hears the "Gospel" only in the testimonies that he has acknowledged as "good spirits." In that sense Käsemann does propose making a choice. In this manner he reaches a middle way between "enthusiasm" and early Catholicism. As a matter of principle the only testimonies in the New Testament he takes seriously *in a positive sense* are those that are and can be "Gospel," that herald the "justification of the sinner." This means renouncing in principle—even if one is unwilling to speak of "a principle"—catholicity in the understanding of Scripture.

But here the Protestant exegete is disavowed by the Protestant dogmatic theologian: Hermann Diem reproaches Käsemann for "necessarily paralyzing [the New Testament's kerygmatic process] by the very fact that he makes it into a history that is not binding on him until he has approved it in critical examination."[36] To be sure, Käsemann is not concerned with the *doctrine* of justification (not, that is, with an "object of faith," a "fundamental dogma," a theological "principle"), but with the *process* of justification; and this can be announced not only in the *Letter to the Romans* or *Galatians,* but also, for example, in a logion of Jesus, in a Beatitude, etc. In *every* testimony that supports the justification of the sinner we are dealing with "Gospel." But it is certain that we are not dealing with "Gospel" in the *whole* New Testament, and that he himself can tell where we are not. In contrast, Diem argues that the Church stood then and stands now behind the New Testament canon, "that the Church has heard the word of God exclusively in the proclamation of these testimonies, and we therefore are likewise to go on proclaiming and hearing it exclusively through these testimonies . . . [The] fact of the canon attests that the Church has actually and unanimously heard the kerygma of Jesus Christ in these testimonies, and that therefore we can and should hear them there too."[37] No doubt, certain testimonies contained in the New Testament may and ought to be evaluated situationally, with some being preferred and some set aside.[38] "But with every such situational evaluation of the individual witnesses the *limits* set by the fact of the canon must be observed. These demand the recognition that even the witness we set aside delivered—in his historically conditioned way, for how else was he supposed to do it?—testimony about Jesus, and for that reason found a hearing in the Church, which means that he spoke as one inspired by the Holy Spirit."[39] Without the tie to the canon the exegete falls victim to "his own subjective arbitrariness, which always creates the danger that, instead of letting the texts speak in their own concrete individuality, he will do violence to their historical uniqueness through a preconceived principle of interpretation, and for that very reason, he will miss them in their testimonial character as a text for preaching."[40]

Naturally, Käsemann would defend himself against the charge of subjective arbitrariness. He does not choose on his own but as he has been touched by the "Gospel." There is no objection to be made against defining a "center" of the Gospel. But we must ask: How does Käsemann explain that he is touched only by these texts and not by others, that he can hear only these texts and not others as "Gospel." This can undoubtedly not be explained on this basis of the New Testament; because even Käsemann says that the New Testament signifies more than just *his* "Gospel." Nor simply on the basis of "exegetical findings," according to which the "Pauline middle course" might be said to impose itself as "Gospel." Because the question is precisely why Käsemann can see only this "middle course" as "Gospel." Can Käsemann invoke more than some kind of Protestant pre-understanding (perhaps unconsciously occasioned by philosophical premises or by a not very credible presentation of the role of Catholicism in history)? Or, more profoundly, can he invoke some final option, in which one perhaps rather finds oneself (Luther's tradition) than places oneself? Then is there in any case a decision *before* one does any exegesis? Isn't that a position in which one can scarcely cite more reasons that would prevent somebody else from choosing a *different* option, and making the exegetical discovery of a *different* center and a *different* Gospel on the basis of a *different* pre-understanding? Once we have abandoned the catholicity of the New Testament, we can no longer appeal to it as a *whole*.

What is left is—against the will of those who practice it—nonetheless a more or less large degree of arbitrariness: "For Luther this center, from which he judged everything, was doubtless Paul or, still more narrowly, his teaching on justification. On the other hand, for

Luther the Gospel according to John was the only 'tender right chief Gospel.' Friedrich Schleiermacher likewise judged and defended this same Gospel to be the essential Gospel on account of its spiritual content. In historico-critical theology at the beginning of this century the "words of the Lord" in the Synoptic Gospels were the standard of authenticity. For Rudolf Bultmann, John's Gospel is definitely the testimony of the valid Gospel as a Gospel of the Word alone and of existential decision in the present—once what are presumably later additions by the Church on the sacraments and future eschatology have been removed. Shouldn't we rather, instead of measuring the New Testament against this sort of norm, measure the critical norm against the riches of the New Testament and accordingly confer on it at best a relative right?" (K. H. Schelkle).[41]

The bold program of establishing "a canon in the canon" demands simply that one be more biblical than the Bible, more New Testamental than the New Testament, more evangelical than the evangelists, and even more Pauline than Paul. Radical seriousness is the intention, radical disintegration is the consequence. As opposed to all *hairesis,* which in its self-absolutizing involuntarily turns into *hybris,* the *catholic* attitude seeks to preserve for itself complete openness and freedom for the *whole* of the New Testament. This often seems less consistent and imposing than the powerfully one-sided creation of a *single* line. Paul alone can under certain circumstances strike us as more consistent and imposing than the whole quite varied New Testament, and the Pauline Paul (purified from sacramentalism and mysticism) again affects us as more consistent and imposing than the whole Paul. But the real Paul is the whole Paul, and the real New Testament is the whole New Testament.

5. Evangelical Catholicity as an Imperative

The catholic stance is to be open on principle in all directions. This liberates the New Testament, excluding no line of thought, whether as a matter of principle or of fact, that is in it. The catholic attitude tries to take the New Testament seriously, without bias, viewing it from all sides. It tries to be catholic, open, and free for the whole, comprehensive truth of the New Testament. The Catholic Church has often been called a *complexio oppositorum* (combination of opposites), in the bad sense, by people who mistook the Church's nastiness (a Church made up of human beings, and sinful ones too) with her nature (a holy Church in the Holy Spirit). But what was often thought of as a reproach can also have a good sense: Käsemann has pointed out that the New Testament itself is a *complexio oppositorum.* The Catholic Church, in other words, has a New Testament orientation when it tries to embrace the *opposita* (not all of them, but those that belong to the New Testament) in a good sense and to understand the *whole* New Testament as Gospel.

The disastrous thing about Käsemann's theology is not that it accepts a "center of Scripture" (however that may be more specifically defined), but that in Protestant exclusivity it makes the "center" the "whole," and eliminates everything else through the "discernment of spirits." The disastrous thing about Diem's theology is not that it puts one or the other witness in the background, depending upon the concrete kerygmatic situation, but that in Protestant exclusivity it too doesn't let certain witnesses speak their entire piece and doesn't take their concerns seriously enough. Diem trivializes what Käsemann has established as the "early Catholic element" in the New Testament: understanding of church office, apostolic succession, ordination, doctrine, etc.

But before Catholics indulge in self-conscious, arrogant exultation over this state of affairs, they might consider the following: To be sure, only the catholic attitude can overcome the Protestant disintegration from the point of view of the Gospel. To be sure, catholicity in the interpretation of the New Testament is a wonderful program. But is it any more than a program? The saying, *"What is Catholic is evangelical,"* can get bogged down and remain a mere formula; in the critical situation of contemporary exegesis and dogmatics it can be understood as an inert, pacifying indicative instead of as an imperative demanding the carrying out of a program. My remarks are not designed to reassure Catholic theologians addressing the problems that have broken out in New Testament studies, but to challenge them to take the Catholic task decisively in hand. Merely *claiming* that what is Catholic is evangelical does not solve the extraordinarily difficult exegetical and dogmatic problems raised by the current state of New Testament research. The Catholic program has to prove its worth by thorough, serious, honest exegetical and dogmatic work that pushes its way into the countless individual questions at issue.

No one can maintain that we Catholics have set a sufficient example of catholicity in interpreting the New Testament. Which one of us would dare to say that we have given other Christians visible proof of that catholic freedom and openness to the whole New Testament? If we had, how would it have been possible for Catholic exegesis over the last centuries continually to find itself bringing up the rear behind Protestant exegesis? How could Catholic exegesis, for all practical purposes, continually take its problems, methods, and solutions from Protestant exegesis? How is it that fundamental exegetical works such as the *New Testament Dictionary (Wörterbuch zum Neuen Testament)* are mostly the product of Protestant exegesis? One should avoid reproaching individual Catholic exegetes on this score. No one would argue that Catholic exegetes are less intelligent or industrious than their colleagues. One thing for sure is that our exegetes were often not allowed full Catholic freedom and openness for dealing with the whole New Testament.[42] Exegesis and dogmatics can meet their great Catholic responsibility not in an atmosphere of anxiety, of totalitarian supervision, and the hypocrisy and cowardice that result from it, but only in an atmosphere of freedom, of sober theological integrity and undaunted objectivity and, precisely because of this, of loyal attachment to the Church.

It also cannot be said that we Catholics have given a sufficiently credible demonstration of catholicity in the interpretation of New Testament ecclesiology. There is no disputing the fact that Catholic ecclesiology, as early as the Middle Ages and especially during the Counter-Reformation greatly overvalued the Pastoral Letters (and the Acts of the Apostles), at the expense of the more charismatically structured community code of the great Pauline Letters. In this way it largely transformed ecclesiology into hierarchology. Even today we are weighed down by this legacy, and the problems to be solved are numerous.[43]

It is, of course, a great deal harder for an exegete to take the *whole* seriously rather than only a part. This is true not only because *every* theologian as a person is in danger of not hearing in the New Testament precisely what he should be hearing, but because for this Catholic path the high exegetical art of differentiation and tracing nuances is especially required. Thus:

— on the one hand there should be no *harmonization and leveling* of contrary statements on ecclesiology in the New Testament out of a systematic search for convenience, which is too lazy to get to the bottom of the various contradictions;

— on the other hand there should be no *dissociation and reduction* of these statements out of a hypercritical attitude that gathers them and sets them in opposition to one another in a purely statistical fashion. This sort of approach finds more satisfaction in ferreting out contraries than in hunting down a deeper unity in the total context of the Scriptures, all of which intend to speak in some form or other about Jesus Christ and his Gospel. Every testimony contained in the New Testament is the expression of kerygmatic history, in which Jesus' message and deeds are handed down in manifold ways so that Jesus may be believed in as the Lord. That is why every ecclesiological testimony in the New Testament must be understood against the background of all of kerygmatic history, as well as from the standpoint of the specific kerygmatic situation that it addresses.

But then isn't Käsemann justified in his suspicion that the *final* Scripture* of this kerygmatic history interprets the whole previous history as a final testimony and thereby decisively defines it? It is true in the Catholic vision of things that this testimony has to be taken seriously too. As early Catholic material it provides the later Church with the necessary continuity between the Apostolic Church of the New Testament and the Church of the "Apostolic Fathers" and the ancient Church as a whole. Nevertheless this cannot mean that Peter's Second Letter has to determine the interpretation of the entire New Testament as *the* crucial Scripture. It is important to notice that we have in this Letter not simply an original testimony but a *derivative* one within the New Testament. Like, say, the Letter of Jude and the Letter of James, the Second Letter of Peter also presupposes other New Testament writings, and these again may presuppose others, such as this or that logion of Jesus. Each new kerygmatic situation compelled the continual reorganization and recreation of the original message, in which the human and theological peculiarities of each new author played a major part. Hence an antagonistic variety was naturally found within the New Testament, as we see in the characteristic fact that tradition has given us not just *one* Gospel or one harmony of the Gospels or even one life of Jesus, but different and often quite conflicting Gospels. But in this whole, complex (not just simple and straightforward) evolution, it is self-evident that the original testimonies take precedence over the *derivative* ones. In the New

* The Second Letter of Peter.

Testament we are *not* dealing with a sort of *Festschrift*, an anthology
of contributions with equal rights (even if not always of equal value).
In the message of the New Testament we are not dealing with a
message from a committee of writers, to which each writer furnishes
the result of his independent research, but with the message of Jesus
Christ, of which all later testimonies can be and aim at being simply
interpretations. Much as the derivative testimonies of New Testament must also be taken seriously, they must at the same time be
taken seriously *as* derivative and not as original. What is significant
here is not just the external temporal nearness to the message of Jesus,
but also the internal objective nearness to the center of the Gospel.
Beyond the temporal nearness, the Letter to the Romans, in comparison with the Letter of James, ought to be credited besides with a
greater objective nearness. The more derivative a testimony is, the
more both exegetes and dogmatic theologians will have to pay attention to the way this testimony deals with the process of salvation in
Jesus Christ: which factors are involved with each of the different
authors in each different kerygmatic situation, encouraging or ob-
structing, strengthening or weakening, intensifying or downplaying.
Thus every testimony in the entire New Testament must be understood from the perspective of Jesus' message and the original focal
points. Hence the later testimonies, such as the Pastoral Letters, must
not upstage the earlier ones, such as the Sermon on the Mount or the
Letter to the Corinthians.

It is the *Church* as the New Testament's people of God that has
handed down the New Testament in an admittedly checkered canon
history, but that means the New Testament as a *whole*. Without the
Church there would be no New Testament. In addition, the Church
was of the opinion that all the parts of the New Testament were
definitely incorporated into the canon as positive testimonies to the
Christ-event (and not just as partly negative programmatic contrasts).
To be sure, it was the early Catholic Church that passed the canon
down to us. But this early Catholic Church demonstrated its catholicity precisely in the fact that it did not exclude Paul, as it logically
should have had it to, were it the early Catholic Church that Protestant exegetes make it out to be. Rather it showed its catholicity by
raising to the canon Paul *and* the Acts of the Apostles, Paul *and* the
Letter of James, in short the *whole* New Testament. In doing so it was
engaging in the discernment of spirits. Catholic theology believes
that the Church did a good job of it and that we could not improve on

it today. The individual exegete cannot do his own discernment of spirits better than by trusting the discernment of spirits carried out by the ancient Church and continued by the later Church that transmitted to us the New Testament as such.

Today, too, the theologian's concrete relationship to the Church will in many cases determine whether he can or cannot accept the whole New Testament, as handed down and guaranteed by the Church, in a spirit that is both trusting and critical. We Catholics are convinced that we do well to join the ancient Church in looking upon the whole of the New Testament as a *fitting* testimony of the revelation event in Jesus Christ, and besides to accord each individual testimony genuine but differentiated acceptance depending upon its orientation to this salvation event in Christ, while taking each one seriously in the theological as well as the practical sense.

It is no accident, then, that in the Catholic faculty of Tübingen the words of the systematic theologian are not disavowed but confirmed by the exegete. "Catholic theology will naturally offer a different appraisal of the testimony of early Catholicism in the New Testament from that offered by Protestant theology. Is it possible to limit the true New Testament message to the one moment, indeed the mathematical point of, say, the Letter to the Romans or the (demythologized) Gospel according to John? In its entirety the New Testament witness to the comprehensive, that is, the catholic, truth lies in abundance. To allow only a part of it to count is choosing—that is, heresy. And if this New Testament in its later sections forms a transition to early Catholicism, then Catholic exegesis will take pains to show that with a truly historical understanding of the text what we have is not a perversion of the original truth, but an authentic and valid evolution. That will not be an obstacle to comparing later texts with earlier ones, to measure the former against the latter, just as all this is done by genuinely critical theology—including the Catholic kind" (K. H. Schelkle).[44]

Ecclesiology is an area where all arguments between Catholics and Protestants necessarily come to a head: Is there room here too for a path to reunion? Yes, there is. It consists in the increasingly serious effort by *Catholic theology* to read the New Testament with *Protestant concentration,* and by Protestant theology to read it with *Catholic breadth.* In this sense Catholics, who are often burdened by too much, and Protestants, who often suffer from having too little, can learn from and help one another. Isn't this at bottom what is happening today, despite all the disputes, again and again, with increasing clarity? The purpose of my remarks and the clear confrontation they delineated was not to close off a discussion, but to call attention as urgently as possible to the great common ecumenical task that lies beyond it. And is it not a hopeful sign that in Tübingen, after thoroughly arguing our case, we keep on sitting together in peace, harmony, and good humor?

6. Postscript 1986

Since the publication of these remarks (in 1962, before Vatican II) a lot of water has flowed down not just the Tiber, but the Neckar as well. The polemic of a young Catholic theologian against (likewise polemically framed) Protestant onesidedness, tightness, and exclusivity was, I should think, necessary. Today there would be many other things to say. In the last quarter century many issues have been settled, on both sides. In the meantime many things have been said differently. *The New Testament as Canon,* edited by Ernst Käsemann in 1970, provides documentation and a critical analysis relevant to the present discussion.[45] On the pages devoted to my article (reprinted in his book) from 1962, Käsemann rejects "doctrinaire purism" and any "principle of selection" with welcome clarity: "On the contrary, both as a historian and as a theologian I certainly recognize its symptoms in the introduction of ordination, the presbytery, the monarchical episcopate, and even control of doctrine out of the concrete kerygmatic situation in Diem's sense as necessary, understandable, and hence interpenetrated by the Spirit."[46]

For my part I gladly agree with Käsemann when he expects me to reject "every theory of legitimacy, so easily unmasked by the historian, in church discipline, . . . which makes a one-time imperative binding for all times, as well as every proposal in systematic theology that robs preaching of its crucial relation to the message of justification and to the crucified Nazarene."[47] And, as a matter of fact, I share Käsemann's basic attitude, as he expects of me: I do "acknowledge likewise a center of Scripture, and would view everything that comes later as an interpretation of Jesus' message."[48] This is just what the expression "center of the Gospel" meant for me then, although the phrase is to be avoided as misleading. Since writing *The Church* (1967) I definitely make my starting point the primacy of Christology and move from there through ecclesiology; not, as Käsemann supposes, the other way around, from the primacy of ecclesiology through Christology. And since the work I did for *On Being a Christian* (1974) I would answer the question about the canon within the canon as follows: *Jesus Christ himself is the center of Scripture.* That means that *he* in person is the Gospel, is the Christian message, is the canon within the canon. In the New Testament everything is to be interpreted from the standpoint of the real Jesus of history, his message, his behavior, and his fate. What this means will become clear in the following chapters.

IV

Dogma Versus the Bible?

Historico-Critical Exegesis as a Challenge to Dogmatic Theology

1. On the Misery of Today's Dogmatic Theology

The misery of contemporary dogmatic theology—Catholic, Orthodox, and Protestant—is the gulf that separates it from historico-critical exegesis. That is why the Catholic New Testament scholar, Josef Blank, in an essay from 1979 programmatically emphasized exegesis as the "basic theological discipline."[1] Unlike some other dogmatic theologians (even in Tübingen) I couldn't see in this argument for exegesis as the basic theological discipline any overreaching or arrogance on the part of the exegete. For, as my theological work progressed, it became to my mind—as the previous chapters have documented—beyond dispute that in the quest for solid ground there is no other way but the one which the New Testament Scriptures themselves point to, on which their authority reveals itself, in which alone they find their inner unity, and which opens up in a new manner with the historico-critical method: the way to the Jesus of history, who was experienced and attested to by the community of his disciples as God's Messiah and the Lord. On this subject it has been shown in addition that this way back "before" the testimonies collected in the New Testament, in other words back to Jesus himself, is possible, despite all we know about our roots in our own historical situation.

Indeed precisely because of this is that way necessary; and in the course of church history, especially in times of internal reform and concentration, people have repeatedly taken it.

So I view the case for exegesis as the basic discipline of theology to be thoroughly justified. I see in it a hermeneutical-methodological logic, which the dogmatic theologian ought to adopt as a matter of principle, although of course it must also be complemented by critical study. This logic flows from the primacy of Scripture, which according to the Second Vatican Council is to be the "soul," the "principle of life" of Catholic theology. The order of the *original* (authentic) tradition of Jesus the Christ *(norma normans),* laid down in the New Testament, as opposed to all *subsequent* church tradition *(norma normata),* must have consequences for defining the relationship between exegesis and dogmatics. The dignity of dogmatic theology—I would prefer the name "systematic theology" (which, needless to say, includes fundamental theology and ethics)—is in no way infringed upon by this, rather it is underpinned by exegesis.

The argument for exegesis as the basic theological discipline, however, ought not to be formulated with a narrow focus on dogmatics (and ethics and praxis). It should rather be defined also as a challenge to exegesis itself—taking into special consideration the history of dogma, theology, and the Church, which must not, any more than the New Testament, be used simply as a "quarry." The "basis" of theology is *not* the whole of it. Dogmatic theologians might therefore frame a more comprehensive thesis, aimed at the exegete's challenge, in something like these terms: *Historico-critically based exegesis calls for a historico-critically responsible dogmatic theology.* This means two things:

(1) For the dogmatic theologian: A critically responsible dogmatics from the perspective of Christian origins can be carried on today only on the foundation of the data concerning the Bible established historico-critically by exegesis. In this sense exegesis must be looked upon not as an ancillary discipline of dogmatic theology but as its basic discipline.

(2) For the exegete: Nowadays the findings that exegesis has arrived at historico-critically (and if possible already systematized) must be subjected to a systematic review that exegetes themselves, in most cases, are hardly capable of doing: against the background of the

history of dogma, theology, the Church, and the world; in the context of the contemporary social and natural sciences; with an eye to the practice of the individual and the Church, as well as to the future of human society as a whole. In this sense exegesis is not a complete discipline of theology, but only a basic discipline, which by its essence remains dependent on the other theological disciplines.

All this means, of course, that an unhistorical dogmatic theology is as antiquated as unhistorical exegesis. A dogmatic theology, which takes insufficient (selective) notice of the results of exegesis, is itself insufficient. A dogmatic theology that, instead of taking a critical approach, remains authoritarian is not scholarly: The scholarly ethos of truth and methodical discipline, critical discussion of the results and critical scrutiny of the problems and methods are required of dogmatic theology just as much as it is of exegesis. Like the Bible (cf. Vatican II), dogma too must be interpreted historico-critically. Like modern exegesis, modern dogmatic theology too must follow and adhere to a strictly historical approach: its truth too must always be anchored in history.

But what serious dogmatic theology nowadays would not ultimately claim to be, in some way, scholarly, critical, and historical? And doesn't that mean that every serious dogmatic theology is somehow on the way to historico-critical responsibility? Thus, in fact, *three possible reactions* to the challenge of historico-critical exegesis increasingly prove to be *three phases of development.* Here, admittedly, the time lag in consciousness (in Rome and elsewhere) has to be taken into account, along with the divided soul in the breast of so many theologians (notably in Germany). There are *three fundamental positions* taken in Catholic theology toward historico-critical exegesis:

— Dogmatic theology can de facto block or ignore the findings of historico-critical exegesis (the Neo-Scholastic conservative phase).

— Or it can go around them, disguise and domesticate them (the phase of speculative harmonization).

— Or it can accept this challenge and modify its own thought accordingly (the phase of historico-critical responsibility). Let me illustrate what I mean with a few important sets of problems.

2. The Sacraments—"Instituted by Christ"?

According to a binding church tradition (Lyon, 1274; Florence, 1439; Trent, 1547), the New Covenant has *seven sacraments instituted by Christ.*"[2] No one disputes that baptism and the eucharist are found as independent sacramental actions in the New Testament and can be substantiated from it. In an appropriate historical, if not a narrow juridical sense (as happened, at the latest, with Thomas Aquinas and the councils mentioned above) they can be considered, along with the authority to forgive sins, as having been "instituted" by Christ, insofar as the oldest Christian community performed them from the beginning while specifically invoking Jesus of Nazareth. But at the same time it is also indisputable that the information given in the New Testament about the other sacraments speaks a different language, and that the traditional proof texts cannot bear the weight of evidence and interpretation they are credited with.

— There is no indication of any independent sacrament of confirmation, as can be shown precisely from Acts 8:14ff. and 19:1ff.

— There is no basis for Christ's having personally instituted an anointing of the sick on the strength of James 5:14ff. (even though a connection is made to Mark 6:13 and 16:17–18).

— There are no adequate references to a sacrament of "holy orders," serving as a condition for and investiture in the functions of church leadership (cf. 1 Tim 4:14, 5:12; and 2 Tim 1:6, 2:2).

— And least of all is there any reference to a sacrament of matrimony, much as Eph 5:21–33 speaks of the great mystery *(sacramentum* in the Vulgate), and although Jesus, according to Mark 10:2–12, forbids divorce.

a) We are familiar with the untroubled *reaction of Neo-Scholastic theology* up until Vatican II. It had indeed heard about these exegetical difficulties, but, unconcerned about—at most annoyed at them and full of mistrust—it insisted that the traditional interpretation was still valid. M. Schmaus was not the only one who continued to follow this line, despite the information from exegesis. As late as 1971 J. Auer wrote, totally unaffected by it, "Thus the institution of the sacrament by Christ is to be inferred[!] for confirmation from Acts 8:17 and 19:6, for extreme unction from James 5:14 ff., for holy orders from 2 Tim 1:6 and 2:2, for matrimony from Eph 5:25 and Matt 19:3–9."[3] The recourse to Scripture thus became quarry-exegesis: a procedure of taking isolated points, out of context, selectively chosen, to confirm one's own position through scriptural quotations. In this way, of course, postbiblical "tradition" can no longer be governed, that is, interpreted or even corrected, by Scripture. Rather, this "tradition" has become the authentic, autonomous interpreter of Scripture, setting de facto biased standards for it. Thus Neo-Scholastic theology basically uncouples the individual statements of Scripture and of the history of the first Christian community. It misuses the original confessions of faith for the purpose of its own legitimation. It presumes, in fact, that it can affirm and legitimize key statements and key normative principles of doctrine independently of Scripture (Scripture and Tradition as two equally valuable sources of faith). Let it be noted, just in passing, that this theology was energetically supported in its hidden struggle against modern exegesis by the Roman Inquisition, from Pius X to Pius XII.

b) In a second phase the reconciliation between sacramental history and sacramental theology, between exegesis and dogmatics, was advanced by means of *speculative harmonization.* Suppose one failed, after all, to prove that the problematic four sacraments had their foundation, like the others, in the Church's origins, and were specifically established in Jesus Christ. In that case one made brisk progress by extending the concept of sacrament, one learned to understand "the Church as the primal sacrament." To begin with, Jesus Christ, "the visible person, who walked through the land of Palestine" is "a visible figure of the invisible Son of God, and hence a sacrament" (O. Semmelroth).[4] And the Church becomes the "sacrament of humanity." Thus the sacraments in the traditional sense, the "individual sacramental actions" (p. 53) become the "differentiation of the one primal sacrament into the multiplicity of the individual sacraments" (p. 54). The effects of these actions, one is astonished to read, impact first of all the Church, "and on a secondary[!] level inner grace." Hence the way leads through the individual sacraments not, by any chance, to Christ, but to the Church as the "primal sacrament" (p. 55). It was no great step from here to Karl Rahner's thesis: "The institution of a sacrament can . . . also take place simply through the fact that the Church has founded the Church with its character as the primal sacrament."[5] The definition of a sacrament is limited then to ecclesiological references. It is "a fundamental act of the Church that really belongs to the essence of the Church as the historical, eschatological presence of salvation . . ." (p. 37). More precisely, it is a sacrament because it is a fundamental and essential act of the Church, not the other way around. Ecclesiology becomes the doctrinal standard for the sacraments exactly at the point where their origins needed to be particularly anchored in Jesus Christ.

This procedure—which at the time was barely tolerated by the "magisterium"—did help to resolve the narrow, legalistic framing of the question by earlier apologetics (which referred as much as possible to words of acts of institution). At the same time, however, theologians were *dodging the hard questions* that as far back as 1520 Luther had raised in *De captivitate babylonica*, and shrinking from the explosive force of modern exegetical research. For if talk of a definite *number* of sacraments is to have any meaning, by what criteria are we to set about barring other church solemnities from the list? If "institution by Christ" is supposed to show that the sacraments in general have a further specific quality not shared by other things the Church does, how can this question then be shorn of all historical references back to Jesus Christ, on the one hand, and of every specifically Christological essential feature? How can one drop the subject with the bland observation that the Church as a whole is established in Jesus Christ? If the point in speaking about the sacraments is that in them Jesus Christ has promised himself to us in a special way, so that the Church can know that it has been empowered to perform just these actions by its Lord in person, how can one then simply flatten out the historical issues and reduce the concept of the sacrament to the structure of the sacramental-in-itself? How can one try to integrate all the aspects of a problem into an ecclesiology whose claim to completeness through sacralization of its contents surpasses all earlier conceptions?

c) But anyone who takes these questions seriously, anyone who concedes that there is still some justice to the traditional understanding of the sacraments, and chooses to look for a positive meaning in the great Protestant-Catholic dispute of the past centuries, will confront—and this sort of third phase is already emerging—the *challenge of biblical criticism.* Such a person, if he is a dogmatic theologian, will pay attention when it is pointed out that there is no "sacrament in itself" in the New Testament, that the community could know in very different ways that it was empowered to perform a certain action, that the number of sacraments depends to some extent on how the term is defined. Furthermore he will listen when he is told that baptism, the eucharist, and the remission of sins can be traced back to an authorization by Jesus Christ of the sort that the other "sacraments" lack. This is true of confirmation, which must be considered as at best a completion of baptism, separated out from it much, much later, and in no way containing a specific sacramental grace; of the anointing of the sick, which is sporadically attested to as a marginal church custom in the New Testament; of "holy orders," which the New Testament is surprisingly late in speaking of and does not at all trace back to Jesus Christ; and finally of matrimony, for whose "sacramentality" that mistranslation of *mysterium* as "sacrament" is responsible.

The attempt at harmonization has shown that the sacramental structure of signs and symbols can be applied—forget for the moment how justly—to other rites as well, even to the Church itself, indeed within the framework of a certain Christology to Jesus Christ himself. That is why the interpretations of the term "sacrament" swing back and forth from an evasive ecclesiological conception to an exclusive Christological one: The Church as a whole becomes the primal or root sacrament, the sacrament of Christ or of the Spirit; or else the title of sacrament is awarded only to Jesus, the Christ. The result is arbitrariness. Hence *the criterion* for the sacramentality of the sacrament must be the object of a *new search,* and is to be found only in a critically responsible exploration of the New Testament on the trail of the notion of "instituted by Christ." In this process one thing must be clear: Even the Church, even her binding dogma cannot do with this qualifier what they will. The only point at issue here is what did Jesus Christ immediately authorize, whatever one understands by that. And this question cannot be answered without submitting to the discipline of history. Thus exegesis becomes in fact a challenge for those who take seriously the priority that faith in Jesus Christ has, that dedication to Christ has over any dedication, however pious, to the Church—even, and especially, in the Catholic domain.

3. Church Offices—
"in the Apostolic Succession"?

Church office: How is it to be explained? What is its nature? How is it passed on? Here too we are familiar with the fundamental difficulties caused by the findings of historical biblical criticism. In contrast to the first set of problems, however, the primary subject of debate is not the exegesis of a few isolated passages in Scripture. Rather what must be considered now is a complex fabric of references, interpretations, and . . . silences about church office, its structure and diversity, its foundations and limitations.

For traditional Catholic ecclesiology *three main problems* arise:[6]

(1) Scripture offers hardly any support for a clerical-sacral interpretation of church office that could justify an essential difference from the vocation and status of the non-ordained. On the contrary, the general mission to *proclaim the Gospel* and the special (apostolic) mission to *found and lead the community* stand in the foreground. Like all offices and functions the office of community leadership is measured in terms of service to the community.

(2) Despite Luke's concept of appointment to church office by the laying on of hands, there is in the New Testament *no uniform theory of an apostolic succession of bishops* that is exclusively bound up with a ritual transmission of authority from the Apostole to his "successor." By contrast the office of the *Apostles* as the first witnesses to the Risen Jesus and guarantors of the true faith is quite precisely defined. Later office holders (community leaders), who can no longer be the first witnesses of the Resurrection, are bound primarily to the apostolicity of their preaching of the faith and to their recognition by the entire Church (for whose propagation they bear responsibility).

(3) Despite the standardization of the structure of church offices in the late writings of the New Testament, it is still premature to speak of a hierarchical constitution, organized into deacons, priests, and bishops, under the primacy of Peter. Rather, particularly in the early years, when numerous offices or services complement the leadership function, we can reconstruct a *plurality of constitutions:* above all a presbyterial (or collegial-episcopal) and at the same time a "charismatic" constitution, in which the preeminent role of a group in

charge of the community, or of individuals (even those authorized solely to celebrate the eucharist) cannot yet be seen.

The responses to these ecclesiological problems differ with the fundamental position taken:

1. Once again *Neo-Scholastic theology* shows no concern. It clings to the traditional understanding of church office, finally laid down as obligatory in Trent, and based on a self-promoting selection of passages from Scripture. For the special priestly character of church office itself, however, the Neo-Scholastics can only refer to Scripture's conviction of a "general" priesthood (1 Pet 2:4–9); that is, of the priestly character of the whole Church and the participation of all the baptized in the sacrifice of Christ (Heb 9:14–15, among others; Rom 12:1, 15:16; Col 1:14). As late as in Schmaus, for example (IV/1, 727), the fact that these passages rather contradict the idea of a special priesthood is not discussed at all. The problem seems to be solved by referring to special powers of the ordained office holders. Only they, and not all the baptized, qualify as "disciples" in the sense of the Gospels: as if they were the only ones who had the commission to proclaim the Gospel (Matt 28:19; Luke 16:15) and the claim to a hearing in Jesus's name (Luke 10:16; Matt 10:40); as if the power to bind and loose had been granted exclusively to the office holders (Matt 18:18); as if only they had the authority to celebrate the Lord's Supper (Luke 22:19) and to forgive sins (John 20:23).

There is certainly no disputing the fact that in the apostolic succession later on other office holders were appointed. They bore a special responsibility for the community and knew they had been assigned to that job in a special way. We have evidence for this in Paul's Letters and in the Acts of the Apostles. On the other hand, Neo-Scholastic theology completely ignores the evidence that the practice of the laying on of hands is found only in Luke and the Pastoral Letters, and even there it does not permit us to infer the later, exclusive theory of succession.

Still it remains true that the New Testament recognizes a variety of constitutions, the *charismatic structure of the community of Corinth,* and the highly adaptable nature of later communities, which met the needs of the time by giving themselves more solid structures, in other words shaped their offices for functional reasons. These findings—which must be taken very seriously—fundamentally contradict the thesis of the institution of the hierarchical order by Jesus Christ himself and thus strike a nerve in the traditionalistic-Catholic understanding of church office. They have been for the most part simply ignored by Neo-Scholastic theology till this day, indeed they have been suppressed by the "magisterium" through "explanations" and other methods. The rule for Neo-Scholastic thought (which still prevails in Rome) holds that whatever must not be, according to traditional doctrine, cannot be the case historically. Nevertheless on this point, too, German theology has led the way to the reconciliation of history and theological thought. How was this done?

b) Once again in the second phase the reconciliation began in a *harmonizing, speculative fashion.* There is no longer any dispute about the fact that church offices can basically be explained in terms of preaching the Gospel and the function of leadership. This has been accepted since Vatican II, which, unlike Trent, points to the historical relativity of the traditional system of the three offices. Theologians have noted and publicly discussed that the priestly terminology of the Letter to the Hebrews and the First Letter of Peter announces the end of priesthood in Jesus Christ, rather than its continuation in the Church. But the exegesis of Rom 5:15–16, for example, can show what sort of ambiguous harmonizing interpretation can come out of such a mediation between exegesis and dogmatics: It is true that Paul does characterize himself in this passage, using cultic imagery, as a "minister of Christ Jesus to the Gentiles." But by his "priestly service" he in no way means a cultic-sacramental activity, but quite unequivocally the service of proclaiming the Gospel. Hence one can put the accent on the Apostle's cultic-priestly activity only against the grain of the text. But that is just what happens not only in Neo-Scholastic theology, but also, for instance, in the conciliatory "Letter of the Bishops from German-Speaking Lands on the Priestly Office," published in 1970 (pp. 25–26), which can be accounted a typical example of overhasty harmonizing in theology. By means of this one achieves a double goal: Both aspects (proclaiming the Gospel and priesthood) are recognized and named, but guarded against, in exchange for a profile according to one side or the other—as would be necessary in the return from traditional doctrine to the New Testament. The message of the New Testament was brought up, without drawing critical consequences for traditional doctrine, and without making allowances for the concerns of the Reformation churches. Direct statements gave way to an abstract manner of speaking that doesn't upset the hierarchy's business-as-usual. The harmonizing interpretation becomes a tool for uncritically stabilizing the status quo.

Let it be noted in passing that here too an evasive *ecclesiology* leads to *domestication* of further problems. Theologians like to talk about the "irreversible evolution" of the understanding and the structures of church office, so that the situation of the Pauline church of Corinth becomes fully irrelevant, and instead of this Luke and the Pastoral Letters (in connection with certain selected passages elsewhere in the New Testament) are exalted as the only theologically relevant proof texts. When opponents sharpen the focus on a problem, they can always be met with the comment that the Church *did* have the right to use the authority granted her by Christ to design a structure of offices that would be valid forever (why so, actually?). The apologists for this mode of argument readily forget that with it they are simply endorsing themselves.

Another speech they like to give, on the *hermeneutical circle*, is used to qualify their own arbitrary solution as good scholarship. For if the shape of the Church had evolved differently, this too could be explained by the irreversibility of such an evolution, and the advocates of this view could bedeck themselves with a wreath of exegetical efforts. Where theory dictates that the history of the Church be uncritically stylized into salvation history pure and simple, the facts of Scripture have obviously had their sting, their organizing and judging function, taken away from them. But isn't it finally time to face the challenge of the theology of church office found in the Synoptics, Paul, and John?

c) It is time, in a third phase, to take note of the *challenge* that lies in a fair exegesis of the biblical passages most often consulted. This was attempted, not only in my book, *The Church* (1967), but also in numerous ecumenical consensus papers, especially the memorandum of the Ecumenical University Institute of Germany, "Reform and Recognition of Church Offices" (1973). We must take seriously the passing of the ancient cult and its categories of priest and sacrificial victim, which is fulfilled once and for all in Jesus; and likewise the resolute rejection of the qualitative difference of priests and lay people in a community of brothers and liberated men and women. We must take seriously in theory and practice the challenge of other statements in Scripture: the refusal of all titles of honor (Luke

22:24–27); the emphatic call—repeated five times in the Synoptics alone—to service, precisely on the part of the "greatest" (Mark 9:33–35 par); the Pauline criteria for the authority of each church office—knowledge of one's own call, service of the common cause, mutual submission—consequently, the duty to frame the leadership offices of the Church in keeping with the function that they have to fulfill. Finally, we must take seriously the insight that—for all the meaning of ordination (even, ecumenically speaking, for those in positions of church leadership)—in the first instance the Church stands as a Whole because of the continuity of her proclaiming the faith in the apostolic succession: that there is also a charismatic way into the office of church leadership, as a consequence of which the claim to stand in the succession of the Apostles cannot be tied exclusively to the succession of laying on of hands.

But the crucial challenge to *repudiate the ideology* of our church offices lies in Jesus' complete disinterest in the erection of an institutional Church and the creation of such offices. Jesus promises the Kingdom of God in his message, not the Church. He is interested in God's will and man's welfare. The Church is a post-Easter community of faith, and as such only something provisory, a help, a center—where it works—for brotherliness and forgiveness that apply to the whole world. The holders of church offices are to be servants in *this* service in a community that appeals to Jesus.

What is the future likely to be? Will the Christian message, will Jesus Christ himself once again become the criterion for church offices in a new and consistent fashion? In any case dogmatic theology and so too the Church is challenged to change its thinking, no more and no less, by accepting the challenge of these fresh insights of exegesis.

4. Jesus Christ—in the Shadow of Dogma?

A last example—it would be hard to find a more topical one—which has been repeatedly mentioned by J. Blank, is the confrontation of New Testament *Christology* with the Christology of the Council of Chalcedon (451). I have spelled out my position here in detail on several occasions, so I can summarize briefly. It would obviously make no sense to refer here to specific passages in Scripture. The subject is just as ubiquitous in the New Testament and resolved in the most different fashion, as Chalcedon can be considered a catchword and abbreviation for a multiplicity of sketches and modifications, confirmations and critical continuations, of the basic concept that found expression in the formula, "true God and true man"; in other words, two natures in the one person of Jesus Christ.

a) There is likewise no need to explain at length that Neo-Scholastic theology, in Christology as in other areas, has not dealt with even the most basic findings of critical exegesis. Its problems have remained those of Hellenistic antiquity and the Middle Ages. It did, of course, try a new focus, quite unhistorically, on the question of Jesus' self-consciousness. But the abundance of research in dogmatic history on Christology and the doctrine of the Trinity, from the Middle Ages back to Augustine, Athanasius and the pre-Nicaean Fathers, has partly hidden the most pressing problem and prevented intensive reflection on the shift—which was already bound up with the beginnings of the Church—of Christology from Jewish to Hellenistic modes of thought, and on the consequences for dogma and dogmatic theology that flowed from it.

b) But even before the Second Vatican Council Catholic Christology had witnessed a phase of *new attempts at mediation* setting in, attempts that deserve recognition, even if, once again, there is no denying their harmonizing character. In his significant essay on "The Problems of Christology Today" Karl Rahner tried to loosen up rigid dogmatic consciousness with respect to the formula of Chalcedon, which he sought to present as a "beginning" and not an "end."[7] Similarly, on the occasion of the fifteen-hundredth anniversary of the Council of Chalcedon (1951), Alois Grillmeier, with a great deal of material from the history of dogma, tried to depict "the theological and linguistic preparation of the Christological formula of Chalcedon" as a supposedly organic development, and thereby prove that there is "no contradiction," but an "inner nearness" between the two "end points," the Bible and Chalcedon.[8] All this took place, needless to say, with no concern for the critical exegesis of Scripture, indeed with no sense for the deeper problems of the New Testament. So it was no wonder that a good two decades later the same learned historian of dogma thought he was obliged to greet a comprehensive attempt to translate New Testament Christology *(On Being a Christian,* 1974) with dogmatic verdicts and the denunciatory formula of a quasi-heretical—or at least banal-sounding—creed. He seemed not to notice how selectively he himself treats the New Testament, how he neglects the Jesus of the Synoptic Gospels, and concentrates everything on John 1:14, so that the internal evolution and weighting of the New Testament is entirely lost sight of. The interest that led such a view even in this "historical" effort at reconciliation was absolutely fixed dogma, which triumphs in every case over history and hence over the data of the New Testament: dogma against the Bible. That explains too the insistence on certain classical Hellenistic formulas and ideas as opposed to the attempt to interpret them critically and constructively from the perspective of their normative and permanently valid Christian origins.

c) But history did not stay put during these attempts at mediation through harmonizing. And one would be well advised in Christology, as in other fields, to attune oneself to the new, third phase, in which Catholic theology has committed itself in a positive manner to the *facts of the Bible, as elucidated by criticism.* Anyone who writes nowadays as a dogmatic theologian about Jesus Christ, therefore, cannot avoid taking note of these facts. And so Christologies have already been devised on a new exegetical foundation. There have also been a great many articles on religious education that show a different sort of historico-critical responsibility than was previously common. A discussion of the method of Christology has thus been set in motion for theology and catechetical practice; and we may hope that it can be pressed forward intensively, objectively oriented, and without regimentation from the outside. For we have here complex hurdles to get over, not just intellectual and philosophical-historical, but emotional as well, that have been built up and have forced their way even into forms of personal piety.

We shall hardly make any progress in this context with slogans like "Christology from below" or "Christology from above," nor with the programmatic phrase of "historical Christology." Theologians have too much virtuosity, particularly in Germany, in domesticating the history of faith—on a supposedly historical scale. In the meantime any Catholic theologian who feels methodically obliged to follow a *"principle of tradition"* even in dealing with specifics, is likewise specifically urged to monitor this tradition as closely as possible for continuity *and* discontinuity. Such theologians may not date the beginning of tradition as late as 325 (the Council of Nicaea) or 451 (the Council of Chalcedon), with Athanasius, Augustine, or even as late as

Thomas Aquinas. Rather they must understand even the binding, widely accepted, historically pregnant and extremely important provisions of Nicaea and Chalcedon from the standpoint of their genesis, and learn to respond critically to them in accordance with the norm of the New Testament message itself.

By this logic, however, the "principle of tradition" is overtaken by the "principle of Scripture" and justified in it. And whatever the "magisterium" may say about it, such a process would be consistently Catholic. Because it finally makes good just that claim by the councils and authorities, whose teaching has binding force: councils and authorities which, as we know, put together no new doctrines, but simply attest to and confirm the agreement of a doctrine with the original "deposit of faith." And this original deposit of faith points to the One who gives his name to everything Christian: *He* in person is the "canon before the canon," the "center of Scripture," the "Gospel" itself.

With such Protestant "concentration," then, even someone committed to our great Catholic tradition—as opposed to merely "received ideas"—will not fall prey to the neoconservative apologetics of the past. Rather he or she will remain open to the fact that every new age can tell the good news about this Christ in an irreducibly new way, so that in principle no one may deny the Christian character of any epoch in church history—neither of the Middle Ages, nor of the present. In these complete processes of life in the church and of the history of theology, hard and fast positions have been broken open from His side, corrections have managed to become necessary and possible, now once more in the upheaval of an epoch the origins of faith can speak to us in new immediacy, the challenging primal shape of Christian faith unexpectedly becomes more lucid and familiar to us today than the ways by which it was mediated over its long history. All of these things surely belong to the healthy and happy surprises of our time.

B.

FUTURE PERSPECTIVES

I

How Does One Do
Christian Theology?

Steps Toward Understanding

The hermeneutical principles laid down in the last chapter dealt with
the interconnection between historico-critical exegesis and historico-
critical dogmatic theology. They found concrete expression earlier in
the elaboration of a consistently historical Christology. In 1974 my
book *To Be a Christian* appeared, followed in 1978 by *Does God
Exist?: An Answer for Today.* At the same time and quite independently from these studies the Catholic dogmatic theologian *Edward
Schillebeeckx* had published his books, *Jesus: An Experiment in Christology* and *Christ: The Experience of Jesus as Lord.* This was followed
in 1977 by *Christ and the Christians: The History of a New Life
Praxis.* [1] The point of departure and the conclusions of both our Christologies, which were written out of the Catholic tradition, seemed to
me to agree on so many points that it is worthwhile to raise the
following question:[2] Is a fundamental consensus on so central an issue
as Christology possible in *Catholic* theology today? A fundamental
consensus, which is also significant for the *ecumene,* since Catholic
theologians have begun critically to adopt the results of Protestant
exegeses that in the meantime have often been inexcusably ignored
or covered up by Protestant dogmatic theologians—precisely in questions of Christology and the doctrine of the Trinity, but also in those of
original sin and the devil. Will the first once again be the last?

1. Vatican II and Its Consequences

Catholic theology has stormy times behind it. The Second Vatican Council proved to be, in theology as in other things, a deeper cleft than many observers had first assumed. The First Vatican Council (1870) had brought total victory for Neo-Scholastic theology, more exactly for the Vatican brand of Denziger-theology that was almost completely controlled by the magisterium and reached its zenith with the almost daily addresses on doctrine, prepared by Roman professors and delivered by Pius XII. The Second Vatican Council (1962–65), however, manifested the incapacity of this theology to deal with the new problems of the individual, the Church, and modern society. Although it did not bring about the disappearance of the theology that prevailed between Vatican I and II, it did put an end to its absolute dominion. The old Catholic plurality of theologies, which had been suppressed by every means during that time, could be seen once more. At the same time, however, the former consensus, which had been really there, even if artificially created, now became a question mark, and it was in no way clear how it was to be rediscovered.

In Vatican II it seemed that the only things at stake were internal church problems and very limited areas of theology: the relationship of Scripture and Tradition (still framing the issue in the old Tridentine terms), ecclesiology in particular and, bound up with that, the questions of ecumenism, Judaism, the world religions, freedom of religion, but finally too, an early approach to the problems of the "Church in the modern world." In the meantime people did not notice that whole other domains of theology had also felt the impact of the new orientation. And the point that first attracted attention in the dispute over the Church, apostolic succession, the structure of church offices, and the eucharist became obvious to everyone in the dispute over infallibility: At stake now were the foundations of the prevalent theology, which evidently neither the positivistic Vatican theology, now thrown back on the defensive, nor the more recent patrological or speculative, mediating theologies could safeguard. Did this mean that a consensus was no longer possible in Catholic theology?

It should be noted that the ones who were pointing out the problems were not the ones who had created them. Radical, basic questions had been broached as early as the Reformation and especially since the Enlightenment. But the dominant "theology of pre-modernity" (J. Kleutgen) had done everything to paper them over—at least until the next crisis. Those manifold theological clashes before Vatican I and then Pius IX's "Syllabus of Errors" (1864), the commotion over modernism and the encyclical *Pascendi* of Pius X (1907), the "nouvelle théologie" and the encyclical *Humani generis* of Pius XII (1950) were, along with the series of purges unleashed in connection with them, the widely visible outbursts of the underground tremor now smashing its way to the surface.

Then in Vatican II, despite all the difficulties, a great deal was achieved on the theological front: for internal church reform, especially in the liturgy, also for relations with the other churches, with the Jews and the world religions, and finally with modern society as a whole. But actual theological reflection on fundamental matters was hindered by the curial apparatus that dominated the council and particularly by the Theological Commission (under Cardinal Ottaviani). Neither critical exegesis nor the history of dogma nor, least of all, Protestant and Orthodox theology had any real say in the discussion. The foundations seemed to be established once and for all with all the defined and undefined traditional doctrinal elements. True, the observer, even without a keen eye for such things, could spot a dangerous moisture in the vaults of the great traditional structure of doctrine, could see the saltpeter efflorescing on the walls. But instead of radically rehabilitating the foundations, the people in charge painted over the corroded patches in a new color. To no one's surprise, shortly after the council the critical spots became visible again, and the saltpeter destruction threatened to damage the upper stories as well.

A *double movement* emerged in postconciliar theology. On the one hand, there was a *centripetal* movement: From the secondary problem areas of ecclesiology and ecumenism critical research pressed on, forcibly impelled to seek out a more solid base, to the primary problem areas of Christology and the doctrine of God. Exegesis had been doing preliminary work for decades with its historical research on Jesus. Its findings demanded ever more imperiously to be admitted into the rigid framework of Neo-Scholastic dogmatic theology. It became increasingly clear how inadequate were the otherwise deserving theological reform movements, both the patristically oriented *"Ressourcement"* (H. de Lubac, J. Daniélou, H. U. von Balthasar) and that of speculative-transcendental mediation (K. Rahner), where modern exegesis was neglected at every stage. On the other hand, there was a *centrifugal* movement: The "modern world," which had been allowed to enter the Church during the the conciliar period, wanted to be acknowledged theologically, and not just in an abstract, general way, but to be taken seriously in its intricacy and ambivalence, and with as much accuracy as possible. Reading the "signs of the times" in theology proved an infinitely more difficult and complex undertaking than the council had assumed. The social upheavals around the end of the 1960s led straight to "political theol-ogy" and then, in Latin America, to "liberation theology."

Meanwhile in our century it was getting increasingly clear that only one kind of theology—and I am speaking here primarily about systematic and particularly dogmatic theology—would be able to survive the future. It would have to dare to try two things at once and would have to manage to achieve this in the most convincing form possible: both "Back to the sources" and "Out to the open sea," or, less poetically and paradoxically expressed: *a theology from the perspective of Christian origins and the Christian center, against the horizon of today's world.*

Does all this go without saying? No, such a theology is essentially different from every other theology that takes the Church's dogmas as the point of departure and goal of systematic theology. Some of those theologies positivistically repeat the dogmas, even though they have become questionable; others try to make them palatable to contemporary men and women in transcendental or some other sort of speculation. For a theology that seeks to think from the perspective of Christian origins and the Christian center against the horizon of today's world, the Church's dogmas will by no means be unnecessary or even impossible, for all the criticism they will have to undergo. They retain their function or, better, they get back their original function. They are not, as in the various forms of Denziger theology, put on the same level with the Christian Gospel; instead they are seen as what they were intended for: as the official helps, road signs, and guardrails on the way through the centuries, designed to protect the Church and the individual and of course the individual theologian as well from misunderstanding.

2. A Comparison of Two Christologies: Edward Schillebeeckx

In the two books on Jesus by Edward Schillebeeckx mentioned above, *Jesus: An Experiment in Christology* and *Christ: The Experience of Jesus as Lord,* the author aimed at providing a theology for the present from the standpoint of Christian origins, just as I did in my books, *On Being a Christian* (1974) and *Does God Exist: An Answer for Today* (1978). It would seem appropriate, therefore, to try to do what some reviewers have requested from both of us anyway: to compare these two theologies a little: not in detail, only in the broad features and above all on the subject of hermeneutics and method. This should be done in the light of Schillebeeckx's "Interim Report on the Books 'Jesus' and 'Christ.'" In it Schillebeeckx explains the assumptions on which he wrote his two books on Jesus. This sort of comparison is all the more tempting, because, although we were both together at Vatican II as conciliar theologians and were active as members of the board of directors of the international theological journal *Concilium,* we wrote our books in complete independence of one another.

Still, for that very reason a comparison of the books is not likely to be easy, because their thematic frameworks in no way coincide: For example, whereas there are only brief sections on grace and justification in *On Being a Christian,* in his second volume Schillebeeckx has developed a broad theology of grace in terms of the New Testament (which is why, once again, the Dutch title is more to the point, *Gerechtigheid en liefde. Genade en bevrijding (Justice and Love, Grace and Liberation).* Whereas in Schillebeeckx the problem of God is addressed primarily in the field of Christology, in my case it is given a philosophical-theological treatment against the whole horizon of the modern period in a separate volume. And while in Schillebeeckx the hermeneutical and methodological questions are presented at length, I go into them only insofar as it is absolutely necessary. Add to this the fact that Schillebeeckx views his two volumes as the prolegomena to a future third volume, a full-fledged Christology, while I hope to take the question of *Justification* (1957) once again, in something like a "Theory of Grace" (cf. *Justification Today,* introduction to the paperback edition [1986]).

But if one starts off from Schillebeeckx's and my own working assumptions, then one can see that for all the differences there is a *fundamental hermeneutical agreement* between us. This seems to me to go far beyond the books I have mentioned. It is supported not only by most Catholic exegetes but also increasingly by the younger, better exegetically trained Catholic systematic theologians; and it might just turn out to be the basis for a new fundamental consensus in Catholic (and not only Catholic) theology, for all the legitimate methodological and objective differences. This basic hermeneutical agreement relates above all to the "two sources," as Schillebeeckx calls them, from which current academic scholarly theology has to draw: "on the one hand from the whole experiential tradition of the great Jewish-Christian movement and, on the other hand, from today's new human experiences shared by both Christians and non-Christians" (p. 13; unless otherwise noted, quotations are taken from Schillebeeckx's "Interim Report," which surveys key ideas of both his books on Jesus, explains them, and defends them against criticism).

Without getting into a dispute over words—so widespread in theology anyway—I would rather speak of theology's "two poles," in order to make the tension within the elliptical, as it were, movement of our theologizing clearer than in the image of the two sources or two streams passing into one another. But let us elaborate now in the light of Schillebeeckx's "Interim Report" what, despite all the irrepressible differences, might be able to form a strong, pathbreaking consensus for *Catholic*—and, in my opinion, *ecumenical* as well—*theology of the future.* To begin with, then, we turn to the first and then to the second pole of *Christian* theology. In both sections, while indicating my basic agreement, I shall also raise a few critical questions.

3. What Is the Norm for Christian Theology?

The first "source," the first pole, the norm of Christian theology is God's revelatory speaking in the history of Israel and the history of Jesus. The following agreements emerge here:

a) *God's revelation and human experience are not simple opposites, rather God's revelation can be perceived only through human experience:* Schillebeeckx quite rightly emphasizes that, although revelation "does not [come] *from* subjective-human experience and reflection," it can "be perceived only *through* human experiences and *in* human experiences" (p. 50). God speaks through human beings. His revelation is not a human product or project. Nevertheless it does embrace human projects, experiences, events, interpretations. Human experiences do not account for God's revelation, rather God's revelation accounts for the human response in faith. Still revelation is not directly and immediately God's word, but is and remains a human word, which already involves interpretation and bears witness to the word of God that humans experience.

In this sense there is no revelation outside human experience, and without the specific experience with Jesus Christ, who gave meaning and direction to human life, there is no Christianity. If for Christian faith Jesus is God's crucial revelation in the history of Israel, then that is because his first disciples experienced him (subjectively) in this way, and because he actually was this (objectively) for them. The objective and subjective factors belong together. "The interpretive experience is an essential part of the concept of revelation" (pp. 20–21). To be sure, the faith of the disciples does not constitute Jesus as God's revelation, salvation, grace. Nevertheless without the experience of faith they could say nothing about him as God's revelation, salvation, and grace. Revelation takes place "in a long process of events, experiences, and interpretations" and "not in a supernatural 'intervention,' like a magic trick, so to speak, although it is still in no way a human product" (p. 21). Thus, to put it metaphorically, revelation comes "from above" (from God), but it is always experienced, interpreted, attested to, and then reflected on and "theologized" by men and women "from below." This leads to the second point:

b) *The human experience of revelation is not interpreted only after the fact, rather it is always given in advance only through human interpretation (means of interpretation):* Once again Schillebeeckx is quite right to point out: "Interpretation-identification is already an internal element of the experience itself, at first unexpressed, later reflexively conscious" (p. 22). Every experience—of love, but also of revelation, salvation, grace—is never given "pure," but interpreted, even if it is not reflected on in advance. Every experience already brings elements of interpretation with it. At the same time it is enriched through further elements of interpretation and finally expressed in language: in specific conceptual or pictorial articulations of interpretation (i.e., means of interpretation), which can have a retroactive effect on the original experience, deepening or even flattening it out. Nevertheless, beyond all concepts and ideas what we are dealing with here is always (more or less conscious) increasingly general structures of interpretation: theoretical models of understanding, on the strength of which one tries to comprehend, order, and synthesize the various experiences. There is no experience, and no faith-statement in the Bible or by the Church, without its interpretive framework, without its model of understanding, without its implicit theory. The influence of experience and theory is reciprocal.

Thus not only the experiences from the history of Israel, but also the experiences with Jesus were presented as already interpreted in advance in different ways by the different biblical authors. The common key experience of salvation from God in Jesus was colored by the Synoptics, by Paulinism and Johannism, by their very different approaches to problems, their ways of imagining, thinking, and speaking, as well as by the interpretive structure of the world they lived in, their social and cultural milieu, their time. They give us pictorial and conceptual articulations and models from a totally different world of experience, which no longer speak to us directly but must be mediated afresh today.

Thus the Christian reality of salvation, to the detriment of Christian faith itself, was confused with specific, time-bound and environmentally conditioned ideas, terms, and models from the experience of the ancient world (e.g., ransoming of slaves, bloody cult sacrifice, the category of a world ruler): "One really cannot oblige the Christian, who believes in the salvific value of Jesus' life and death, to believe for all time in all these readings or interpretations. Images and interpretations that used to be meaningful and suggestive can become irrelevant in another culture" (p. 25). In the New Testament greatly differing means of interpretation were adopted with the greatest freedom: "That gives us too the freedom to make a new representation of this experience of salvation that we have with Jesus, and to write it down in the key words taken from our contemporary modern culture with its peculiar problems, expectations, and afflictions, even if they too are subject to criticism from the expectation of Israel, *as* it was fulfilled in Jesus. Still more, we must do this, *in order to* remain faithful to what the New Testament Christians experienced of salvation in Jesus, to what they proclaimed as gospel and therefore promised to us" (p. 25). This leads us to the third point.

c) *The source, norm, and criterion for Christian faith is the living Jesus of history.* Through *historico-critical research on Jesus, Christian faith is historically justified in the face of today's problematic consciousness and protected against both unchurchly and churchly misinterpretations.* Schillebeeckx is right when he says, "Not the historical image of Jesus, but the living Jesus of history stands at the beginning and is the source, norm, and criterion of what the first Christians *interpretively experienced* in him. But precisely in view of this structure of the earliest Christian faith a historico-critical investigation can clarify for us how the concrete contents of early Christian faith were 'fulfilled' through the Jesus of faith" (p. 44).

Historical probing into the Jesus of history is possible thanks to the New Testament source, and necessary because of advanced modern awareness of the problem. For Christianity is based not on myths, legends, or fairy tales, and not merely on a teaching (it is not a book religion), but primarily on a historical personality: Jesus of Nazareth, who is believed as God's Christ. The testimonies in the New Testament—kerygmatic reports—do not enable us to reconstruct the biographical or psychological development of Jesus, but then this is not at all necessary. Yet they do make possible something that *is* urgently necessary today for both theological and pastoral reasons: to get a fresh view of the original outlines of his message, his way of life, his fate, and so of his person, which have so often been painted over and concealed in the course of the centuries. The modern person will find it possible to follow the *itinerarium mentis* of the first disciples from the baptism of Jesus until his death, in order to understand why they acknowledged him after his death as the living Christ and the Son of God. Only from the standpoint of his preaching and way of life does his execution too become understandable, do the cross and the resurrection escape being formalized into an abstract "salvation event."

There must be no contradiction between the Christ of faith and the Jesus of history. The Christ of faith must be able to be identified as the Jesus of history. Obviously, historico-critical research on Jesus can and does not seek to prove that the man Jesus of Nazareth is really God's Christ. Recognizing Jesus as Christ always remains the venture of believing trust or a *metanoia.* But historico-critical research on Jesus can help us to see that the Christ of faith whom we believe in is really the man Jesus of Nazareth and not someone else nor, by some chance, no one at all. All too easily faith in the true Christ becomes superstitious belief in an imaginary Christ or a mere code figure or symbol. A theology conscious of its responsibilities has to take seriously the doubts of so many contemporary men and women about the traditional image of Christ. Its job is to defend the Christian faith, not only against the attacks of unbelief but also against distortions and false conclusions on the part of the Church. Projections by belief or unbelief are subject to critical comparison with what the historical Jesus really was. Thus we have *fides quaerens intellectum historicum* —a faith seeking historical understanding—and at the same time *intellectus historicus quaerens fidem*—historical understanding seeking faith. A believing interpretation of Jesus that has no need at all to hide the interests of faith has to be a historically plausible interpretation.

Only the theology that takes into consideration the problems posed by history itself, and answers them to the limit of its ability, is a theology equal to the demands of a contemporary awareness of the problems (at least as we find that awareness among people who have gotten a Western education in both the West *and* the East) and is in this sense a scholarly theology that is truly up to date. For this reason we have no choice but to apply the historico-critical method (in the comprehensive sense) strictly in order to find out what were the established facts, what is known with scientific certainty or great probability about the Jesus of history. That is why the biblical canon and church tradition are not simply canceled, but the history of dogma does have to begin in the beginning, precisely in the New Testament.

4. The Consensus on Historico-critical Exegesis

I can agree completely with this brief summary of Edward Schillebeeckx's key hermeneutical principles. They fully concur with the argument I have formulated in this book and with the case I have worked out in my publications ever since *The Church* (1967). Edward Schillebeeckx, once a dedicated follower of Thomism, has admirably taken the same path or the search for solid ground: the path that the New Testament Scriptures point to, on which their authority reveals itself, on which alone they find their inner unity, and which opens up in a new way through the use of the historico-critical method—the way to the Jesus of history, who was experienced and attested to by the community of disciples as the Christ and Lord.

Thus Schillebeeckx too tries to translate into reality the program that I—in retrospect, similar to him—formulated in this way, and that might perhaps represent a column to help support a future fundamental consensus in Catholic theology: *Exegesis with a sound historico-critical base calls for a historico-critically responsible dogmatic theology.* After all, it has been shown that the findings of historico-critical exegesis must not be hindered or ignored (Neo-Scholastic conservatism), nor evaded, disguised, and domesticated (historical and speculative harmonization); rather they must be accepted and systematically worked up (historico-critical responsibility).

According to Vatican II, Scripture is to be the "soul," the "principle of life" of Catholic theology, and the historico-critical method is fundamentally affirmed by the same council. Am I deceiving myself when I see indications in the work of other Catholic theologians too that we are moving into this phase of historico-critical responsibility? Can a seriously responsible systematic theology, working from the standpoint of Christian origins, operate on any other basis except the facts of the Bible as historico-critically mediated by exegesis—even when this demands an extra measure of effort from the theologian?

In fact, if unhistorical exegesis is definitively outmoded today, then so is unhistorical dogmatic theology. And if the Bible has to be interpreted historico-critically, the same holds even more for postbiblical dogma. A theology that, instead of critically questioning the "data," openly or secretly remains authoritarian, will, despite its talk about scholarly standards, hardly manage to satisfy the demands of scholars in the future.

5. What to Do in the Jungle of Hypotheses?

Edward Schillebeeckx characterizes both the Catholic and Protestant response to his two books on Jesus as "on the whole positive" (p. 10). There was basic agreement despite all the criticism on details, especially from the exegetes, Germans included; there was fair criticism from systematic theologians such as M. Löhrer and P. Schoonenberg; and there were countless misunderstandings, of course, on the part of individual German systematic theologians. Some theologians seem unable to read well. Schillebeeckx often "rubbed his eyes" (cf. p. 94) when he saw how he had been understood. He rejects certain interpretations and insinuations as "groundless," "false," "incomprehensible," indeed as "science fiction," along with labels like "liberalism," from critics like W. Kasper, W. Löser, and L. Scheffcyk. Could it be the ongoing shock of the Reformation that causes Catholic dogmatic theologians, precisely in the land of Luther, to feel called upon—in this discussion too—to come forward as defenders of orthodoxy, without any genuine readiness to understand the issues? Here is what Schillebeeckx says about the "unrest" of the systematic theologians who "have no idea what to make of the critical findings of today's exegesis: "One cannot raise the autonomy of one's own perspective to the level of the uniquely legitimate theological possibility, so that one cannot muster up any understanding for other possibilities. No one needs theologians to add their contribution to the growing polarization of the parties, as if one theology was more concerned, and another less, with providing theological protection for complete, unabridged Christian faith. Obviously what we have here is far more a 'pluralism of anxieties!' " (p. 114).

One will have to concede to Schillebeeckx that, for all the concern over orthodoxy, the other "concern, to convey the Good News in an unabridged but at the same time understandable manner" is just as valid and "at certain times can be even more urgent" (p. 10). This does not mean, of course, even for Schillebeeckx, that there aren't *problems* here that *must be discussed* seriously and fairly. Methodological and objective clarification strikes me as necessary precisely for the sake of the highly desirable basic consensus, so that *secondary differences* do not mask the primary consensus or call it into question.

This may be briefly illustrated by an example, which is mentioned both in the serious exegetical and systematic criticism of Schillebeeckx's successful major work and in the author's "interim report" (see pp. 46–57): the systematic working up of the *exegetical Q problem* (analogous points might be made about the related hypothesis of a Palestinian prophet-Christology (see pp. 77–87). Schillebeeckx does not have, as those German dogmatic theologians accuse him of having, a biased "predilection" for the sayings source (Q) used by both Matthew and Luke, but Q does play a considerable role in Schillebeeckx's historical reconstruction of the original layer of the Christian *kerygma*. Because this collection of the words of the Lord contains nothing about Jesus' death and resurrection, Schillebeeckx concludes from this that the first Christology, strongly molded by the Jewish spirit, must have been not a paschal Christology (about the crucified and risen Jesus) but a *parousia* Christology (about the Jesus who was carried away and will come again).

Now this historical question should not, of course, be immediately blown up, as the dogmatic theologians named above do, into a *problem of faith,* and its solution ought not to be prejudiced out of dogmatic anxieties, because what must not have happened cannot have happened. What *did* happen? This question must be answered in an unprejudiced way as a *historical question.* We may assume as historically certain the existence of a sayings source that was lost early on. We can also take for granted the existence of Christologies that differed from one another, at least within a certain framework, during pre–New Testament and New Testament times. But doesn't postulating from the hypothetical Q-source, not just a Q-editor, but a Q-community, and even later on "surviving" Q-communities mean piling on top of a hypothesis further unverified hypotheses, which naturally begin to teeter more preciptiously? Yet isn't this to misread the literary character of this source, which represents after all only a collection of the words of the historical Jesus and which has a particular historical credibility precisely because it contains nothing about a soteriology of the cross or a Christology of the resurrection?

But, however one answers the question of Q, I mentioned this example only to raise the basic methodological issue of the relationship between exegesis and systematic theology: Is it theologically correct and—something very important for Schillebeeckx too—pastorally helpful, if the systematic theologian builds up his presentation on hypotheses that are scarcely verified and defended only by individual exegetes, oversubtle hypotheses perhaps, of the sort that are continually being advanced in the history of research on Jesus—and then sooner or later corrected? The *systematic theologian* should, it seems to me, *avoid betaking himself into the exegetical jungle of hypotheses,* where he then would have to officiate as an arbitrator between individual exegetes. He is not competent to do this. It is too easy to dismiss broad swatches of his systematic presentation as a purely hypothetical matter.

Still, what to do, given this exegetical jungle of hypotheses now staring us in the face? Schillebeeckx is right: As a systematic theologian one need not wait in every case for a general consensus of exegetes, which is often long in coming. And an isolated exegete may often prove in the end to be the pathfinder, who turns about to be right in the face of opposition from a host of his colleagues. Nevertheless, it would seem to me methodologically more correct in the normal situation—where a question must be decided systematically not absolutely—that the systematic theologian builds as far as possible *on secure exegetical results, supported by the broad consensus of critical research.* This consensus is already impressive enough in the research on Jesus. Wherever possible, the systematic theologian will leave unexplained exegetical questions open. (I have done this in *On Being a Christian,* for example in discussing the problem of the title "Son of Man.") With respect to the Q-community Schillebeeckx says that this question "to a certain extent" is meaningless for systematic theology. "As far as substance goes, this actually means little" (p. 56).

And so what has been said about the fundamental hermeneutical consensus remains in full force. Schillebeeckx deserves unbounded admiration for the objectivity, expertise, and intensity with which he has labored over the facts of the Bible in the light of the historico-critical approach, for the sensitivity to differences and alertness to the current scene that he has shown at the same time in translating the past into the present. Which brings us to the second pillar of a possible ecumenical consensus in Catholic, or rather Christian, theology.

6. What Is the Horizon of Christian Theology?

The "second source," second pole, or horizon of Christian theology is none other than our own human world of experience. The following areas of agreement emerge here:

a) *What is at stake here is our everyday, common, human, ambiguous experiences:* not, as in earlier theology, the elitist experiences of intellectual clerics; not continually new and naturally quite temporally conditioned academic systems and methods. Rather, as Schillebeeckx stresses, we are dealing "with our everyday experiences, with the vital consciousness of men and women in the world, with their deepest problems with meaning, life, and society" (p. 14): in other words, universal-human experiences of Christians and non-Christians, to which the social and natural sciences also make important contributions.

Nowadays these experiences are seldom if ever unambiguously religious. They are instead ambiguous experiences. In the secular world, amid the contemporary crisis of faith, we can detect a break between tradition and experience, between the Christian tradition of experience and today's individual and collective experiences. But the reasonable response to this is neither a retreat by theology and the Church into private inwardness nor a flight into the purely political nor a nostalgic longing for a bygone "Christian" society. The religious dimension of human existence—not to be equated with specific institutions and dogmas—fascinates men and women now as it always did, and it is precisely in our secular, scientific, technological world that man experiences his alienation afresh.

b) *These human experiences require a meaningful, religious, Christian interpretation:* The vague, undirected, ambiguous experiences that often lead a person up to a boundary (final meaninglessness or transcendental meaning?) are dependent on interpretations that establish their meaning. But only a new, comprehensive, integrating experience can mediate such an interpretation for the individual with previous experiences: and that is religious experience. But how does one come to a religious experience?

The secular person nowadays rarely has religious experiences "from above," as it were, in the form of passive-solemn occurrences, but rather, for all their immediacy and spontaneity, more through reflection than used to be the case. As Schillebeeckx rightly remarks, "The modern person reflects on specific experiences and interprets them, often groping carefully along, in a religious sense. The ambivalent experiences that he has are both positive (in the direction of infinity) and negative (in the direction of finity). They confront the contemporary person with a decision, that is, they are a summons to and an experience with these experiences" (p. 15).

This sort of religious "experience-with-experiences" does not, however, take place in the abstract through an isolated individual, but always concretely in a specific culture and religious tradition of experience, be it Christian or Buddhist or whatever. But when does this religious experience with ambivalent human experiences become an experience of Christian faith? "Whenever anyone in the light of what he has heard about Christianity, *in* this experience-with-experiences comes to the conviction: 'Yes, that's how it is; that's it.' What is proclaimed by the churches in their message as a possibility for life, which can also be experienced by others, and what can be provisionally called for them only a 'heuristic project' (H. Kuitert), finally becomes *in* this experience with experiences (within the given heuristic project) an altogether personal act of Christian faith—a personal conviction of belief with a concrete, Christian faith content" (pp. 16–17).

c) *Theology has to establish a critical correlation between the Christian tradition of experience and contemporary experiences:* Fewer and fewer people nowadays accept the Christian credo on the mere authority of others, but only in and through an experience-with-experiences that is interpreted in the light of the Christian history of experience, as mediated by the Church. That means, according to Schillebeeckx, "that catechesis and preaching must not only cast a light on today's human experiences, but that they also must show as responsibly, exactly, as suggestively as possible what the Christian orientation toward existence can mean concretely for the men and women of our time" (p. 17).

It is not enough to "apply" an already familiar, supposedly time-less, eternal message. Rather that message has to be newly "trans-lated" into our world of experience. We have already heard that each present-day situation is an internal constitutive element in the under-standing of God's revelation. Even the word "God" can be used meaningfully only when it is experienced as a liberating answer to our real problems in life. Hence in preaching today there must be no "sink or swim" approach. Preaching will not help the contemporary person with an alien conceptual system, and certainly not with a catechism of experience that makes no reference to the history of Jesus.

Back in the reflections on the first pole of Christian theology it became clear that neither can we simply adopt today all the interpre-tive means once used to explain the salvific significance of Jesus, nor may we simply make the Jesus of history, his message, his way of life, and his destiny into anything we like, even a simple code figure for our own human experiences. No, theology that serves Christian preaching is interested in establishing not just any sort of relationship but a "critical correlation" between the Christian tradition of experi-ence and our contemporary experiences. And this sort of critical correlation, says Schillebeeckx, demands three things: "1. an analysis of our present-day world of experience and—2. a tracing of the con-stant structures of Christian experience, which the New Testament and later Christian tradition of experience tell us about, and—3. the critical interrelation of these two 'sources.' For these elements of the Bible will have to structure the present-day experiences of Christians, as they also structured in a Christian fashion the particular world of the various New Testament authors. Only then is there continuity in

Christian tradition. This continuity, therefore, also demands that we pay attention to changes on the horizons of the issues" (p. 63).

I can agree completely with these basic hermeneutical principles of Edward Schillebeeckx, which I have once again briefly summarized. And I am surely not mistaken to assume that when Schillebeeckx, for his part, could declare his agreement on the following *ten guidelines for contemporary theology,* as I formulated them on the occasion of the appearance of *Does God Exist?* (1978) and as they will be stated in this book in another context (cf. pp. 204–5 below).

7. Critical Correlation Without Critical Confrontation?

Nothing will change in the basic consensus that we have ascertained, if we raise some questions about Schillebeeckx's three demands for "critical correlation," which may be understood less as critical strictures than as suggestions challenging him to develop his thinking further.

a) *On the analysis of our present-day world of experience* (cf. 67–72): This sort of analysis is, of course, inevitable for contemporary theology, and can take place in a thousand ways. But that is just where the whole difficulty lies: How are we to capture analytically this modern world of experience, with its unprecedented complexity, which has been multiplied over and over by the social and natural sciences? We have seen empirically that theologians, and especially "political ones," easily succumb to a double temptation: either to want to look out over this enormously wide and complex world from a quasi-divine bird's eye view, *sub aspectu aeternitatis,* and then pass judgment on it, or in all too earthly fashion simply endorse a specific, one-sided political-social analysis with its corresponding preprogrammed conclusions. Is the theologian at all capable of providing an "analysis of our contemporary world of experience"? And so the briefly sketched analysis in the "Interim Report" (as opposed to *Christ: the Experience of Jesus as Lord)* seems to have turned out too global and a little biased: True as it is to say that Western society "stood and stands beneath of the banner of 'utilitarian individualism' " (p. 68), whose central value is an often purely formal freedom, still at the same time the point must be elaborated that we find ourselves today facing altogether different problems than those in the times of Hobbes, Locke, Adam Smith, and classical liberalism. Not only do hundreds of millions of people, from the banks of the Elbe to the China Sea suffer under the reification of the socialist collective and state socialism and thirst for nothing more than bourgeois freedoms, but in Western Europe, in North America, and, with the spread of industrialization, in the Third World as well, people from all levels of the population are growing anxious in the face of more state presence, bureaucracy, anonymous forces, regimentation, and the threat to individual freedom in all areas. Precisely here in Schillebeeckx's concentration, which I share, "on the one hand on our ineradicable expectation of a humanly viable future, and on the other hand on the equally persistent anxieties that we all have about this future" (p. 68) these contrary movements would have to be included in an analysis of our world of experience.

In short, our present-day world of experience must be present in theology, but not necessarily in the form of a panoramic analysis (economics, politics, sociology, philosophy); rather in the form of a presence—naturally one that has been treated countless times—of our modern experiences, the present-day feeling of life and contemporary impulses. I think a salient example of this is the way Schillebeeckx, in his second volume, discusses the problem of suffering ("critical remembering the suffering human race") and the question of redemption and emancipation. We can also by and large agree objectively with his conclusions with regard to the relations between salvation history and profane history, salvation from God and self-liberation, Christian faith and politics.

b. *On tracing the constant deep structures of Christian experience in the New Testament and later tradition* (cf. pp. 63–67): Schillebeeckx has determined the following "four formative principles" to be "constant structures" in the various New Testament Scriptures: (1) a key theological and anthropological principle, (2) Christological mediation, (3) ecclesiological history and practice, (4) ecclesiological fulfillment. In other words one might also say, In all the New Testament Scriptures the issue is God and humanity, as they are seen in Jesus Christ and experienced in the community of faith, with a view to fulfillment.

Needless to say, I have nothing against constants in the New Testament Scriptures and nothing against erecting theological systems. But one wonders after all whether it is necessary to speak of God and man, of Jesus Christ and the Christian community, of creation and fulfillment in terms of "four formative principles" and "constant structures," as if these principles and structures were what held the different New Testament Scriptures together, as opposed to one very concrete person with his history. In any case I would have misgivings about saying, in the face of the manifold questions and problems here, that "the various New Testament authors did nothing except[!] continually give a different formulation, starting from the beginning, to these four factors, to compose them anew as it were, without becoming unfaithful to the basic history" (p. 64). I would say, rather, that the New Testament authors keep speaking to us anew of God and man, the community and the world in the light of the concrete person and history of this Jesus, without troubling themselves about any sort of structures or principles—even these four, which, one could say, can be found just as naturally everywhere in the New Testament as once the Aristotelian Scholastics could find the four causes everywhere in their world (a similar case is the "four New Testament credo-models" or "credo-trends" (pp. 82–87).

But this question, perhaps more terminological than anything else, should not be drawn out too long. I merely wish to warn against systematizing and formalizing the Bible's history and message overmuch, which could all too easily lead to a new Scholasticism. The fact that constants can be systematically developed from the facts of the Bible as historico-critically ascertained, and that these constants can serve as criteria for judging later theology and the Church, can only be welcomed. And this is precisely what Schillebeeckx has intended for his third volume. As a man whose career has made him outstandingly well versed in patristic and medieval theology, he will certainly show his *adversarii*, who constantly talk about religion, who really knows church tradition. But it is clear to the connoisseur how thoroughly even the first two volumes have been written in the context of the church community and out of a knowledge of its great tradition. Furthermore it will be possible to do theology today, following the model of the great theologians in the patristic period and the Middle Ages, without always having to repeat the whole traditional evolution of doctrine before one gets to say one's piece.

c) *On the critical interrelation of the two "sources"* (cf. pp. 72–76): No one will argue when Schillebeeckx ascribes to the old (biblical) experiences a "critical and transforming power" and a "productive and critical power" to the new (contemporary) experiences (see p. 27). Both experiences in fact have a *reciprocal* hermeneutic meaning that fosters understanding and thus is also thoroughly critical. But what happens when biblical and contemporary experiences contradict each other, and contemporary "experiences" once again present us with a "leader" or some sort of political "salvation movement" or similar modern "achievements"? In that case which experience should settle the matter for the person deciding first-and-final questions? Biblical and contemporary experiences do not always click neatly into one another (see pp. 73–74). Quite often *conflict* arises. If so, mustn't the critical "correlation" necessarily turn into a critical "confrontation"?

In the face of this conflict, which is always positive, it seems important to me to sharpen Schillebeeckx's criteriology. In first-and-final human questions, Schillebeeckx would certainly agree, the special Christian experiences or, rather, the Christian message, the Gospel, Jesus Christ himself, *acquires a normative meaning*. Particularly if we go along with Schillebeeckx's distinction between the time-bound ways of interpretation and the saving reality itself, we can make this point clear: The center of Scripture, the Christian message, the Gospel is he himself in person, the one who was experienced by the first Christian community as the Christ and was originally attested to in the New Testament—the living Jesus as he stands for God and man. And that is why for Christians the original testimony of this Christ, the New Testament in other words, is and remains the *norma normans* for all postbiblical tradition. This latter can (especially in binding statements made to the whole Church, certainly share in that normative character too, but by its nature only in a derivative way *(norma normata)*. We may note in passing that in this context Schillebeeckx too finds himself facing the crucial question of Catholic theology: infallibility.

But let us break off at this point. It ought to have become sufficiently clear what the path is that we must continue to follow to a new basic consensus—not a total consensus—in Catholic and, wherever possible, ecumenical theology: the centrist path between churchly opportunism and unchurchly separatism, in candid scholarship, with unshaken faith in the cause we represent, and out of hope for a fair settlement of the differences on all sides.

II

Paradigm Change in Theology and Science

A Fundamental Historical-Theological Clarification

1. In Search of Connections

During the 1960s it became increasingly clear to me that the crisis of contemporary theology was not a matter of isolated symptoms but a foundational crisis. In Catholic theology church officials had begun—already under Paul VI, but in a faster pace since 1978 under John Paul II—setting up the signs pointing to a restoration. A group of Catholic theologians who were critical of the system and intent on ecumenical breadth went increasingly on the defensive. Why should an ecumenical reform theology be forced onto the defensive? To understand this, one has to look beyond individual persons, events, and symptoms of the situation.

The analysis of paradigms developed by the physicist and historian of science *Thomas S. Kuhn* helped me to see the contemporary crisis in a larger historical context: as conflict and controversy not just involving various theologians and theologies but large-scale paradigms.[1] Here was the question: Despite all the reverses on individual issues, isn't there today a theology that can rise to the challenges of a new paradigm? What I had done in particular analyses in the quest for consensus, was now, we hoped, to be achieved in a broader theological context for contemporary theology as a whole—at our International Ecumenical Symposium, entitled "A New Paradigm of Theology," which took place at the University of Tübingen in 1983. This symposium had no wish to force upon theologians any rigid, uniform, monolithic unified paradigm of theology and the Church. It was assumed in advance that, today as in the past, every paradigm of theology and the Church (understood as a unit) contains a *plurality* of divergent schools, divergent intellectual orientations, indeed *divergent theologies*. This was, as always, an expression of creativity and vitality, but also of conflict and disputes.

Nevertheless the efforts at this symposium were aimed at breaking through the surface of diverging theologies and seeking for a *common point*. For there is no gainsaying the fact that:

— Much as theologians like Irenaeus, Clement, and Origen, Tertullian and Cyprian, Athanasius and the Cappadocians were different in their theological approaches, attempts to find solutions, and conclusions, they very much shared—as we can see in retrospect—convictions of their time that were fundamentally different from the apocalyptic-eschatological paradigm of the original Jewish-Christian first community.

— And much as, prompted by Augustine, Anselm and Abelard, Thomas and Bonaventure, Scotus and Ockham went methodologically different ways and arrived at results that were partially different, indeed irreconcilable, still as a whole they mirrored the fundamental model of understanding of their epoch, the Middle Ages. This medieval paradigm was essentially different from the primitive Christian-apocalyptic model of understanding, but also from that of the Greek and early Fathers of the Church.

— And much as Luther, Zwingli, and Calvin engaged in theological disputes with each other, still they were united precisely by what was irreconcilable with the medieval—as distinguished from the Eastern—typically Roman Catholic model for understanding the Church and theology.

— And much as, with the beginning of the modern period theology dispersed, under pressure from the new rationalistic-empirical philosophy and natural science, into contrary schools, it was clear to both Semler and Reimarus, Schleiermacher and Baur, Ritschl, Harnack, and Troeltsch, that theology could no longer be done as it had been in the age of the Reformation or of Protestant orthodoxy.

Here original innovation finally developed everywhere—in discontinuity and continuity—into tradition. Of course, such great processes of historical change could also be ignored. Then tradition led to traditionalism. Then people tried, as they are still trying, *to preserve* or *restore* with fresh embellishments their old familiar *model of understanding:*

— In this way theologians in the domain of Greek or Russian orthodoxy could become apologists for the ancient ecclesiastical-Hellenistic model. The key words here are *paradosis, traditio,* and *patres.*

— On the Catholic side theologians then became Neo-Scholastic champions of the Medieval (or Counter-Reformation) Roman Catholic system and of a Denziger theology. The key words here are *ecclesia, papa, magisterium.*

— On the Protestant side theologians became defenders of a biblicist Lutheran or Calvinist orthodoxy, a Protestant fundamentalism. The key words here are the Word of God and inerrancy.

— Nowadays theologians can also speak of a liberal traditionalism, if they have not taken note of the shift to the Post-Enlightenment, to postmodernity. The key words here are rationality and history.

Such great comprehensive models of understanding theology and the Church in the face of epochal, broad-scale temporal upheavals can be called "paradigms," after Thomas S. Kuhn, and the replacement of an old model of understanding by a new paradigm candidate can be termed "paradigm change." I should like to call these great epochal paradigms or basic models *macro*paradigms, to clarify and distinguish them from lesser kinds: macroparadigms, because they include again a great number of *meso*paradigms for different sections of theology (the two-natures doctrine for Christology, the Anselmian doctrine of satisfaction for soteriology) and still more *micro*paradigms for many individual questions, over which the various theologies have to grapple.

We are *not* dealing here with the propagation of a naive, optimistic faith in progress (whether idealistic or Marxist, positivistic or Social Darwinist), but neither with a skeptical-pessimistic devolutionary kind of thought (backsliding from the Gospel), but rather with a *dialectical understanding of the history of theology and the Church,* which always brings with it advancement and decline, progress in knowledge and forgetfulness, continuity and discontinuity: at once a relativizing negation, a preserving affirmation, and a continuing transcendence.

The intent of our conference at Tübingen was not to justify Kuhn's analyses. Rather we were interested in taking up the indisputably correct and important fundamental ideas of Kuhn from the history and theory of science and to the extent that they applied in the realm of the humanities, and more specifically theology, to ask how we might find enlightenment and certainty for ourselves about the *situation of contemporary theology*. From the sketch presented to the symposium (see below) at least one thing becomes clear: In the twentieth century we have on our hands a competition, indeed a conflict-ridden dispute, not only of divergent theologies but of divergent paradigms as well. This conflict is the result of the time lags between the major models of understanding with which theologians or representatives of the Church are or were working with in each case. And from this analysis of the overlappings and superimpositions of different macroparadigms I am convinced that Kuhn's theory of paradigms can be extraordinarily enlightening. This is how contemporary theology assures itself of its origin and its future. In this way it can also do historical justice to whatever paradigm holds for a given epoch. And since we are dealing here with paradigms, basic assumptions that have been long in ripening, are deeply rooted, profoundly influential, often conscious and often unconscious, the dispute between the so-called "progressives" and "conservatives" in the various churches is often so hard, and seemingly so irreconcilable.

In the meantime in our century, evident to all of us in the wake of the First and Second World War, *new approaches to solving* problems in theology and the Church have developed that seek to respond adequately to the enormous sociocultural revolutions of our time. And once again the question arises:

Much as Karl Barth, Rudolf Bultmann, and Paul Tillich, much as both the Niebuhrs and Walter Rauschenbusch differed in their approach, method, and consequences, nevertheless they agreed not only in their critique of the Roman Catholic system and of Protestant orthodoxy, but also in their criticism of Enlightenment devotion to reason and progress, of cultural Protestantism and historicism, in short in their rejection of nineteenth-century liberalism. Shouldn't all these great theologians, therefore, despite all their divergences, be viewed together within the framework of a new, that is to say modern-post-Enlightenment paradigm of theology and the Church, which seems to setting the intellectual rhythm of our time?

— *Where then do we stand,* we who have to do theology today with Auschwitz, Hiroshima, and the Gulag Archipelago at our backs?

— For all their differences what unites the proponents of dialectical and existential theology, of hermeneutic and political theology, of process theology, feminist, black, and non-Western liberation theology?

— What, then, are the common conditions of possibility for all of us in doing theology today, which, beneath the surface of diverging theologies, hold modern-post-Enlightenment theology together all over the ecumene?

That means: Our symposium was not seeking consensus for specific doctrines and dogmas, but a consensus for a definite theoretical-practical understanding of theology today.

We were looking not for a rigid canon of unalterable truths, but a historically changing canon of basic conditions that demand to be met if theology is to take its place in today's world seriously, if it wishes to be in tune with both the age and the Gospel. The following remarks served as one of the three keynote papers.[2]

2. The Theoretical Framework

Traditional *theology* of all times and all churches has always been extremely distrustful of novelty—a category given new prestige in our time by the Marxist philosopher Ernst Bloch: The *innovators*— they are the heretics, the enemies of the Church and often of the State. Seduced by Satan and their own doubts, stubbornly persisting in their pride and obstinacy, these unbelievers have come under the verdict of damnation, they must be persecuted with all means possible, defamed, and liquidated, if not physically any longer, then at least morally . . . But I do not wish to concern myself here with the history of Catholic—and in some cases Protestant—heretics. I wish to turn to intrinsic problems, and first of all to the *intellectual-theoretical* problems. The theory of science is interested in the science of science and the theory of theory. It will, however, quickly become clear that what is at stake here is not just *theory* but the *practice* of

PARADIGM CHANGES IN THE HISTORY OF THEOLOGY AND THE CHURCH

An essay in periodization and determining of structure

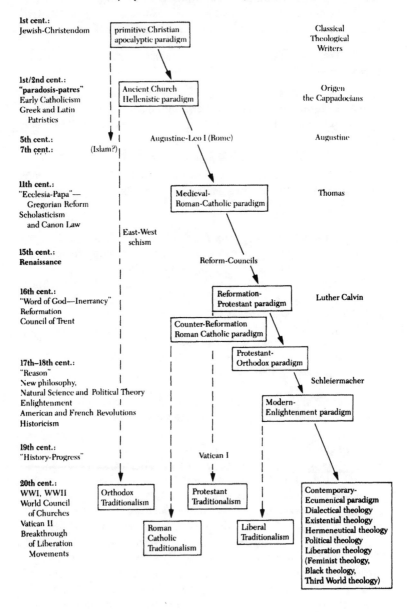

1st cent.:
Jewish-Christendom

primitive Christian
apocalyptic paradigm

Classical
Theological
Writers

1st/2nd cent.:
"paradosis-patres"
Early Catholicism
Greek and Latin
Patristics

Ancient Church
Hellenistic paradigm

Origen
the Cappadocians

5th cent.:
7th cent.: (Islam?)

Augustine-Leo I (Rome)

Augustine

11th cent.:
"Ecclesia-Papa"—
Gregorian Reform
Scholasticism
and Canon Law

Medieval-
Roman-Catholic paradigm

Thomas

East-West
schism

15th cent.:
Renaissance

Reform-Councils

16th cent.:
"Word of God—Inerrancy"
Reformation
Council of Trent

Reformation-
Protestant paradigm

Luther Calvin

Counter-Reformation
Roman Catholic paradigm

Protestant-
Orthodox paradigm

17th–18th cent.:
"Reason"
New philosophy,
Natural Science and Political Theory
Enlightenment
American and French Revolutions
Historicism

Schleiermacher

Modern-
Enlightenment paradigm

19th cent.:
"History-Progress"

Vatican I

20th cent.:
WWI, WWII
World Council
of Churches
Vatican II
Breakthrough
of Liberation
Movements

Orthodox
Traditionalism

Protestant
Traditionalism

Contemporary-
Ecumenical paradigm
Dialectical theology
Existential theology
Hermeneutical theology
Political theology
Liberation theology
(Feminist theology,
Black theology,
Third World theology)

Roman
Catholic
Traditionalism

Liberal
Traditionalism

theology, not just an innocuous general analysis but a highly dramatic history and present that must be analyzed.

How does science arrive at novelty? What does it mean when theology talks about something new? Is this just a typical squabble among theologians, as non-theologians sometimes think, especially after the most recent quarrels? For good reason the term *rabies theologorum*, theological rage, has become proverbial: a clear sign that philosophical and religious arguments can cause individuals emotional, altogether existential agitation, they can get into the bloodstream as it were, far more than political or aesthetic disagreements. And certainly far more than, say, scientific arguments, which, many scientists claim, not without pride, run their course quite calmly and rationally. But are they really altogether so *rational?* I wonder: Do *subjective conditions and presuppositions,* standpoints and perspectives really play no role in mathematical-scientific perception and research? Is science so different from theology on this score? Can subjective elements be fully eliminated in favor of a pure objectivity?

We should not deceive ourselves: A comparison between scientific and theological quarrels may make it clear how much is at stake here for theology: how the great confrontations are not simply a matter of squabbling, nor of intrinsic, necessary tensions. Perhaps—as in crucial arguments over science—we are witnessing the replacement of one theological "paradigm" or model of explanation by another, newer one. That in any case is how the situation looks when we view it from the height of the *contemporary discussion of the theory of science,* a discussion that—after logical positivism and critical rationalism—has entered a new, third phase, where it begins to be fruitful for the humanities and for theology in particular, once again immediately interesting and fruitful. The at first unusual comparison with the natural sciences—and especially with their hard core, physics and chemistry—can help us to develop a more intense awareness of the problem of innovation in theology.

For all the methodological differences, the *natural sciences and the humanities* must once again be seen more in their *connectedness.* Some methodological contraries set up as principles—such as "explain" for the sciences versus "understand" for the humanities—have to be viewed as out of date. For every natural science too has a horizon of understanding, has a hermeneutical dimension, which is now seen more clearly today by humanistic students of hermeneutics such as Hans-Georg Gadamer: Nowhere, not even in natural science, can the human subject, the researcher himself, be eliminated in the name of absolute objectivity. The information obtained by the scientist and technician has already been hermeneutically elaborated: It has already been limited to answering the question posed of it. And finally modern physics, in connection with the theory of relativity and quantum mechanics, has called attention to the fact that the findings of natural science are valid in themselves but only under quite specific conditions and not under others. Even in physics experiments, the method alters the object; it always reflects only one perspective and only one aspect.

It was *Karl Popper* who as early as 1935 in his book *The Logic of Scientific Discovery* analyzed the rules of the game according to which scientific hypotheses and theories are obtained. His finding: New scientific theories are not obtained by being positively proved to be true, not validated through testing or *verification*. That was the thesis in the 1920s and 1930s of the logical positivism of the Viennese school, centered around Moritz Schlick and Rudolf Carnap, who with his program of an antimetaphysical "scientific view of the world" (together with the earlier Ludwig Wittgenstein) shaped the first phase of the modern theory of science. Positive verification of general scientific propositions—for instance, that *all* copper in the world conducts electricity—is not at all possible.

New scientific hypotheses and theories, said Popper, come about not through verification but through *falsification*, through refutation: The discovery, say, of black swans in Australia refutes, "falsifies" the universal proposition that "all" swans are white and allows us to infer the general existential proposition "There are nonwhite swans." Therefore a hypothesis or theory may be considered true, or rather "proved," when it has stood the test of all previous attempts at falsification. Thus science appears to be a continually ongoing process of trial and error, which does not lead to the secure *possession* of truth but rather to progressive *approximation* to truth, a process in other words of continual alteration and evolution.

The question, of course, that was posed with increasing clarity in the face of Popper's penetrating logical analysis was this: Science, to be sure, is no subjective and irrational undertaking, but is *logic enough for understanding it?* Is this "logic of scientific discovery," which consists in constant falsification on the basic of strictly rational testing, enough to explain progress in science?

No, this became clear in the *third phase* of the theory of science: logical-critical penetration is not sufficient (as people working in the sciences had already been long convinced). Historical-hermeneutical reflection is also needed (just as it is called into play in the history of theology and dogma). What is needed above all is psychological-sociological investigation (hitherto still largely absent from theology). What we have then is an investigation *into science* that represents a union of the *theory, the history, and the sociology* of science.

From abstract, positivistic logic and linguistic analysis the way led over the past fify years through countless internal corrections to a renewed seriousness about history, the social group, and the human subject. And what comes out of such a comprehensive effort at explanation, as far as our problems are concerned?

3. What Does Paradigm Change Mean?: Thomas S. Kuhn

Crucial new hypotheses and theories are generated in natural science neither simply through verification (as the Viennese positivists thought) nor simply through falsification (as the critical rationalist Karl Popper suggested). Both views are too mechanical. New discoveries arise through a highly complex and usually long, drawn out process of *replacement of a previously valid model of explanation or "paradigm" by a new one.* They arise through something that is neither fully rational nor fully irrational—and in any case more revolutionary than evolutionary—a *"paradigm change."*

This is theory that the American physicist and historian of science *Thomas S. Kuhn* (whose thinking was prompted by James Conant, a president of Harvard—and before that an honorary senator of Tübingen), presents in a book that has already become a classic in the new research on science, *The Structure of Scientific Revolutions.* I am glad to admit that it was this theory that led me to a deeper and more comprehensive understanding of the theological ramifications of *problems of the growth of knowledge,* of evolution, progress, and the emergence of novelty, and along with all that of current arguments on these issues.

I would like to adopt Kuhn's terminology only to a limited degree, without insisting on the words "paradigm" or "revolution." "Paradigm"—originally meaning simply an "example," "typical example," "pattern" for further experiments—has proved to be quite ambiguous. For my part I would equally prefer to speak of *models* of interpretation, explanation, or *understanding*. By paradigm I mean— as Kuhn comprehensively defined it, in a review of the discussion (in "Postcript," 1969): "an entire constellation of beliefs, values, techniques, and so on shared by the members of a given community" (Kuhn, p. 175).

To avoid misunderstandings, Kuhn himself speaks lately of a "disciplinary matrix," which for him embraces "symbolic generalizations, models, and examples."[3] On the discussion between Kuhn and critics from the Popper school see the collection edited by I. Lakatos and A. Musgrave, *Criticism and the Growth of Knowledge.*[4] On the relevance of the new paradigm in the various disciplines cf. G. Cutting, *Paradigms and Revolutions.*[5]

Stephen Toulmin, another leading representative of the third phase, remarks in his fundamental work, *Human Understanding: The Collective Use and Evolution of Concepts,*[6] that the expression "paradigm" (which denotes more than a "conceptual system," was introduced for certain basic patterns of explanation as early as the middle of the eighteenth century by the Georg Christoph Lichtenberg, professor of natural philosophy at Göttingen. After the downfall of German Idealism Lichtenberg had great influence on Ernst Mach and Ludwig Wittgenstein, who adopted the expression "paradigm" as a key to understanding how philosophical models or patterns serve as "molds" or "brackets" to guide our thinking in preestablished and sometimes unsuitable paths. In this form the expression made its entrance into general philosophical discussion and was first analyzed by a student of Wittgenstein, W. H. Watson, by N. R. Hanson, and by Toulmin himself. Finally the expression arrived in the United States in the early 1950s.

In his foreword Toulmin formulates his "central thesis," his "deeply based conviction:" In science and philosophy alike, an exclusive preoccupation with logical systemacity has been destructive of both historical understanding and rational criticism. Men demonstrate their rationality, not by ordering their concepts and beliefs in tidy formal structures, but by their preparedness to respond to novel situations with open minds—acknowledging the shortcomings of their former procedures and moving beyond them" (pp. vii–viii).

Toulmin agrees with Kuhn in that he restores the neglected connection between conceptual changes and their socio-historical context, without fusing the two: "Writing as a historian of science, he

(Kuhn) was able to do a useful service, by re-emphasizing the close connections between the socio-historical development of scientific schools, professions, and institutions, and the intellectual development of scientific theories themselves" (p. 116). In short, this is a less formalistic and more historical "approach" (as opposed to "self-sufficient, anti-historical, logical empiricism inherited from the Vienna Circle" (p. 126).

To be sure, there is a dispute between Kuhn and Toulmin about whether we have to speak of "revolutionary" or "evolutionary" changes. I shall return to this question. But more important, it seems to me, is the basic agreement between both authors that "paradigms" or "models" change. Whatever term we choose for our specific theological task, it must be understood widely enough in order to include not just concepts and judgments but "an entire constellation of beliefs, values, techniques, and so on."

Of course, I openly confess that it is no small venture to consider in a single chapter the richly documented work of Kuhn (and Toulmin), which have up till now scarcely been noticed in the writings by theologians on the theory of science, as well as to report about the highly complex, internal theological evolution, to which Kuhn himself—unlike Toulmin, a person by nature alien to the humanities—has thus far paid no heed. Still the bare fact of the continuing hermeneutical discussion in both Catholic and Protestant theology about valid methods and principles for solving problems should be a sign that we are in the middle of a theological revolution, and that there is a desperate need for further reflection here. Precisely in the situation of contemporary theology we find reflection on a new paradigm, within the framework of the theory-practice discussion in Europe (e.g., Jürgen Habermas, Karl Otto Apel) and in America (along with Kuhn and Toulmin, others such as Richard Bernstein) more necessary than ever. Both the hermeneutical and the political implications of the paradigm change were treated in keynote papers by David Tracy and Matthew Lamb. But the historical analyses of C. Kannengiesser (on Origen and Augustine), S. Pfürtner (on Thomas and Luther), B. Gerrish (on modernity according to Troeltsch), and M. Marty (on modernity and postmodernity) were also important.[7]

4. Macro-, Meso-, and Microparadigms

In *physics* we can now distinguish between a Ptolemaic, a Copernican, a Newtonian, and an Einsteinian macromodel. Couldn't we make an analogous distinction in *theology* between a Greek-Alexandrian, a Latin-Augustinian, a Medieval-Thomistic, a Reformation, and one or several modern-critical interpretive models?

For our purposes it may help to use the terms "paradigm" and "model" interchangeably, but then to distinguish between *macro-, meso-, and micromodels (paradigms)*.

Thus in *physics*, there would be macromodels for general scientific solutions (such as the Copernican, Newtonian, or Einsteinian model), mesomodels for the solution of medium-range problem areas (such as the wave theory of light, the dynamic theory of heat or Maxwell's electromagnetic theory), and micromodels for scientific solutions of detailed problems (such as the discovery of X-rays).

The theological analogy for this would be macromodels for general solutions (the Alexandrian, the Augustinian, the Thomist, the Reformation model), mesomodels for the solution of intermediate problem areas (doctrine of creation, grace, the sacraments), and micromodels for solutions of detailed problems (doctrine of original sin, the hypostatic union in Christology).

Kuhn, it is true, speaks only of "science." But he sees, although with some skepticism, that this set of problems also arises for the humanities. In fact he concedes that he himself has many times applied insights to the sciences that are more familiar to the historiography of literature, music, pictorial art, and politics. On the other hand, the problems of the "hard" sciences open up new aspects of thought to the humanist and especially the theologian.

I am speaking of a *"model"* or "paradigm" to stress the provisory character of the pattern, which holds true only under specific presuppositions and within specific limits, which does not on principle exclude other patterns, but *always has an only relatively objective grasp of reality, from a certain perspective, with certain variables:* The scientist's data are never "naked" and experiences never "raw," but always subjectively mediated and interpreted. Every act of seeing takes place a priori in a (scientific or prescientific) model of understanding. Even very well scrutinized "classical" theories like those of Newton or Thomas Aquinas have proved inadequate and in need of overhauling. There is no reason, then, to absolutize a method, a blueprint, or model. Instead we have every motive for an unrelenting new search, for permanent criticism and rational supervision: on the way through pluralism to ever greater truth.

5. How Does Novelty Come into Being?: Parallels from Natural Science and Theology

All this still sounds rather abstract, but it can be concretized in view of our central question: Where are there parallels between the progress of knowledge in natural science and in theology, where are the differences? The differences are more striking. That is why I shall try in this section—and the whole piece is an experiment that challenges the reader to think along with me—to work out clearly, in the first instance, definite parallels, similarities, and *analogies* in order to broach in the next section the primal essence of theology. There are five links in the chain of reasoning:

a) We can start off with an observation that Kuhn makes about the natural sciences: In practice students of science accept certain models of explanation less because of proofs than because of *the authority of the textbook* they are using *and that of the teacher.* In olden times this function was fulfilled by the famous classics of science, such as Aristotle's *Physics* or Ptolemy's *Almagest;* in modern times the texts would be Newton's *Principia* and *Optics,* Franklin's *Electricity,* Lavoisier's *Chemistry,* Lyell's *Geology,* etc.

Christian theology, which from the beginning distinguished itself both mythic-cultic "theology" (i.e., legends and pronouncements of the gods) and from the philosophical "theology" (the doctrine of God) of the Greeks, begins right in the New Testament with Paul. Alongside the oldest apostolic witnesses, great teachers, something like the "classics," remain of the highest importance for theology: Irenaeus, for example, the most eminent theologian of the second century, the man who, in the process of defending the Church against Gnosticism, put down in writing the first overview of Christianity. Then in the third century there was Tertullian in the West and above all the Alexandrians Clement and Origen in the East, who did theology in a sweeping confrontation with the culture of their time. That is why theology must always be understood as a "dialectic of challenge and response" (D. Tracy).

Theological textbooks in the strict sense came into being once theology constituted itself in the Middle Ages as a university discipline: That is why theological paradigms or models of understanding have become especially comprehensible since then. In the *East*, of course, systematic works like *John Damascene*'s (d. ca., 750) *Pegè gnóseos* (Source of knowledge), and especially its third part, the "Exposition of the Orthodox Faith," had long before offered a summary of Eastern theology. As one of the few Byzantine presentations of systematic theology, this work has exercised a lasting influence all through the Middle Ages till the present day in both the Greek and the Slavic East.

In the *West* Latin theology, bearing the stamp primarily of Augustine, was transmitted to the Scholastics through the *Sentences* of *Peter Lombard* (d. 1160), which consisted for the most part of quotations from Augustine. In this way Augustine, together with a predominantly Neo-Platonic body of thought, was the master, all the way into the thirteenth century, over Scholastic philosophy and theology, in both method and content.

Thomas Aquinas (d. 1274) was at this time still a highly controversial theologian: attacked and branded a heretic by traditionalistic (Augustinian) theologians, who considered him a modernist, he was recalled from Paris by his own Dominican order and in the end solemnly condemned by the church authorities who had jurisdiction in Paris and Oxford for advancing a *"thèologie nouvelle,"* even though the order then took him under its protection. Not until immediately before the outbreak of the Reformation did his *Summa theologiae* succeed in finding adherents outside the Dominicans. The first commentary on the entire *Summa* came from the pen of the classic interpreter of Thomas and opponent of Luther, Cardinal Cajetan; and only in 1526 did Francisco de Vitoria, the father of Spanish Scholasticism, introduce Thomas's *Summa* as a textbook at the University of Salamanca. Louvain followed later with two chairs in Thomism and seven-year courses in the *Summa theologiae*. As of 1924, it has been calculated, a total of ninety commentaries had been written on the whole *Summa* and 218 on its first part.

A similar point could be made—though on a much smaller scale —for the Reformation world with works like *Melanchthon's Loci,*

Calvin's Institutio, and for the Anglican Church with *Hooker's Laws of Ecclesiastical Polity:* all classics and textbooks that made history. There is no mistaking the fact that, as in science, so in theology too, there is something like Kuhn's "normal science": research that is based on one or more scientific achievements of the past, achievements "that some particular scientific community acknowledges for a time as supplying the foundation for its further practice" (Kuhn, p. 10). These great theoretical structures serve the everyday work of science as an "example," as a "pattern," as a "model of understanding," as a "paradigm."

And this holds whether in *physics* the paradigm be Ptolemaic or Copernican astronomy, Aristotelian or Newtonian dynamics, the corpuscular or wave theory of light; and whether in *theology* the paradigm be the Alexandrian or Augustinian or Thomistic or Reformation, Protestant-Orthodox or a more recent doctrine. Anyone who—even as a student—wants to "join in the conversation" in given science has to have intensively mastered the appropriate model of understanding, the macromodel and the meso- and micromodels that go with it. And here is the remarkable thing: True novelty is not very welcome within the established model either in the natural sciences or in theology. Why? Because it would change, upset, and possibly destroy the model. Normal science is quite intent on using all available means to confirm, make more precise and secure, and extend the scope of its model of understanding, its paradigm. But this is a *process of evolution through accumulation,* a slow acquisition of more and more knowledge.

Hence normal science is in practice ultimately *not* interested in falsification, which would of course endanger the model, but in *solving the problems that still remain.* That is why it tries to confirm its own model, to integrate into its structure new phenomena, counterexamples, and anomalies as they emerge—if it doesn't actually first deny or suppress them. Then it tries to modify or reformulate as well as possible its established model. The case of Galileo is equally interesting for theology and physics on this score. Not only in theology, but in natural science as well, discoverers of new facts or anomalies that threaten the usual model are often morally discredited at the outset as "disturbers of the peace" or even simply gagged.

Thus analogies between science and theology show up with regard to normal science, and so we can state a (provisional) *first thesis* on our problem of how novelty comes into being. Later, as with all the subsequent ones, we shall have to make some distinctions in it:

> As in natural science, so in theology there is a "normal science," with its classic authors, text books, and teachers, that is characterized by
> – a cumulative growth of knowledge,
> – a solving of remaining problems ("puzzles"), and
> – resistance to everything that might lead to the alteration or replacement of the established model of understanding or paradigm.

b) We should not be too hasty to criticize this normal science: We all practice it and are intellectually dependent upon it. Nevertheless, does science really get done by the slow but irresistible triumph of progress over a multiplicity of errors? Do the scientific disciplines or those of theology develop only in such a way that they take a step closer to the truth inch by inch?

No doubt, this all too simple notion of "organic development" is widespread, even among scientists. And among theologians (especially Catholics) it was given a theoretical elaboration as early as the nineteenth century by John Henry Newman and above all (thanks to the influence of Hegel) by the Catholic school of Tübingen. Finally it was made popular in Rome—to explain the new dogma of Mary's Immaculate Conception: the whole thing was an organic development?! I would like, however, to draw attention to the following historical counterexamples that show us not simple development, but *crises:*

— In the sixteenth century what was the point of departure for *Copernicus*'s revolution in astronomy? It was the manifest crisis of Ptolemaic astronomy, which along with other factors was the major reason why astronomers could no longer manage the discrepancies and anomalies that were recognized with increasing clarity: a persistent incapacity on the part of normal science to solve the puzzles assigned it, especially the long-term prediction of the position of the planets.

— In the eighteenth century what was the presupposition for *Lavoisier*'s fundamental breakthrough in chemistry? It was the crisis of the prevailing theory of phlogiston, which attempted to explain why bodies burn (supposedly because they were enriched with phlogiston). But because it failed to explain (in all its various proliferating versions) the gain in weight that was increasingly more often observed in the process of combustion, Lavoisier finally began to ignore the existence of such a warmth-energy-substance and recognized combustion as oxygen absorption. The foundations for a new formulation of all of chemistry had been laid.

— And in the nineteenth and twentieth centuries what preceded *Einstein*'s theory of relativity? It was above all the crisis of the prevalent ether theory, which could not explain why despite all the instruments and experiments it was impossible to observe any movement, current, or impact of ether (no "ether wind" of any sort). That is why Einstein began simply to ignore the notion of such an inert medium for carrying the forces of gravity and light waves ("light ether"), and was able to posit the speed of light as equally great for all reference systems, uniformly moving toward each other.

But enough examples from science. Are there similar processes in *theology*—crises in theology?

As early as *New Testament times* various Jewish and Hellenistic schemata for interpreting the one Christ event began to appear either simultaneously or successively. These schemata intersect most notably in the work of Paul, the Apostle of the Jews *and* the Greeks. One of the first critical situations that early Christianity had to deal with was the nonfulfillment of the immediate apocalyptic expectations: Christians looked for an early arrival of the Kingdom of God, but it did not come. This Jewish-apocalyptic model of the proximate *end* (Christ as the *end* of time) was quietly replaced—especially in the writings of Luke, the Pastoral Letters, and the Second Letter of Peter —by a focus on salvation history: the early Catholic interpretive model of Jesus Christ as the *center* of time, with a Church that was obviously going to have a longer duration. This was a Church, besides, that now increasingly forgot its Jewish-Christian origins and became more and more Hellenized and institutionalized.

But this deep penetration into the Hellenistic world led to an *identity crisis*, as manifested especially in the second century in Gnosticism, which was all too unconcerned with the historical origin of Christianity and inclined toward an unhistorical-mythical theology. In response to this life-threatening challenge several theological models were worked out in succession within the Church:

— in the second century there developed first the new philosophical theology of the *apologists,* who by borrowing from popular philosophy and invoking the Hellenistic-Johannine Logos (seen as active everywhere in the world) tried to make a rational defense of the identity and universal validity of Christianity:

— then around the end of the second and the beginning of the third centuries there was the theology of *Irenaeus.* His thought was oriented to the Bible and salvation history, and had recourse to Scripture and apostolic tradition in his opposition to the Gnostic mythologies;

— finally in the middle of the third century (parallel to Tertullian in the West) there was the theology of the *Alexandrians* Clement and Origen, who boldly assimilated all previous efforts (including Gnostic ones) and in dialogue particularly with Neo-Platonic philosophy evolved the first fully articulated, widely influential, long prevalent macromodel of theology. The structural elements of this Greek theology, which was both cosmopolitan and ecclesiastical, historically responsible and philosophically reflective, were the biblical canon, the *regula fidei* ("rule of faith), and Neo-Platonic thought. Origen's method of expounding Scripture—allegorical, symbolic, intellectual-pneumatic, prompt to reinterpret the literal text—won the day in theology, overcoming the objections of the school of Antioch, with its more Aristotelian and historical-grammatical orientation. That is, a theological model had been sketched out that helped pave the way for the decisive turn of events that came with Constantine the Great. In the fourth century it was corrected and developed further primarily by Athanasius and the Cappadocians (Basil, Gregory Nazianzen, and Gregory of Nyssa), until it became the paradigm of Greek orthodoxy.

In the West the theology of *Augustine* was a very different sort of thing, for all its similarities the Greek approach to exegesis. Augustinianism became the other macroparadigm with a long-term influence. It came into being—amid the downfall of the Roman Empire—first of all on account of Augustine's personal crisis, his turning away from dualistic Manichaeism and academic skepticism, as well as his turning toward the faith of the Church, to Neo-Platonism, to allegorizing, to Paul, to Christian asceticism, and finally to the episcopate. Still, the determining factors in the specific development of his theology were two crises in the history of Church and theology: the *Donatist* crisis, which had a profound impact on Augustine's—and then the whole Western world's—understanding of the Church and the sacraments; and the *Pelagian* crisis, which played a crucial role in forming the theology of sin and grace, all the way down to the Reformation and Jansenism.

A further example: For a man like *Thomas Aquinas,* the most modern theologian of the thirteenth century, what was the occasion for his novel decision to place a higher value on reason versus faith, the literal sense of Scripture versus the allegorical-spiritual one, nature versus grace, and philosophy versus theology? What prompted, then, his grandly designed new theological synthesis, which was destined to shape both Spanish Scholasticism as well as the Neo-Scholasticism of the nineteenth and twentieth centuries? It was the *crisis of Augustinianism,* provoked by the broad dissemination and reception of the whole of Aristotle's works in Christian Europe. This led not only to the confrontation with an immense abundance of more recent ideas, especially in science, but also with Arabic philosophy, which was likewise oriented toward Aristotle. Theology was now constituted as a scholarly discipline at the university and in a new form: Thomas, who was methodologically strict and dialectically adroit, found a place for Platonic-Augustinian thought in his extraordinarily unified system. He never engaged in polemics with Plato or Augustine, but he had no hesitation in basically reinterpreting their ideas or even in magisterially discarding them when they did not suit him.

Furthermore, what was the point of departure, in the sixteenth century, for *Martin Luther*'s new understanding of the Word of God and faith, the justice of God and the justification of man, his revolutionary biblical, Christocentric reconception of the whole body of theology, rejecting allegory and grounded in rigorous linguistic-grammatical exegesis? This was the crisis of *systematic-speculative Scholasticism*—itself part of the larger crisis affecting the late medieval church and society. By piling up rational conclusions Scholasticism neglected the basic truths of faith as well as its existential character.

Or, then again, what was the point of departure for *historico-*

critical theology, which was decisively launched in the seventeenth and eighteenth century with the German Enlightenment? This school wanted to cling to the historicity of Christian belief, in opposition to all pietistic biblicism and, at the same time, all deistic natural theology. It aimed at giving a critical account of biblical faith in a spirit of strict modern rationality and freedom. In deliberately undogmatic exegesis the doctrine of literal inspiration was abandoned and replaced by equating the Bible, on principle, with other literature and by expounding Scripture in unconditional accordance with philology and history. The point of departure was undoubtedly the *crisis of Protestant orthodoxy,* which broke out at the end of the denominational era and its "wars of religion": This Lutheran and Calvinist orthodoxy had—once again falling back upon Aristotle—built up and extended a Protestant-Scholastic model of theology, but lived to see its collapse, when at the time of the great epochal shift toward modern philosophy and the modern image of the world Aristotelianism ceased to be the standard form of thought for all the sciences. Connected with this was the emancipation both of philosophy and the individual sciences and disciplines, as well as, ultimately, of the state and society as a whole from the authority of theology and the Church (secularization). That liberation led to continual new revolutionary thrusts in philosophy and the sciences and, in the end, to a new comprehensive understanding of theology: a new modern-critical paradigm.

What I have sketched out here in a sort of generalized typical outline are—as far as their causes, beginnings, and evolution are concerned—needless to say extremely complex processes affecting the community of theologians. They were scarcely ever the work of one man alone and certainly never took place overnight. It is an irony of history that in theology just as in the sciences *normal science itself involuntarily contributed to the undermining of the established model.* This was because, as it became increasingly more refined and specialized, it brought additional information to light that did not fit the traditional model and complicated the theory:

— The more, for example, astronomers studied and corrected the movements of stars on the basis of the Ptolemaic world system, the more they produced material to refute it.

— And the more Protestant orthodoxy invested in the methods of Neo-Aristotelian science, the more by this very fact it provoked the unscientific "simple" biblicism of Pietism and, on the other hand the unhistorical, rational natural theology of the Enlightenment.

— And the more the Neo-Scholasticism of this century sought to provide security for certain speculative theses—for example, concerning the constitution of the Church, the primacy and infallibility of the pope—by means of historical research, the more it helped to bring to light contradictions that led to subverting them.

And thus in science and theology the replacement of a model of explanation was preceded as a rule by a *transitional period of uncertainty*, in which faith in the established model began to waver, patterns of thought were seen through, bonds loosened, traditional schools dwindled, and a host of competing new approaches made their appearance. Catholic theology, which had remained far behind modern developments and Protestant theology, went through this sort of transitional situation during the Vatican II era. The classic Scholastic differences between, say, Thomists and Scotists, or Thomists and Molinists, no longer played any role, and in their place appeared a whole series of new competing approaches, which even now make the future of Catholic theology look highly uncertain.

Thus, for all the complexity and multiple causes at work in the evolution of every theology, one thing has become clear enough: New models of theological interpretation do not simply come into existence because individual theologians tackle heated issues or sit down at their desks to construct new models, but because the traditional interpretive model has failed, because the "problem solvers" of normal theology, in the face of a changed historical horizon, can find no satisfying answers for new major questions, and "paradigm testers" set in motion a "extra-ordinary theology" alongside the normal variety.

A crisis is surely not an "indispensable prerequisite" for a paradigm change, as Kuhn first argued in his book. But rather, as he more cautiously put it in his 1969 postcript, "the usual prelude, supplying, that is, a self-correcting mechanism which ensures that the rigidity of normal science will not forever go unchallenged" (p. 181).

With regard to the emergence of novelty in theology I would therefore like to formulate a provisional *second thesis:*

As in the natural sciences so in theology the awareness of a growing crisis is generally the point of departure for a crucial change in certain previously valid basic assumptions and finally for the breakthrough of a new interpretive model or paradigm: Where the available rules and methods fail, they lead the search for new ones.

c) Up till now we have presented only the point of departure for the replacement of a paradigm: some crisis. But how does such a *replacement* take place in the realm of science? Here too Kuhn's observations from the history of the natural sciences can be helpful. A replacement requires not only that the old paradigm be in a critical condition, but that a *new one arrive on the scene.* The new paradigm, intuitively recognized, has most often already been around for some time as a specific system of common rules and findings of research. The new astronomy, the new physics, the new chemistry, the new biology, the general theory of relativity make it clear that the decision to give up an old model is simultaneous with the decision to adopt a new one. The model to be replaced needs a worthy, credible model to succeed it before it can make its exit. It needs a new *"paradigm candidate."*

If one is ready, the replacement does not simply take place through a continuous "organic" development, not, in other words, through the usual cumulative process of normal science. After all, we are dealing here not with an adjustment in the course being followed, but with a change to a different course. Call it a "scientific revolution" or not, it is a *scientific upheaval,* a fundamental reshaping of an entire science, with its concepts, methods and criteria, often with grave social consequences.

With respect to the great upheavals in *natural science* all this calls for no long explanation. More important in this case too is the application to *theology.* As we have seen, theology as well from time to time experiences decisive changes, not only in the limited micro- or mesodomain, but also in the macrorealm. As with the change from the geocentric to the heliocentric view, from the chemistry of phlogiston to the chemistry of oxygen, from the corpuscular to the wave theory of light, so when one theology changes to another,

— established, familiar concepts change;

— norms and criteria that determine the admissibility of certain problems and solutions undergo a shift;

— theories and methods are shaken.

In short, the *paradigm or interpretive model* changes, together with the whole complex of different methods, problem areas, and attempted solutions as hitherto recognized by the theological community. Theologians accustom themselves, as it were, to another kind of seeing: seeing in the context of a different model. Many things are now perceived that were missed before, and some things too may be overlooked that used to be in people's line of sight. A new vision of man, the world, and God begins to prevail in the domain of theological scholarship, where the whole and its details appear in a different light.

Thus in times of epochal upheaval theology takes on a *new shape,* which spreads into literature. To take only comprehensive systematic outlines, compare Clement of Alexandria's *Paidagogos* and Origen's *Peri archon* with Augustine's *Enchiridion* or *De doctrina christiana,* or those works again with the medieval summas, and the latter finally with Luther's programmatic writings of 1520 or his Great Catechism.

As we have seen, the first theological upheaval occurred as far back as New Testament times, when the model of apocalyptic expectation taken over from Judaism was unobtrusively replaced by a Hellenistic notion of salvation history, which conceived Jesus Christ as the center of time. That model, which received its first full treatment from *Clement* and *Origen,* who understood the whole history of humanity as a grand educational process *(paideia)* continually leading upwards: The image of God in humanity, covered over by guilt and sin, is restored in humanity and brought to fulfillment through the pedagogy of God himself: according to God's *oikonomia* the incarnation of God as man is the presupposition for man's becoming God. This implies a considerable alteration in the total constellation of theological presuppositions, concepts, convictions, values, and patterns of behavior. The primary salvation event now seems to be less the cross and resurrection, as it was in the New Testament, than the Incarnation.

This kind of theological upheaval also occurred in the West when that originally very secular man, that intense thinker and sharp dialectician, *Aurelius Augustinus,* set to work converting into theology his spiritual-intellectual experiences, his early sexual and his later ecclesiastical life. Like the Greeks he sought to create a synthesis between Christian faith and Neo-Platonic thought. But the individual details and the overall picture had changed as a result of his personal career and his later anti-Donatist and anti-Pelagian positions:

— There was a mysterious-uncanny double predestination of some to bliss and others to damnation;

— a new, sexually determined understanding of sin as original sin;

— a new theology of history focused on the City of God and the City of Man (secular state);

— a new, psychological relationship between Father, Son, and Spirit, proceeding from the one unalterable divine nature . . .

All in all this was an epochal new macromodel that lasted almost a millenium. The Greeks understandably have looked on it to this day with the greatest mistrust, even though the comprehensive and thoroughgoing patristic unity of reason and faith, philosophy and theology remained preserved.

Another epochal theological revolution occurred again amid great battles in the case of *Thomas* and much more so later with *Luther.* All these are examples that likewise shed light on just how much each of these paradigm changes had specific *social and political preconditions and* at the same time important social and political *consequences:* highly ambiguous consequences, of course, whether it was the Hellenistic Christian concept of *paideia* for the Byzantine churches or Augustine's doctrine of two states or kingdoms for the Middle Ages, Thomas's papalistic ecclesiology or Luther's new understanding of justification, the Church, and the sacraments for the new age. And after Luther or the Lutheran and Reformed orthodoxy we could go on, as already indicated, with the theological upheavals of modernity.

For our purposes, however, these instances from the history of theology suffice now to formulate a provisional *third thesis:*

As in the natural sciences so also in theology an old model of understanding or paradigm is replaced when a new one is ready.

b) This has now indirectly made a point clear that was already noted in the beginning: The history of all the great theologians shows that nothing new has prevailed in theology (and in the Church) without opposition, battle, and personal sacrifice. But we must now spell outmore precisely the subjective circumstances accompanying this paradigm change, with a view to comprehensive scientific and scholarly research. We take it for granted that in the case of theologians a whole host of miscellaneous factors comes into play when they decide —whether as initiators or supporters, in any event generally in a rather long, complex process—in favor of a new model of explanation. This could be superabundantly documented from Augustine's *Confessions* and Letters, as well as from Luther's life history. It is also sufficiently familiar in the case of Origen (from Eusebius's *Ecclesiastical History)* and Thomas Aquinas (especially with regard to the Dominican order). But Kuhn also documents the fact that with natural scientists Popper's "logic of discovery" is only one of many factors at work, and again Kuhn accompanies his evidence with some observations that theologians will find altogether comforting.

A *first* observation: Not only the theologian, but the natural scientists as well has *doubts about his faith* at times of great crisis; namely, when normal science and its traditional system leave him in the lurch, and he goes off on a quest for novelty. "It was as if the ground had been pulled out from under one, with no firm foundation to be seen anywhere, upon which one could have built." This was said not by a theologian about theology, but by a physicist—Albert Einstein— speaking of physics.

"At the moment physics is again terribly confused. In any case, it is too difficult for me, and I wish I had been a movie comedian or something of the sort and had never heard of physics." That was how the later Nobel laureate in physics Wolfgang Pauli spoke in the months before Heisenberg's paper on matrix mechanics showed the way to the new quantum theory (quotations from Kuhn, pp. 83–84). We all know that in this sort of critical situation, when no new way has been found, not only do theologians lose their faith in theology and choose another profession, but scientists—though, of course, the historiography of science scarcely mentions this—lose their faith in science and likewise look to another calling.

A *second* observation: Not only in theology but also in science, *nonscientific* factors likewise play an important role. There is a mixture of "objective" and "subjective," of individual and social factors: The origins, career, and personality of the people involved play a role here, but often so do the nationality, reputation, and teachers of the innovator; and finally too the attractiveness—not seldom contingent on aesthetic features—of the new model of explanation: the consistency, lucidity, efficiency, but also the elegance, simplicity, and universality of the proposed solution.

A *third* observation: Kuhn himself has not remarked how greatly *religious convictions* can influence supposedly purely scientific decisions, though this is true not only with the great theologians, but also with the great astronomers, from Copernicus to Newton. In fact during his last decades a great silence gathered around the greatest physicist of our century, Albert Einstein, because he felt could not go along with the new epochal shift that physics had taken with quantum mechanics. He felt he ought not to go along with it—for religious reasons, as we can see in his correspondence with Max Born. His famous remark about the Old Man who doesn't play dice with the universe, is no joke, but the expression of a specific religious conviction: To his last days Einstein believed in the pantheistic-deterministic God of Spinoza, something that obviously remained hidden from Born during their discussions.

A *fourth* observation: Not only in theology but also in science, in the light of the new model of understanding something like a *conversion* is demanded, though it cannot be rationally compelled. We are speaking now less about the initiator, the person who (on the strength of a sudden intuitive experience or of a long, laborious maturation process) proposes a new model, but rather of the "receivers," who have to decide for or against it. The representatives of the old and new model—this must not be underestimated—live in different worlds, different intellectual and linguistic domains. Often they can barely understand one another. Translation from the old language into the new one is necessary, but at the same time there must be a new conviction, a conversion.

To be sure, convincing objective grounds for such a conversion are important. After all, we are not dealing here simply with an irrational process. Nevertheless even good reasons cannot force anyone to convert. Nor are we dealing with a purely rational process. In the final analysis what is at stake is—in the nonreligious sense of the word—a "faith-decision," or rather a "vote of confidence": Which model will come to terms better with the new problems and at the same time preserve the most old solutions to problems? To which paradigm will the future belong? This is not so easy to say. And because we are ultimately dealing with a question of trust, the discussions between the two schools of thought and linguistic worlds are often less rational arguments than skillful attempts at wooing, persuading, and converting the other side. For both parties have their own lists of problems, their priorities, norms, and definitions, their ultimately incommensurable standpoints: let the other man adopt my so very convincing standpoint, let him accept my premises, which are different in each case. Thus the adoption of a new paradigm depends upon the decision of the individual scientist whether he wishes to make this standpoint, these specific premises his own. And doing that is precisely what makes the decision hard; because this is no purely theoretical question.

A *fifth* observation: Not only on theology but also in science a new model in its early beginnings has only a *few and mostly young advocates:*

— Copernicus was thirty-four years old when he elaborated the heliocentric systems.

— Newton, the founder of classical physics, formulated the laws of gravitation at the age of twenty-three.

— Lavoisier, the founder of modern chemistry, was twenty-five years old when he submitted to the Secretary of the Académie Française his famous sealed notes casting doubt on the predominant phlo-giston theory.

— Einstein put forward his special theory of relativity when he was twenty-six.

And as far as *theologians* go:

— The first Christian scholar to do methodical research, Origen, successfully undertook, at the age of eighteen, the labor of carrying on Christian education among the cultivated classes, a task that had been neglected since Clement's advancement in Alexandria.

— At the time of his "final" conversion Augustine was thirty-two, and Aquinas not yet thirty when he began his commentary on Peter Lombard's *Sentences* in Paris from an Aristotelian perspective.

— Finally, Luther was thirty-four years old when he proclaimed his theses on indulgences to the public.

But we can drop all the numbers. Kuhn is surely right to say with regard to natural science *and* theology that only with time will more and more scientists convert to the new paradigm and then intensively press on their new research into it. It is not just out of senile stubborn-ness, but because they are altogether wedded to the established model, that most experienced older researchers of the established model put up lifelong resistance to the new one. And it takes then a new generation—as no less a figure than Charles Darwin expressed with almost depressing clarity in the Foreword to his *Origin of Species*—until finally the great majority of the scientific community goes over to the new model of explanation. And in the final analysis it does not depend upon this researcher or that one but on the scientific community as a whole, where a new model prevails or not. Max Planck's well-known remark in his *Scientific Autobiography* holds even more truth, perhaps, for theologians than for physicists: "A new scientific truth tends to win acceptance not because its opponents become convinced and declare their conversion, but rather because the opponents gradually die out and the upcoming generation has already become familiar with the truth."[8]

Still enough material ought to have been adduced by now to formulate a provisional *fourth* thesis:

As in natural science so also in theology both scientific and non-scientific factors play a role in deciding whether a new paradigm will be adopted or rejected, so that the transition to a new model cannot be rationally compelled, but may be described as a conversion.

e) A last question remains that must be answered briefly: Is it then so certain that the new theological paradigm, the new model of understanding, always prevails? I would say that as in the great scientific quarrels, so too in theology there are three possible ways out of a crisis:

The first possibility: The new model of explanation is absorbed by the old one. Against all probability normal science proves its capacity to assimilate certain new discoveries and to improve the traditional model, without having to give it up; for example, as with Augustinianism after Thomas, or Thomism after Luther. This means:

The *Augustinianism* of the Franciscan school, which increasingly embodied even Aristotelian ideas, was picked up in modern "Scotism" and finally ended in Ockhamism, to which Luther probably owed the early features of his theology.

Thomism, too, managed to maintain itself far into the modern period (and particularly in relatively closed-off regions like Spain), although, of course—because it ignored modern science and philosophy—it changed from the theological vanguard of the thirteenth century to the rearguard of the seventeenth and (with the Neo-Thomism fostered by Rome with every means available) the nineteenth and twentieth centuries. Only with Vatican II did Thomism largely lose its dominant position in the Catholic Church.

The *second possibility:* The new model of explanation prevails against normal science and replaces the old one. This means, concretely, that scientific books, popular presentations, and comprehensive interpretations that were based on the previous model now have to be rewritten, in whole or in part. What once was originally the new, now becomes old. What began as a heretical innovation quickly turns into an honorable tradition.

All this can be observed both in the scientific and the theological macroparadigms. We should note here that the textbooks normally present primarily the received *results* of the scientific upheaval, on the other hand they often obscure the fact and the proportions of this upheaval. To that extent a textbook on physics or chemistry and often even a textbook on dogmatic theology or ethics creates a rather deceptive impression of progress in the field. Such textbooks in many ways render the revolution, the upheaval invisible, and present it simply as an e-volution, as an extension of traditional knowledge: Thus we get the impression of a cumulative growth of normal physics, an organic growth of normal dogmatics.

The *third possibility:* The problems and possibly too the conditions of the time balk against radically new approaches, and the problems are provisionally "placed in the archives." The new paradigm is put on ice.

This kind of storage in the archives can be a purely scientific process. But the theology and the Church it was often carried out with force, through the Inquisition. But this leads directly from the analogies to the differences between science and theology, and these are the object of the next section.

The series of analogies can be concluded with a provisional *fifth thesis:*

As in the science so also in theology it is hard to predict, amid the great arguments of the day, whether a new model of understanding or paradigm will be absorbed by the old one, or the old one replaced or stored in the archives for a longish time. If it is accepted, the innovation solidifies into tradition.

"It is harder to smash prejudices than atoms," Albert Einstein said once. And I would add that once they are smashed they release forces that can move mountains perhaps even in the Church. Still, we have already gathered enough food for thought, with respect to the structural similarity between science and theology in the generation of novelty. Now the question arises: With all these paradigm changes and new conceptions doesn't theology, doesn't Christian truth itself, fall prey to historical relativism, which refuses to acknowledge the concerns of Christianity and allows equal truth and validity to every paradigm? This problem may not greatly preoccupy the scientist, but it is of the greatest consequence for the Christian theologian. It was not for nothing that I spoke of "provisional theses": A *more theological counterpoint* is overdue and will be set up in the following section when, in discussing the five theses developed with the help of Kuhn, we will deal with the function of Christian theology, with the Christian understanding of truth, and with what paradigmatically distinguishes a modern, critical ecumenical theology today. We shall face the question: Is there a paradigm change at work, or a *total break?*

6. A Total Break? The Question of Continuity

The first point to be considered here is this: In the natural sciences, despite all the scientific revolutions, there is in no way a total break. Rather in each paradigm change, with all the discontinuity, there is still a *fundamental continuity.* Thomas Kuhn stresses that paradigm change involves "handling the same bundle of data as before, but placing them in a new system of relations with one another by giving them a different framework" (p. 85). The transition, for example, from Newtonian to Einsteinian mechanics does not involve the "introduction of additional objects or concepts," but only a "displacement" of the conceptual network through which scientists view the world" (p. 102). "Whatever else he may see then, the scientist after a revolution is still looking at the same world. Furthermore . . . much of his language and most of his laboratory instruments are still the same as they were before" (pp. 129–30).

We have to say still more: There is, after all, a common language for theoretical discussion, and there are also procedures for comparing results. Thus the "conversion" from one paradigm to another is not necessarily an irrational act, it does not lack arguments to justify the change of standpoint, it is never an absolute break with the past. Stephen Toulmin is right: "One must realize that paradigm changes are never as complete as the full-fledged definition maintains; that competing paradigms never really boil down to totally mutually incompatible world pictures; and that the theoretical discontinuities in science conceal deeper, subterranean methodological continuities."

This in fact is my conviction: If we wish to understand the evolution of *theology,* we have to avoid choosing not only between an absolutist and a relativistic vision, but also between a total continuity and a total discontinuity. Each paradigm change shows at the same time continuity *and* discontinuity, rationality *and* irrationality, conceptual stability *and* conceptual change—in short, evolutionary *and* revolutionary elements. And if anyone dislikes speaking about "revolutionary changes," then he can speak of *drastic* (and not just gradual) or *paradigmatic* (and not just conceptual) *changes* that, needless to say, include gradual and conceptual alterations.

In the historical sciences and *theology* far more than in the basically nonhistorical natural sciences, which mention their founding fathers and heroes only marginally and in introductions, the issue is *not* to *rediscover a tradition,* but *rather* to *reformulate tradition,* in the light, of course, of a new paradigm: "Novelty for its own sake is not a desideratum in the sciences as it is in so many other creative fields. . . . As a result, though new paradigms seldom or never possess all the capabilities of their predecessors, they usually possess a great deal of the most concrete parts of past achievement and they always permit additional concrete problem-solutions besides" (Kuhn, p. 169).

For theology the problem of continuity naturally presents itself with altogether greater profundity. For we are looking here for something that Kuhn avoids mentioning until the very last pages (p. 182) of his book—the "truth." Indeed, we are looking for the "truth of life" or —as Wittgenstein said—the "problems of life." The natural scientist in general takes a less direct departure from the problems of life: "Unlike the engineer, and many doctors, and most theologians, the scientist need not choose problems because they urgently need solution and without regard for the tools available to solve them" (Kuhn, p. 164). And because the theologian is more immediately interested in the problems of life, he must care more about recognition not from the "experts," but from a broader public: Even "the most abstract of theologians is far more concerned than the scientist with lay approbation of his creative work, though he may be less concerned with approbation in general" (Kuhn, p. 164). Kuhn then, as a scientist, has no answer to the obvious life question about where the gigantic process of development, both of science and the world in general, is headed: "Inevitably that lacuna will have disturbed many readers" (p. 171). But he also has no answer to the vital question about the Origins: "Anyone who has followed the argument this far will nevertheless feel the need to ask why the evolutionary process should work" (p. 173).

As a matter of fact, we run up here against the *limits of science,* which remains bound in its judgments to the horizon of our experience in space and time. Perhaps we are also coming up against the limits of the humanities and the social sciences and—if Kant is right— the limits of philosophy itself, insofar as it is a science of pure reason. Life questions about the Whence and Whither of the world and man, hence about first and last interpretations and standards, values, and norms, and so in general about a first and final reality: These are questions of a certainly not irrational, but altogether reasonable, believing trust or trusting faith. As far as they are concerned, *theology* as a "science"—theology as thinking speech or reckoning about God (Augustine, *De civitate Dei,* vol. III, bk 1: *"de divinitate ratio sive sermo")*—is responsible for these questions: responsible, of course, in a way corresponding to their own method. For, like questions of nature, questions of the psyche and society, of justice, politics, history, and aesthetics, so too must questions of morality and religion be treated in accordance with a particular method and style that fits their object. What does this mean?

7. Differences Between Theology and Science

For *Christian* theology, which is unconditionally scientific still less than other scientific disciplines, it is characteristic that the *Christian message,* as originally attested to in Scripture, was handed down by the Christian community through the centuries and is still proclaimed today—is its *presupposition* and its *object.* For that reason Christian theology, for all its scholarly rigor, is essentially defined by its relation to history, *historicity.* Christian theology is interested in a profoundly historical truth. Precisely insofar as it was historical, it distinguished itself from the beginning (1) from *un*historical-mythological "theologies," that is the sagas and sayings of the gods of the mythic poets and cult priests (Plato was the first one to use the word *theologia* in this sense and at the same time to criticize it, (2) from *super*-historical-philosophical "theologies," that is the natural doctrines of God taught by the philosophers.

This needs to be scanned more closely. Christian theology is quite definitely a thinking account of the truth of *Christian* faith, of the faith in other words, that is concerned with the cause of *Jesus Christ* and hence with the cause of God and at the same time the cause of man. This Jesus Christ is neither an unhistorical myth nor a superhistorical idea, doctrine, or world view. He is rather the historical Jesus of Nazareth, who according to the testimonies in the New Testament is the standard for believers of all times and all churches, as the Anointed One of God. The original *faith-testimony of this Christ Jesus* forms the basis of Christian theology.

But still, doesn't this exclude in advance any critical scholarly work from the picture? By no means. Just as, for example, the historian or the expert on constitutional law has no other history or constitution to interpret, in critical loyalty, except the one given in fact, so the theologian—at least if he wants to be and remain a Christian theologian—has no other testimony to faith than those originally written down in the Old and New Testament, which was transmitted through the ages in continually new linguistic shape and always has to be retranslated for contemporary men and women.

To that extent, now Christian theology is not *only,* like the natural sciences, *connected to the present and the future.* It is also not *only,* like every historical discipline (the history of literature, art, philosophy, the world), *oriented to tradition.* Beyond all that it is in a quite specific sense *oriented to its origins:* The original event in the history of Israel and of Jesus Christ, and hence the primal testimony, the Old and New Testament documents, remains for it not just the historical beginning of Christian faith, but at the same time its continual reflexive point.

And this above all is what, despite all the parallels, still shows us important differences *between a paradigm change in natural science and one in theology,* Christian theology. The five provisional theses, with which I have tried to explain the emergence of novelty in theology, hence have to submit to some distinctions:

a) On thesis 1 concerning *normal science:* For theological normal science classic authors, texts, and teachers are important. They provide the established theological macromodel, along with its meso- and micromodels in a systematic form that is easy to appropriate. But unlike the situation in the natural sciences, they are granted at best only secondary, derivative authority. This is true also of all conciliar and theological authorities, which normal theology continually invokes and which can always be only the "normed norm" *(norma normata)*.

The primary norm, the *norma normans,* which controls all other norms (including councils and the popes) is the primitive biblical witness. According to the Catholic view of things (Vatican II) this has to be the "soul," the "principle of life" of every theology. The theologian can invoke this primitive testimony of the Bible at all times. And because theologians have in fact continually done this—in mediated immediacy—the great paradigmatic schools have always been paralleled by constantly creative individuals and groups who have gone their own way and who could yet never be denied the title of "theologians" (the criteria differentiating a genuine mediation of immediacy will be discussed later). They have—think of, say, the Dutch and German mystics of the late Middle Ages, or of Pascal, Bérulle, and the École Française of the seventeenth century—developed their own theological model apart from the mainstream of theology by invoking the primal testimony. That already gives us something to say about thesis 2.

b) On thesis 2 on the *crisis as the point of departure:* In theology too a crisis can be unleashed by certain historical and sociopolitical factors or by developments within the sciences. But, more than that, it can at a given moment in time—as in the case of Luther and other "reformers" in antiquity, the Middle Ages, and the modern period— make a breakthrough by means of an immediate, altogether personal experience of the original Christian message.

The primal Christian testimony—which theology has never fully gotten abreast of has continually revealed an inspiring force that continually troubles and towers over theology, that has in fact shown in cases where the Church and theology had become all too hardened a downright revolutionary explosiveness. Then under the circumstances even older, forgotten paradigms came back, and backward glances turned into new vistas. Think of the appeal to the Paul of the Letter to the Romans in Augustine, Luther, and Karl Barth, whose consequence in each case was a "theology of crisis." Think too of the rediscovery by Johannes Weiss and Albert Schweitzer of Jesus' preaching about the coming Kingdom of God at the end of time.

Thus the Gospel itself—naturally always in the context of the great contemporary-historical developments—appears here as the direct provocation of theological crisis, as the reason for discontinuity in theology, as the impetus for the new paradigm. This leads to the third thesis.

c) On thesis 3 concerning the *paradigmatic upheavals:* This same *primal* testimony of Christianity is also for theology and the Church a permanent *foundational testimony.* It can be the occasion not only for theology's entering a crisis, but also for the fact that in the theological upheaval a new paradigm *does* arise, but not simply through a total replacement or total suppression of the old paradigm.

Now of course in the natural sciences there has been controversy over Kuhn's pressing the point that in scientific revolutions (e.g., Einsteinian versus Newtonian mechanics) the new model completely replaces and suppresses the old one. In theology, at all events, the primal, basic Christian testimony—which is common to the "old-fashioned thinkers" and the "new-fashioned thinkers," the "problem-solvers" of normal science and their opponents, the "paradigm testers"—deliberately takes care that the old paradigm is not fully repressed. This means that, in principle, elements of the old paradigm can be taken over into the new paradigm, unless they contract the primal, basic testimony. In this way steps have been taken in advance so that, not only between Origen and Augustine, but also between Augustine and Thomas, and even between Thomas and Luther, an upheaval does not lead to a total break; what happens, rather, is that with the common bond of Christian faith a certain amount of common theological ground is also preserved. Think, for example, of the affirmation of justification through faith alone not only in Luther's commentary on the Letter to the Romans, but also in the commentaries of Thomas, Augustine, and Origen.

To be sure, the Christian message (Gospel, faith) on the one hand, and Christian theology (doctrine, scholarship) on the other, must be distinguished. But they cannot be fully separated, for two reasons: On the one hand, even the New Testament Scriptures themselves always offer the Christian message in specific and very different linguistic guises and schemata; on the other hand the post–New Testament theological models always aim at expounding one and the same Christian message. That is why there were more than opportunistic reasons, there were thoroughly serious and objective reasons, why great theologians—including Luther—always had been nervous about rejecting the previous school of theology outright, and about speaking of their new theological insights as if they had discovered previously unknown stars. In this context too we can understand why people even felt an aversion toward the word "revolution" in theology.

All this means that a drastic, paradigmatic upheaval can take place in Christian theology—if it is to be and remain Christian— always and only on *basis* of the Gospel, and ultimately *on account of* the Gospel, but never *against* the Gospel. The Gospel of Jesus Christ himself—much as the testimonies to him must be deeply probed by means of historico-criticism—is no more at the theologian's disposition, to rule on its truth, than history is for the historian or the Constitution for the constitutional lawyer. The Gospel itself appears here as the reason not only for discontinuity, but for continuity in theology: a theological paradigm change is thus based on the permanence of the Christian message. And from there we move to thesis 4.

d) On thesis 4 concerning *conversion and extra-scientific factors* in paradigm change: This thesis is intensified rather more when looked at specifically from the viewpoint of theology. For, unlike the situation in the sciences (where such things have happened, of course), there is always the danger in theology that the scientific decision for this or that paradigm will be made into an existential decision for or against the cause of faith itself.

The "decision to believe" (in the nonreligious sense), the "vote of confidence" for or against a theological paradigm, is then overblown into a "decision to believe" (in the strictly religious sense) for or against God and his Christ. And Protestant Fundamentalists or Catholic traditionalists demand conversion to the "Gospel" or to "Catholic doctrine" when the only conversion is to a (perhaps long outdated) theological paradigm. The theological opponent is then necessarily made over into the heretic or unbeliever, becomes either un-Catholic or un-Protestant, indeed is turned into a potential Antichrist and atheist. This leads to a tightening of the argument in thesis 5.

e) On thesis 5 concerning the *three possible upshots of a quarrel* over a paradigm: When theology and the Church *reject* a specific model of understanding, then that rejection easily becomes a condemnation, and discussions lead to excommunication: The Gospel and theology are identified, the Church's essence is equated with the Church's system, the contents of faith equal the shape of faith. Conversely, we see with the same identification that

— When a model of understanding is, however, *accepted* and turns from innovation to tradition, once again it becomes easy to make over a theological interpretation into a truth of revelation; the *theologoumenon* becomes dogma, tradition becomes traditionalism.

— When a model of understanding is finally *put in the archives,* this can often be a purely scientific process. But it was precisely in theology and the Church that it was often carried out with force and repression: contrary to all human rights there was persecution of heretics, the Inquisition, physical or psychic burning at the stake of opponents, or simply suppression of discussion.

Even the great theologians we have named—Origen, Augustine, Thomas, Luther—did not escape, at least posthumous blame, or even condemnation. Consider the following:

‛ — Origen, for example, had a rather serious conflict with his bishop, Demetrius. After his death he was—with the progressive solidifying of church doctrine after the Council of Nicaea—accused of heresy by Epiphanius and Jerome, and in the sixth century he was condemned by pope Anastasius, then by the Emperor Justinian (who had most of his works destroyed), and finally by the Fifth Ecumenical Council of Constantinople.

— Quite early on, then above all around the time of Jansenism, and all the way into the twentieth century, there were warnings of all sorts issued against Augustine, whose authority must not necessarily be preferred to that of the magisterium. (Perhaps these warnings were not unfair with regard to his teaching on double predestination and the irresistible working of grace). Later, Augustinianism simply went under.

— The condemnation of Thomas in 1277 (three years after his death) by the bishops of the two leading universities of Christendom, Paris and Oxford, has been characterized as the "the most momentous condemnation of the Middle Ages" (van Steenberghen), through which the further free development of theology was for a long time stopped cold.

— Everyone knows what the condemnation and excommunication of Luther meant and still means today.

Still, the question can no longer be put off: Which paradigm, which model of understanding is appropriate to today's theology? I shall attempt to sketch it out carefully, offering no all-comprehensive hermeneutics (we have already spoken in detail of Scripture, Tradition, and the magisterium), but some guidelines (especially in regard to the constants of a new theological paradigm).

8. A Critical Ecumenical Theology

a) *Heuristic criteria:* I mention here a few crucial presuppositions of the new paradigm, which are applicable not just to theology, but which ought to be understood as heuristic criteria that determine any sort of genuine human research. These criteria are especially important in shedding light on the process of mediation, in which the original biblical testimony is continually actualized in new situations throughout history. Precisely because these criteria determine all human research, the paradigmatic approach cannot be used to legitimize a traditionalistic or fundamentalist theological sectarianism (as in "We have a different paradigm—'Christian,' 'biblical,' 'Catholic'—from the one the 'world' has"). I cannot develop fully here the heuristic character of these presuppositions. Instead I will only state briefly the relevance of these very basic human attitudes for theology. Theology must be

(1) A true (not conformist or opportunistic) theology: a thinking account of faith that seeks and says Christian truth in truthfulness. And this by all means to serve the *unity* of the Church. For there can be no true Church without a true theology.

(2) A *free* (not authoritarian) theology: a theology that can meet its responsibilities without hindrance from administrative measures and sanctions and can profess and publish its reasonable convictions, following the best lights of its knowledge and conscience.

And all this again to serve the *authority* of the Church. For there is no free Church without a free theology.

(3) A *critical* (not a traditionalistic) theology: a theology that is free and true, that knows its obligation to the scholarly ethos of truth, to methodological discipline, and the Church's supervision of the way it poses all the issues, of its methods, and results.

And this entirely to serve the "edification" of the Church, its construction in this society. For there can be no critical Church in this society without a critical theology.

(4) An *ecumenical* (not a denominational) theology: a theology that sees in every other theology not an opponent but a partner, is bent on understanding instead of separation, and this in two directions: inwards for the realm of the inter-church and internal church ecumene, and outwards, for the domain of the extra-ecclesiastical, non-Christian-world ecumene with its different regions, religions, ideologies, and sciences. This sort of ecumenism corresponds to the transcultural, universalistic aspects of paradigm analysis in theology and other disciplines.

And this is entirely meant to serve the *mission* of the Church in this society. For there can be no ecumenical Church without an ecumenical theology.

b) *Historical presuppositions:* This paradigm of a true and free *critical ecumenical theology* is now, of course, not something that has to be discovered today or presented in a completely new proposal. In the face of the major twentieth-century theological figures, such as, for example, Albert Schweitzer, Karl Barth, Rudolf Bultmann, Dietrich Bonhoeffer, or Paul Tillich—not to mention those who are still living—this would be ridiculous. This sort of paradigm rather "grows to maturity" (Kuhn too is familiar with this term in the context of scientific evolution) over a rather long period; and nowadays not the least of its tasks is to embody the decisive theological impulses emitted by the theologians we have just named. It is by now a generally accepted notion that the end of confessional thinking in the seventeenth and eighteenth centuries, and the rise of modern thought with the Enlightenment, German Idealism, and Romanticism meant a great, epochal break for theology. An abundance of the most varied experiences has since then come into contact with this *theology of modernity* and often entered into it and fundamentally changed its understanding of humanity, society, the cosmos, and even God. Theology has been changed—to indicate the areas briefly—by permanent findings in

(1) modern *science*, which from Copernicus to Darwin and Einstein shows us the place of man in the cosmos, the creation

and evolution in the world, and so the creator and "evolver" himself in a wholly different light;

(2) modern *philosophy,* which from Descartes, Kant, and Hegel all the way to Heidegger, Whitehead, and critical theory give us a new understanding not only of reason, freedom, the historical and social nature of man, but also the historicity and worldliness of God;

(3) modern *democracy,* which—beginning with the American Declaration of Independence and the Bill of Rights and with the French Revolution—has led to a new understanding of individual freedom, of human rights, but ultimately too of social justice, and of the state, society, and thus of the Church as well;

(4) modern *criticism of religion,* which discovered the always possible misuse of religion for anti-human alienation (Feuerbach), for the stabilization of unjust social structures (Marx), for the moral degradation of man (Nietzsche) and for infantile regression (Freud);

(5) the modern *humanities and social sciences,* which especially since the nineteenth century have led us to understand the individual, his psyche (consciousness and unconsciousness), his behavior, and his social nature in a concrete and highly nuanced fashion altogether different from what was possible in the days of Aristotle, Augustine, Thomas, or Martin Luther;

(6) modern *exegesis and history,* which since Spinoza, Simon and Bayle, since Reimarus, Lessing, Semler and Strauss has taught us a critical new understanding of both the history of Israel and the history of Jesus of Nazareth, the history of the Church and the history of dogma;

(7) the modern *liberation movements,* which back in the nineteenth century fought against purely formal freedom (only for the "bourgeois"), against sexism, unjust social structures, against racism, imperialism, and colonialism, so as to mete out full justice to women, colored peoples, and the Third World.

These, then, are some (not all!) of the historical elements and developments that have to be considered for a modern theological and truly ecumenical paradigm. By a glance at them we have gotten to know the heuristic criteria and historical presuppositions of the new theological paradigm. The only theology adequate to the modern period is one that is critically/constructively engaged in the experiences of the modern person. If we now—amid the flow of history—look for some constants of the new paradigm, we can sum up all that has been said as follows: The first constant of the new theological paradigm has to be the contemporary world of experience.

9. Horizon? The World (First Constant)

Thus we have already pointed to the one pole or, more exactly, the *horizon,* of the paradigm of a modern ecumenical theology. In other words there can be no timeless or "worldless" theology. This horizon can only be *our own present-day human world of experience:* all the historical and current experiences that make up our ambivalent present-day reality.

Reality? Yes, that is everything real, is everything that is: all being, the totality of beings, the existing act of being itself. Naturally I cannot go into a detailed analysis here of what reality is. Reality cannot be defined a priori. The All-Comprehensive cannot by definition be defined or demarcated. I will only briefly call attention to what is concretely meant here by this multilayered and many-dimensional term, so that what we say will not be abstract or devoid of content.

The reality that theology has to deal with is in the first instance the *world* and everything that makes up the world in time and space, the macrocosmos and microcosmos with all their abysses. The world in its history, in past, present, and future. The world with matter and energy, with nature and culture, with all its wonders and terrors. Not the world where "all's right," in any event, but the real world in all its questionableness: with all its concrete conditions and natural catastrophes, with its concrete misery and all its pain. Animals and men in a struggle for existence: delivered up to emergence and extinction, "eating and being eaten." The whole world, in its ambivalence, which is so hard to accept, as Dostoyevsky describes it in his novel *The Brothers Karamazov:* "Yet would you believe it," says the skeptic Ivan Karamazov to his young brother Alyosha, who has faith in God, "in the final result I don't accept this world of God's. Although I know it exists, I don't accept it at all. It's not that I don't accept God, you must understand, it's the world created by Him I don't and cannot accept" (tr. Constance Garnett).

Reality means, as far as this world goes, especially the *human beings,* the men and women of all social strata and classes, of all colors and races, nations and regions, the individuals and their society. Human beings: the farthest away and above all the closest neighbors, who are often the most remote to us. The men and women with all their human, all-too-humanness. No ideal human race: at any rate, with everything thrown in, everything that we would prefer to exclude when we hear the *"Seid umschlungen, Millionen"* (Be embraced, you millions) and the *"Kuss der ganzen Welt"* (kiss of the whole world) in Schiller's "Ode to Joy." Humanity also includes the people who can make our life a hell on the grand or a minor scale: *"L'enfer, c'est les autres"* (Hell is other people) is the main thesis of Jean-Paul Sartre's drama *No Exit,* expounded by the three protagonists who are damned to stay together in one room with the light forever turned on: Sartre analyzes the failure of being-together in his great philosophical work *Being and Nothingness* from every angle.

Above all *I myself* am reality, I who can become an object to myself. I myself with mind and body, with my inclinations and behavior, with my strengths and weaknesses. No ideal person, in any case, but an individual with his heights and depths, day side and night side, with everything that C. G. Jung calls the "shadow" of a person, with everything that the person has cast off, suppressed, and repressed and what Freud tried with all the tools of analysis to lift into consciousness and make acceptable. I am a person who is always disintegrating into the various social roles that he has to play in society, who also always has to fulfill specific social functions that society expects of him. Often people have an easier time accepting the world than themselves, as they are or were made by others. "I'm not Stiller," begins the novel *Stiller* by the Swiss writer Max Frisch, who tells the story of a man who stubbornly refuses to accept himself because he wishes to escape from the images that others have made of him; because he wants to cast off the roles that others force him to play; because he suffers from the fact that he cannot be the way he wants to be, but the way he is supposed to be. Against this background problems of identity and role-playing so characteristic of modern man, a person's self-acceptance becomes a serious difficulty. Jung said that "the simple [however] is always the hardest. In reality being simple is the highest art, and thus self-acceptance is the quintessence of the moral problem and the core of an entire world view."[9]

This much then should be clear: The reality of the world, humanity, and myself reveals itself most profoundly in its *ambivalence:* Success and failure, beauty and ugliness, fortune and misfortune, weal and woe, sense and nonsense. And the point is not to malign the world, so that theologians can bring their God into play all the better, but to take an unprejudiced inventory of what is there. Theology does not make reality, it interprets it.

If we wish to sum up all these thoughts in a short *sixth thesis* we can say

> The first constant, the first pole or horizon of a critical ecumenical theology is our present-day world of experience with all its ambivalence, contingency, and changeableness.

Only a theology that does its work against the background of today's horizon of experience, only a strictly scholarly and, precisely because of this, a cosmopolitan and up-to-date theology: only this sort of theology, it seems to me, deserves a place today in the University amid all the other sciences and disciplines. Only this sort of theology is a truly ecumenical theology, which has laid aside the still widespread denominational ghetto mentality and can combine the greatest possible tolerance toward extra-ecclesiastical and generally religious phenomena, toward the simply human with the task of elaborating what is specifically Christian. Which brings us to the second pole of a present-day paradigm of modern theology, which has, so to speak, moved elliptically from one pole to another and back again. Hence there is tension, not only between both poles, but constant movement in "critical correlation" (Paul Tillich). If we want no *"world-less"* theology, we also want *no "god-less"* theology.

10. What Standard?
The Christian Message
(Second Constant)

Given the broad horizon of such an ecumenical theology, given, in particular the contradictoriness of so many experiences, individual and collective, historical and everyday, the great question arises: In the face of all this what should theology adhere to? What is its *criterion?* We have already given the basic criteriological answer to this:

Insofar as ecumenical theology wants to be Christian theology, its criterion, its first norm, can be none other than the *Christian message*, on which it builds on as its ultimate foundation: The primal and fundamental Christian testimony, as it has found expression in the Old and the New Testament Scriptures, is the basic norm of ecumenical theology. If the universal temporal and spatial horizon manifests the *Catholic* dimension of such ecumenical theology, then the orientation toward the primal and fundamental Christian testimony (the Gospel) manifests its *Protestant* dimension; and only in linking together the Catholic and Protestant dimension, blending Catholic breadth with Protestant depth, is truly *ecumenical* theology possible.

We do not hesitate, in the context of the Old and New Testament testimony to speak of *God's word and revelation*, which appeal to the *faith* of the individual. We want no time-less or world-less theology, and no god-less theology either. But this must not be understood mythologically or fundamentalistically, but historically: For God's revelation does not fall down from heaven, like the Qur'an, for example—as strictly orthodox Muslims think—which was dictated word for word to Muhammad by an angel, and for that reason must also be literally accepted, repeated, and applied all the way down to the regulations of an archaic penal code. No, it has become increasingly clear that God's revelation takes place in and through the history of Israel and of Jesus of Nazareth, and is understood in and through the *experiences* that believers have had, in very different ways, in this history with their God. And the Old and New Testament Scriptures are thus not directly, not immediately, God's Word, as, for example, the Qur'an explicitly claims to be. They are and remain human words that attest to the Word of God and have already interpreted it in highly individualistic ways.

For that reason it bears repeating that we are dealing with experiences from the history of Jesus and experiences with Jesus that have already been interpreted by the various biblical authors each in his own way, sometimes deepening, sometimes flattening out. The common key experience of salvation in Israel and Jesus as coming from God is never given "pure," but always through varying modes of interpretation, through varying sorts of concepts and images, schemata and models of understanding. These can be concepts such as "Son of Man" and "Son of God," images such as the descent into hell and the ascent into heaven, individual schemata such as bloody sacrifices of atonement and ransoming of slaves in the doctrine of redemption, whole models of understanding such as the apocalyptic vision of the end of time or the Church's view of salvation history: They all derive from a *past* world of experience and language, which for the most part no longer speaks directly to us. That is why they must all be mediated anew, must be distinguished in order to get a better understanding of the subject matter itself, must sometimes even be replaced. In any event the crucial point is that through all the texts the substance itself, the Christian message, the Gospel, can once again be heard afresh *and* understood. So we need a theology that is both timely and appropriate. Only when the Jewish-Christian tradition of experience, when even words like God, salvation, and grace are connected with our *present-day* experiences, can we experience for ourselves what was experienced in the Bible. Theology, then, is interested not just in a simple "application" of a supposedly eternal doctrine, but rather in the "trans-lation" of a historical message from the world of past experience into our present-day world of experience.

To that extent theology is facing a great task of *critical correlation,* which often enough takes on the form of a critical *confrontation:* to relate our own experiences to the experiences of the Christian-Jewish tradition, and to interpret them in the light of the history of Jewish-Christian experience, indeed in the case of contradiction to correct them. For when biblical and contemporary experiences fundamentally contradict one another, when contemporary "experiences," such as in the Third Reich, once more present us with a "leader" from the Right (or Left), with some sort of political "salvation movement," or similar "achievements": What then should decide the issue in the crucial first-and-last questions affecting man and humanity? The biblical experiences, the Christian message, the Gospel, Jesus Christ himself. For this Christ Jesus is in person the "essence of Christianity," the "Christian message," the "Gospel" itself, indeed God's "Word," "made flesh."

We can sum up this section in a *seventh* thesis:

The second constant, the second pole or the basic norm of a critical ecumenical theology is the Jewish-Christian tradition, which in the final analysis is based on the Christian message, the Gospel of Jesus Christ.

These, it seems to me, are the essential structures of a new paradigm of theology: a theology against background of the contemporary world of experience, critically grounded in the Christian message. That is, so to speak, the *"cantus firmus"* of this book. This is a theology that in a new age tries to be at once:

(1) "Catholic," that is, constantly concerned with the "whole," the "universal" Church, *and* at the same time "Protestant," strictly intent on Scripture and the Gospel;

(2) "traditional," that is, always responsible to history, *and* at the same time "contemporary," passionately addressing the questions of the present;

(3) "Christocentric," that is, decidely and distinctly Christian, *and* still "ecumenical," oriented to the "ecumene," the whole "inhabited earth," all Christian churches, all religions, all regions of the world;

(4) theoretical-scholarly, engaged in the study of doctrine and truth, *and* at the same time practical-pastoral, taking pains with the life, the renewal, and the reform of the Church.

In this chapter I have tried as precisely as possible to sketch out the main features of a slow-ripening paradigm of a critical ecumenical theology. I am well aware that only the practical-theological implementation can decide about the effectiveness, convincingness, and truth content of this sort of new paradigm. But amid all the problems and difficulties faced by theology, the Church, and society, I would like to hope that—despite all the differences—a path has been opened here to a *basic consensus* in theology: not a uniform theological school, not an all-comprehensive theory, not an exclusive method, but a theological paradigm that allows different methods, theories, schools, and theologies.

III

A New Basic Model of Theology?

Disputable and Indisputable Points

Do we need today, *is* there today something like a new paradigm or basic model of theology? That question was the starting point of our International Ecumenical Symposium in Tübingen in 1983, which discussed the theological situation of the most varied theological schools, countries, and continents and from all possible standpoints. Despite all the different theories, methods, and structures, indeed despite different theologies, are there universal constants that every Christian theology must presuppose if it wishes to be an intellectually responsible account of the Christian faith?

The draft papers for this symposium, the papers presented at the Symposium itself, and, finally, the discussions undertaken there made it clear that for all the divergencies there are also convergencies with regard to the dimensions of a new theological paradigm.[1] In taking up the contributions of my colleagues from the University of Chicago, above all by Stephen Toulmin, Langdon Gilkey, Martin Marty, Anne Carr, and David Tracy; of my Tübingen colleagues, Jürgen Moltmann, Eberhard Jüngel, Norbert Greinacher, Rüdiger Bubner, as well as the work of J. B. Metz (Münster), Gregory Baum (Toronto), Leonardo Boff (Petrópolis), Jean-Pierre Jossua and Claude Geffré (both from Paris), Josef Blank (Saarbrücken), Edward Schillebeeckx (Nijmegen), John Cobb (Claremont), Elisabeth Schüssler-Fiorenza

(Notre Dame), and Mariasusai Dhavamony (Rome), I have tried to take both the discussions held at the symposium, as well as the dimensions of the new paradigm that they elaborated, and synthesize them for discussion.

1. *"Paradigm": A Controversial Concept*

No doubt we were handicapped by the fact that Thomas S. Kuhn, although invited, unfortunately could not be present at the symposium because of special circumstances. Because of this, the philosophical "opposition" to the concept of paradigm was well represented, but the professional theoretician, the "defender," failed to speak for his own cause.

For it was only to be expected that the *concept of paradigm* would be the subject of controversial discussion—among theologians, for whom it was largely something new, but also among philosophers. The keenest critic of Kuhn's theory of paradigms, the philosopher Stephen Toulmin, made no secret in the debate of his skepticism about the word "paradigm." Nevertheless, it became clear that despite their different methodological approaches (Toulmin's more piecemeal approach goes more into the detail of the development of concepts and judgments, whereas Kuhn's paradigmatic approach was more sweeping, interested in the total constellation of convictions, values, and patterns of behavior), the two men have a great deal *in common.* Negatively, the rejection of antihistorical logical empiricism and its formalistic approach, as we still find it in Karl Popper with its source in the Vienna school. There people are interested only in the alteration of concepts and in the logical connections in the progress of knowledge and science.

Positively, Kuhn and Toulmin are linked by their affirmation of the unity of the theory, the history, and the sociology of science, and hence the reflection on the intellectual evolution of scientific theories in the context of the social-historical evolution of scientific schools, professions, and institutions. The discussions clearly showed that when one adopts the term "paradigm" in theology in a nuanced fashion, the objective differences of opinion over the term shrink to a minimum, practically to the simple question of whether the *word* paradigm is a happy choice or not (as Stephen Toulmin admitted in departing, "Between you and myself there is only *one word,* nothing else").

Now the *issue* we were all concerned about is too important to be turned into a quarrel over a word. In the meantime, however, a word *is* needed. And instead of the word paradigm (basic model) there were hardly any other suggestions that proved to be more convincing, including the term "structural hórizon" (Geffré). On the contrary, we could see that in the final analysis the term did seem usable; moreover, the term became increasingly clear the more material we brought in to explain the issue, and, among us, the initial skepticism gave way. We were dealing with wide-sweeping, deep-rooted alterations in the history of theology and the Church. And then the evidence showed that for these "epochal shifts" (Gilkey called them "continental shifts") one could hardly find a better expression than that of change, from which a *new "paradigm"* emerges (for the Hellenistic-Byzantine Imperial Church, for the Latin Western papal Church, for the Reformation, for modernity or the Enlightenment, for the post-Enlightenment or post-modernity).

The *presupposition* here, of course, is that this term maintains, on the one hand, its breadth and elasticity, but on the other hand its specificity and precision, which was brought out clearly in the draft papers. If "paradigm" is used for every possible situation, the term becomes threadbare. Not *everything* can be a paradigm. Not every theory, not every method, not every hermeneutics, not every theology is ipso facto a paradigm. A paradigm in the precise sense is—as the draft papers echoing Thomas S. Kuhn's definition, had it—"an entire constellation of beliefs, values, and techniques, and so on, shared by the members of a given community."

It was important that no one raised any objections against two points: first the fact of epochal upheavals, which shape the history of theology, the Church, and the world as a whole; second, the proposed *periodization* (see the schema on p. 128), which largely follows the familiar periodization for world history, church history, and the history of theology, much as we presupposed—and indeed had to presuppose (Moltmann)—only the previous history of Christianity (hitherto ignoring other domains of culture and religion).

The discussion often led to talk about the *crises* in the history of theology and the Church that led to the paradigm change (for example, Metz emphasized the replacement of Jewish Christianity by Hellenistic Christianity, others spoke of the crisis in the early Middle Ages and the East-West schism or the continually cited two great crises of the Reformation and early modernity). Still in this report I wish to limit myself to the factors in the contemporary crisis that could serve to outline a new paradigm (a post-Enlightenment or postmodern paradigm), for which we still cannot come up with the key term. Certainly there is a lot more that might be said about the active mechanisms here, the concurrent scientific and nonscientific factors, about the necessity of conversion in the transition to a new paradigm and the uncertainty of the outcome in a dispute over paradigms.

This much at least is certain: Neither the individual theologian nor theology as a whole can simply create a paradigm. Rather, a paradigm takes shape in an extraordinary complex of various social, political, ecclesiastical, and theological factors. It grows out of them and matures in them. In the course of this highly complex process, which need not always take such a dramatic course as it did in Luther's case, but which definitely includes not only gradual but drastic, and, precisely, paradigmatic changes, the individual theologian will sooner or later face the question of whether the *paradigm of theology* still corresponds to the *paradigm of his time*. He will thus be presented with the decision of what paradigm he wants to work with. Once and for all he will have to choose—and lay bare his loyalties, his ties, and his interests.

2. Clarifications

Before I spell out the factors of this crisis in detail, here are a few fundamental determinations that our discussion produced:

(1) The "given society" (Kuhn) in which the theological paradigm change occurs is the *community of theologians* (scholarly or not, theologians at a university or in a base community, professional writers or lay people, men or women), in the context of the *community of believers* (hence in the Church in the broad sense of the word), against the background of the human community as a whole (in other words, human society).

(2) The *paradigm of theology* has to be seen in the context of the paradigm of the *Church* against the background of the paradigmatic changes in society as a whole: Hence the history of theology, the Church, and the world have to be analyzed in connection with each other, and *not*—as was continually stressed, especially by Boff, Dussel, and Metz—from a Eurocentric perspective.

(3) The *subjects* of theology and its *locales*—this point frequently came up—can therefore change (Baum, Boff, Greinacher, Jossua, Metz): not only the university but the base community can be a place for theology. Not just the academic—and only the male of the species —but women and nonacademics can be its practitioners.

(4) *Theology* cannot simply take over a paradigm from *science* or gather from it something like the raw material for the construction of a new theological paradigm (as Thomas Aquinas did with Aristotelian physics or Protestant theologians did with Descartes and Newton). To be sure, theology must not ignore the findings of science either, as both Neo-Scholastic and Protestant fundamentalist theologians do. Rather the dialogue between science and theology has to take place on the basis of equal rights (Toulmin): Then on the one hand the limitations of the natural sciences (including behaviorism and psychoanalysis) will become evident; on the other hand, however, the "current meaning" of scientific ideas and analyses (which must be explored in patient, piecemeal examination) will be made fruitful for theology.

(5) The philosophical debate with the theory of paradigm change forces theology for its part to clarify the *relation between rationality and irrationality* (strictly in accordance with theological and nontheological factors), particularly (Bubner says)

— the relation between *reality and speech,* empirical experience and theory, facts and perception;

— the problem of *periodization* through paradigms: only through the new does the normal become the old; the old, the new, and threshold of eras come into existence side by side and in conjunction; the division of time into strata cannot be done by time itself nor from some suprahistorical standpoint outside of time, but can be undertaken only immanently and relatively;

— the problem of the *dialectic of knowledge and history:* the internal scholarly history of theology and its external marginal conditions cannot be separated, but have to be seen in context. Theology can neither be explained by social factors nor can it be simply abstracted from them. The rule holds for theology too: In the end no theory is the master of its conditions, but within the framework of this dialectic of knowledge and history it is no longer totally at their mercy.

(6) The *criteria* for a new paradigm will need to be discussed further in the future. An important mode of specifying the criteria, as found in Kuhn, is constituted for theology by the capacity for perceiving and processing crises (Metz): Crises are an interruption in the usual connections in life and thought, so that in the Church and theology the world before and after is no longer the same.

3. The Present-day Crisis: What We Don't Have to Argue About Any More

(1) The loss of the 400-year-old political-military and economic-cultural predominance of the West (Europe and then America) since the Second World War and the *discovery of other* political-military and economic-cultural *centers of power* (Gilkey): *polycentrism* (Metz).

(2) The deep ambiguities of the basic forces, potentially just as *creative as destructive*, of our culture in both West and East—the forces of *science, technology, and industrialization.* Technological-industrial culture bears within itself a fatal potential for destruction: destruction of the environment and the possible destruction of humanity through atomic overkill (Blank, Cobb, Gilkey, Metz, Moltmann, Schillebeeckx).

(3) Along with cultural polycentrism, *social antagonism*—exploitation and suppression, racism and sexism—offers the central challenge in our century for theology, the Church, and society (Boff, Carr, Cobb, Gilkey, Metz, Moltmann).

(4) A visible *jolt has been delivered to the fundamental symbol system of modern culture,* which stands beneath the sign of the myth of *progress*—scientific, technological, industrial, as well as political and social progress. An optimistic modern view of history (supported by progressive theologies and ideologies from both the liberal-democratic and the socialist-Marxist camp) was followed by a widespread pessimistic disorientation, hopelessness, anxiety about the future (Gilkey et al.). Needless to say, this is characteristic above all for the modern industrial affluent societies, not necessarily for all Third-World countries (Cobb).

(5) We can make out critical developments, especially momentous for theology, within the framework of the modern paradigm from the changed and now precarious position of the *book*, of the role of the *university*, of theology as a discipline in the humanities and from the position of the Christian community (Marty): Books, universities, theology, and community are all of them endangered by opposing pressures: both by *hypermodern* differentiation and specialization, by individualization and pluralism, as well as by *antimodern* reactionary suppression of differences and regimented uniformity, by "hunger for wholeness" and totalitarian tendencies, secular as well as religious. Many impulses for the frequently sterile kind of theology one finds in the universities are coming today from the outside (Baum, Jossua, Schüssler-Fiorenza).

(6) The loss of the West's political-military and economic-cultural hegemony has also been accompanied by a *jolt to the hegemony of Christianity* as the "one true," "beatific," or "absolute" religion: For the first time we are witnessing an encounter between Christianity and the other *religions on the level of roughly equal rights"* (Cobb, Gilkey). This implies

(7) a *loss of credibility among Christians and secular post-Christians,* when Christianity is still looked upon as the a priori "higher civilization" (presumably because it promotes the development of science and technology or brings with it individual freedom, equal rights for women, and family stability). Instead of this, on the Christian side nowadays people are genuinely prepared to listen and to learn from the other religions (Cobb, Dhavamony, Gilkey).

(8) *Historical catastrophes* like the two world wars, then Auschwitz, Hiroshima, and the Gulag Archipelago, along with recurrent mass starvation in the Third World, have made us aware that idealistic theological constructs of history are no longer possible. Theology must rather be done in the face of these concrete plural *histories of human suffering* (Metz). It is these histories of pain that make an "option for the poor" (Boff) seem so urgent, remembering that the poor are not only the materially needy but also those who suffer physically and psychically (Marty).

(9) Among the plural histories of suffering belongs the pain of millions of *women,* who have been dominated, beaten, raped, tormented, and destroyed through all the centuries of patriarchal pre-

dominance. Few developments in this century have shown so clearly the depth of the upheaval separating the old from the new paradigm as the *new awareness by women* of their identity, equality, and dignity. For this new women's consciousness the old paradigm, as it has been handed down until today in the textbooks of theology, church history, and canon law, has simply collapsed (Carr, Schüssler-Fiorenza).

4. Four Dimensions of the Postmodern Paradigm

Points of view that must be considered and translated into reality in all the areas and themes of theology and the Church:

a) The biblical dimension

(1) The problem of *continuity* with a paradigm change requires special reflection in Christian theology, insofar as even in a new paradigm *the old Gospel* and none other has to be expounded afresh for our time (Schillebeeckx). The meaning of Christian tradition, of the Gospel, of faith in God in Jesus Christ—this was continually stressed on all sides—is the one *constant* that holds up throughout and must prevail in every paradigm change by theology and the Church (Jüngel).

(2) *Witness for the Gospel* and its implications are particularly necessary in a "time of troubles," which is no longer borne along by a secular faith in progress, but threatened by anxiety over the future, shaken institutions, and the possibility of every sort of lethal conflict (Jüngel, Gilkey).

(3) The meaning and necessity of the *historico-critical method* for an up-to-date interpretation of Scripture and the texts of Christian tradition were clearly affirmed (Blank, Ogden, Kannengiesser). The role of Scripture in the new paradigm remains a critically liberating one. Biblical hermeneutics has to be carried out in continuity with historical criticism since the Enlightenment, however much today's hermeneutical instruments may have been refined. Nobody wanted to go back to biblical hermeneutics that was rigidly anti-Enlightenment and fundamentalist or reductive in a post-Enlightenment

dogmatic style (something like the just published German *Catechism for Adults*).

(4) The Gospel of the God who reveals himself in Jesus Christ can no longer be preached today without our becoming aware of the problems of patriarchal symbolic language: What is theologically relevant about Jesus Christ as the Son of God is not his maleness but his humanness. God himself should no longer be thought of and proclaimed in exclusively masculine metaphors as Father, Lord, and Judge, but inclusively by *incorporating the experiences of wives and mothers* (Carr).

(b) Historical dimensions

(1) In a post-Enlightenment-postmodern paradigm of theology, *time* is not to be understood as simply *linear* but *historical:* The three dimensions of time—past, present, and future—are not to be seen as a linear succession, but in their dialectical interplay as a web of time (Moltmann).

– It must not, however—as liberal humanism is in danger of doing—lead to an absolutizing of the present and an absolutism of the human subject, and by that route to a universal relativism.

– Rather historical criticism has to consider the relativity of its own present and its subjective standpoint. In place of universal relativism we have the relationism of a universal network of connections.

(2) *History and nature* must not be torn asunder in an ahistorical notion of nature and a nature-less notion of history (Moltmann):

– The man-nature relationship must not, as has become usual in modern science, technology, and industrialization, be seen and put into practice as a master-slave relationship.

– Rather human history is to be synchronized with the history of nature, in order to arrive at a new viable symbiosis between human society and the natural environment.

(3) In a common world and a common world history, whose subject is *humanity as a whole,* there is only one common future or else no future. World peace becomes the condition for the survival of the human race. To that extent the new

paradigm must be a "paradigm of humanity" in the face of indescribable inhumanity, a paradigm profoundly stamped, penetrated by humanity, which, of course, is rightly grounded and founded only in *God's* humanity, as shown in *Jesus of Nazareth.*

(4) The history of this humanity has hitherto been written largely as a history of and with men. The history of the majority of humanity, namely of women, was widely ignored and even in part suppressed. Women rightly demand the *integration of women's history into history itself:* both as regards the history of the suppression of woman and the history of her activity and creativity in society, the state, and the Church throughout the centuries (Carr).

c) Ecumenical dimension

(1) In view of the manifold political, economic, and military threats to the one world and to the common future of humanity the *transition from particularist to universal thinking,* from a *"theology of controversy"* to an *"ecumenical theology"* is an absolutely necessary desideratum. Denominational Christian traditions are not to be perpetuated, but to be received with a view toward what they contribute to an ecumenical community of all Christians. An ecumenical style of thinking is called for, in which particular-denominational elements can be understood not as a realization of the whole, comprehensive Christian truth, but as a part of it. This inner Christian ecumene can, for its part, become a model for a future ecumene of religions and cultures (Moltmann).

(2) Given the problem of the *multiplicity of religions* and religious relativism, the right way must be found to understand and interpret the *uniqueness of the Christian faith* (Dhavamony): a "relative absoluteness," which has countless consequences for the understanding of revelation, Christology, justification, the Church, eschatology, and social practice (Gilkey).

(3) The *Indian* (Chinese, Japanese, African, Latin American) "way of reading the Bible" is not only legitimate, but necessary: Only in this way can westerners be enriched through the

spiritual, moral, and aesthetic values of the other religions and cultures (Dhavamony).

(4) The ecumenical dimension of the new paradigm includes an ecumene not only between the churches, religions, and cultures, but also an *ecumene between the sexes* (Carr): "In Christ not only the difference between masters and slaves, Hellenes and barbarians, but also between men and women is 'sublated.' " In a new paradigm of theology and the Church the further solidification of an inferior position for woman, and in particular the further denial of her churchly ordination, would be downright absurd (Carr).

d) Political dimension

(1) A peculiar feature of the new paradigm of theology is its *fundamental political dimension* (Metz): The relationship between theory and practice in theology should no longer be determined by a division of labor between practical theology, social ethics, or even Christian social doctrine on one side and systematic theology, dogmatics, and church doctrine on the other. The whole of theology must learn to think politically and practically. Thus a political-practical hermeneutics is demanded, one that critically opposes all attempts to politicize religion (as a means of legitimizing and stabilizing certain arrangements of power and domination).

(2) No one disputed or now disputes the fact that theology in its new paradigm has an essential political dimension. What *was* disputed was whether, by chance, European—or rather West German—political theology or instead Latin American liberation theology could be the new universal paradigm. It was questionable whether a single theology could make this total claim, especially when these are theologies that otherwise mistrust all universal "imperialistic" claims to validity.

(3) As I review the situation I myself would like to stand by the viewpoint that was expressed in all the draft papers: *Within the one* post-Enlightenment, postmodern paradigm or basic model *various theologies* (theological orientations, schools, locales) are possible; they may compete with each other to see which can best form the paradigm, its presuppositions and consequences. A hermeneutical and a political theology, a

process theology and the different approaches to liberation theology (feminist, black, Third World, etc.) can coexist and compete within the framework of a contemporary post-Enlightenment, postmodern paradigm of a Christian (ecumenical) theology. In any case the new paradigm needs world-political perspectives, so that the different continents (not just Latin America) and the different religions (not just Christianity) have to be taken into the equation.

The important thing is that we theologians of a new paradigm—confronted with firmly rooted, tough, and long-lived traditionalistic paradigms (and especially now with the Roman Inquisition once more in full swing against theologians and bishops)—do not lose sight of our common cause. All reciprocal theological provocation and confrontation, justified and necessary as it is, should not lead to self-promotion, pushing for particular interests, to isolation and separation. It should lead rather to reciprocal spiritual penetration, to mutual enrichment, and to transformation all around, in order to unite all those whose interest in a postdenominational, postcolonialistic, postpatriarchal, in short *postmodern paradigm* is rooted in concern for the comprehensive liberation of humanity, for what Edward Schillebeeckx has aptly called the "cry for what is human."

Work in Christian theology must go on, despite all the obstacles and hindrances. It must become more precise, concrete, rich in facts and materials. The theory of paradigms is only a hermeneutical framework, and not until it is implemented in a material, historical fashion, as well as through analysis of contemporary conditions, will all its luminous power be seen—and not only for Christianity. Hence one could think of *applying the analysis of paradigm change to other religions*, to Judaism, Islam, Buddhism, Hinduism, and the Chinese religions. A beginning was made in this direction in January 1984 at the University of Hawaii, where a symposium—inspired by the Tübingen symposium and led by Professor David Chappell—took place with the central topic, "Paradigm Changes in Buddhism and Christianity." This is a subject that will bear further evaluation (cf. Chapter C II).

IV

Theology on the Way to a New Paradigm

Reflections on My Own Career

"The things in my books that come from myself are false, Madame," the philosopher Hegel is supposed to have said to one of his open-mouthed admirers. And if the philosopher cannot be intent on *his* system and *his* truth, still less can the theologian, who is allowed to reflect on *God's* Word and *God's* truth. That is why I hesitate to use these pages to outline "my" theology, as I have been asked to.[1]

There is, of course, yet another reason. Since writing my dissertation almost thirty years ago up until my latest books I have greatly preferred to seek to integrate other theologies into my work rather than to separate myself from them. I have done this in the awareness that the theologian has the weakest of claims to infallibility, that a theology must never become a closed-off system but must continually be sketched out anew: not just an "outline of theology," but a "theology in outline." Thus for me personally, *theologia semper reformanda* —theology has to be constantly reformed.

1. The Paradigm of Catholic Traditionalism

I never learned the *iurare in verba magistri*, to swear an oath on the words of a teacher, although I did learn the business of learning day in and day out. For learning, too, needs to be learned in theology.

And learning here doubtless means more than memorizing doctrines, theses, and dogmas. Needless to say that is the sort of learning I started out with as a twenty-year-old in theology—and I don't regret it. Studying for seven long years thesis after thesis—ultimately I had to know a hundred theses by heart for the final examination in philosophy and a hundred in theology—that was the core of my theological training in Rome. All the teaching was in Latin, of course, always marked by strict terminological discipline, clear intellectual structures, and logically consistent argumentation: first the *status quaestionis,* then the terms, then the opponents, finally the arguments for and the objections against. All in all, with Latin lectures and thousands of pages to be conned, a hard school, which in the examinations allowed no talking around the subject in one's mother tongue, which demanded the verbatim texts not only from the Bible but from conciliar and papal definitions, and even when it came to the speculative doctrinal heights of the Trinity, inspiration, or predestination forced the student to engage in conceptual vivisection.

As far as form and substance went, this theology was oriented toward *medieval Scholasticism:* Along with the powerful Roman bishops, it was Augustine above all, the great genius of Latin patristics, who, beginning with the doctrine of the Trinity and moving all the way to doctrine of the sacraments and the state, had initiated the medieval paradigm in theology and the Church: that "total constellation of convictions, values, and patterns of behavior, etc. that are shared by a given community." And it was then—after the ultimate triumph of Roman centralization in the West with the Gregorian reform at the beginning of the second millennium and the consequent break with the Eastern Church—in the thirteenth century that Thomas Aquinas, who despite a universal range of interests was an independent thinker, built up with methodical discipline and didactic ingenuity that grand philosophical-theological synthesis whose unity had never been matched. The *Summa* became the classical expression of the *medieval* and specifically *Roman Catholic paradigm* (cf. the schema on p. 128). Thomas gave Augustinian theology not only a decidedly Roman orientation, but also—with the help of Aristotelianism—a thoroughly rational basis: Right down the line he distinguished between a double order of knowledge and being (a natural basis and a supernatural superstructure), two powers of knowledge (natural reason, faith through grace), two levels of knowledge (natural truth—the truth of revelation granted in grace), two "sciences" (philosophy and theology). A thoroughly two-tiered system, each level clearly distinguished and yet in no way opposed to the other, but the lower section directed toward the upper, higher level.

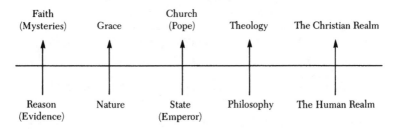

| Faith (Mysteries) | Grace | Church (Pope) | Theology | The Christian Realm |
| Reason (Evidence) | Nature | State (Emperor) | Philosophy | The Human Realm |

This Roman Catholic paradigm of theology was totally different not just from the Jewish Christian apocalyptic paradigm of early Christianity, but also from the Greek Hellenistic paradigm of Byzantine Christendom. In the late Middle Ages it fell into a crisis that—after vain attempts at Reform—led to the revolutionary paradigm change of the Reformation and to the second great church schism. In the course of the Tridentine Restoration, however, it was strengthened and rebuilt into the *Counter-Reformation paradigm,* and, theologically, found a special forum in Spanish Baroque Scholasticism. Although it was increasingly threatened and thrust into the shadows by modern intellectual and political tendencies especially in northern Europe—modern philosophy and science, the Enlightenment, the American and French Revolutions—this medieval-Counter-Reformation paradigm was renewed in the Catholic countries during the nineteenth century with the help of theology and politics, textbooks and new editions, encyclicals and the Inquisition, externally modernized through still more rational analysis and still less biblical theology, and finally given a dogmatic sanction by Vatican I (1870) and legally sanctioned through the Code of Canon Law (1918).

Even in its own view of itself, this Neo-Scholasticism—in which we were trained in the days of Pius XII and which has maintained its powerful ideological bastion to this day in the Office of the Roman Inquisition (A. Ottaviani, F. Šeper, J. Ratzinger)—had no intention whatever of offering a "new" theology. Instead, it aimed to restore the "old time theology" (J. Kleutgen), that same medieval-Counter-Reformation theology. In the spirit of Romanticism and the Metternich Restoration it tried to impose the medieval-Counter-Reformation paradigm on the whole Church in the grand style (Neo-Scholasticism, Neo-Romanticism, Neo-Gothic art and architecture, Neo-Gregorianism). In the meantime, Thomas (condemned in his day as the champion of a "nouvelle théologie") was made into the *"doctor communis,"* the "common teacher" of Christendom. The intellectual avant-garde of the thirteenth century became, of course, the rear guard of the nineteenth and twentieth centuries, which took a defensive posture in arguing with all means possible for a rational-deductive theology of "conclusions" and against the modern world-image and modern science (1950: Pius XII's encyclical *Humani generis* as a new "Syllabus of Errors," and at the same time the definition of the Assumption of Mary).

Of course, studying this sort of theology guaranteed one a thorough familiarity with at least the Roman tradition. And anyone who has followed all the chains of reasoning of Scholasticism and Neo-Scholasticism—particularly in its confrontation with modern philosophy—will have a better understanding of many things in theology, the Church, and the magisterium up to the latest papal pronouncements. No doubt the theological clarity aimed at here could exercise a certain fascination, could even for a while make one believe one had a solid, unshaken foundation—first of all in philosophy and in theology too—under one's feet, upon which one need only go on building.

But as soon as you got even a short distance from them, you noticed how little these Neo-Scholastic theses often said, how much they passed over in silence; how remarkably selective, literally "heretical" they basically were. The biblical profession of faith in Father, Son, and Spirit had turned into a higher conceptual mathematics, and the message of the Christ Jesus into a bloodless Christ-theory. The Sermon on the Mount of Jesus, the Nazarene, played just as little a constitutive role as his deadly conflict with the hierarchy and theology.

As a matter of fact, the most important thing here was not the Christian message, joyful, liberating news, but a *sana doctrina,* sound Catholic teaching: Roman Catholic doctrine as a juridically formulated dogmatic law, hedged about with churchly punishments, with which the theologian had to deal the way the jurist deals with his articles. That means, just as the legal positivist rejects every principle that does not derive from positive law and looks upon existing law as the beginning and end of law and justice, so dogmatic positivism takes the official documents of the councils and the popes as the beginning and end of theology, indeed of God's revelation. He makes, for instance, Heinrich Denziger's *Manual of the Church's Doctrinal Decisions (Enchiridion kirchlicher Lehrentscheidungen)* from the Marian Year, 1854, into an unquestionable dogmatic law book that, undergirded with Scriptural quotations, dispenses the theologian from critical reflection on the foundations, and in exchange for that obliges him to the *sacrificium intellectus* (the sacrifice of the understanding)— from the doctrine of the Trinity through Christology all the way to the infallibility of the pope.

In point of fact, Neo-Scholastic Denziger theology makes this "Denziger" the key to the whole structure of dogmatics. Whatever fits into it counts as proper to the Church, whatever doesn't is either not proper to the Church or irrelevant. And this with no regard for whether the language of contemporary men and women is understood or not, whether the exegetical basis for many propositions corresponds to the current state of research, whether proofs for the theses are believable or seem like answers to objections in the form of shadowboxing. This is all the more reason why the kerygmatic situation is ignored, and preachers and catechists get stones instead of bread. The letter rules in place of the spirit so that, as reality quickly changes, the mechanical application of the laws of faith fails and leads to a crisis of faith: Is it honestly true?

Under these circumstances many people in preconciliar days felt it as a liberation when in the middle of the golden cage of the Neo-Scholastic system a theology emerged that tried to avoid the difficulties of that purely positivistic interpretation of dogma by means of a "speculative" interpretation. For me this theology was bound up above all with the name of Karl Rahner.

2. Speculative Escape Routes?: Karl Rahner

After the Second World War it was primarily the great Frenchmen Yves Congar, Henri de Lubac, Jean Daniélou, Henri Bouillard, and Teilhard de Chardin who towered over the edifice of Catholic normal theology and called it into question. Congar's work always struck me as exemplary for ecclesiology and church reform, Teilhard's for the reconciliation of theology and science—despite (and because of) all the inquisitorial measures taken against his efforts in connection with the encyclical *Humani generis* (1950) and the suppression of the worker priests (1953). Nevertheless, we German-speaking students pricked up our ears when finally a German dogmatic theologian dared to criticize the Denziger approach and to say that in the Catholic interpretation, too, dogmas had a temporal relativity, that there was not only a history of how dogma evolved, but of how it was forgotten, that even solemn conciliar definitions of the person of Christ ("true God and true man") could be not merely an end, but at the same time a beginning of theological thought. For that reason dogmas should not only be repeated, but also given a new "understanding" in a new age.

In other words, in Rahner's theology the dogmatic formulas, for reasons of formal orthodoxy, are still maintained literally and verbatim (and Rahner himself later edited Denziger, making only minor alterations), but often enough the whole tenor of the text was reinterpreted. For a long time, schooled as I was by Aristotle, Thomas, Hegel, and Heidegger, I have admired Rahner's lofty dialectic, just as I have affirmed (and still do affirm) a concern for the unity and continuity of the Church expressed so diversely in this interpretation of creeds and doctrinal propositions. Isn't this a brilliantly successful way to interpret a formula "dialectically" so that the language remains (and that is the main thing for "conservatives"), but the content is remolded (which is what the "progressives" are interested in)?

This sort of formal conceptual dialectic in the interpretation of dogma did not have to be illogical, and generally it wasn't. It sufficed that the terms were no longer understood in their old sense to make it possible to interpret their content in a contrary direction. To be sure, for some unprejudiced observers, who could see through a sometimes rather obscure method, this process seemed to be contradicting historical truth and scholarly integrity. Thus, for example, all the heretics and schismatics, the Jews, Muslims, Hindus, and even the atheists (in good faith), who according to the infallibly defined dogma, "Outside of the Church there is no salvation," had to go into the "eternal fire," suddenly became "anonymous Christians," every one of whom could already belong to the (Roman Catholic) Church and (needless to say) receive eternal salvation. Then the Tridentine dogma, that all seven sacraments were instituted by Christ, was turned into a vague statement about the institution of the Church (and so "implicitly" of these seven sacraments) through Jesus Christ. Then the absolutist definition of papal primacy by Vatican I changed into an implicit statement about episcopal collegiality . . . Could all that, I wondered, be exegetically and historically justified?

But as far as the medieval theological paradigm was concerned, Rahner's hypothesis of a "supernatural existential" that falls to the share of every (natural) individual, remained just as anchored in standard Neo-Scholastic thinking as the solution (promptly condemned by Pius XII) of his fellow Jesuit Henri de Lubac, according to which a natural desire for the eternal beatific vision of God *(desiderium naturale beatitudinis)* fell to the share of every human being. Both ideas derived from the Catholic transcendental philosophy of Joseph Maréchal; at the time they were hotly contested apparent surmountings of standard Thomism, but today they are largely forgotten, along with the whole natural-supernatural terminology. In the debate over infallibility (1970) Rahner came down on the side of the Curia and solemnly declared himself a "system immanent" theologian. Hindsight then enabled everyone to recognize him for what he was, the last great (and stimulating) Neo-Scholastic.

But what other way was there to go about it? What sort of a foundation should theology have, when even church dogmas were so much in need of interpretation? Any young theologian looking for a new foundation could find in Karl Barth's *Church Dogmatics* a theology that had few equals in its commitment to Holy Scripture, in the depth of its interpretation, the artistic shape of its execution, and the intellectual and linguistic power of its formulas.

3. A Theology of Crisis: Karl Barth

In Protestant theology, after a phase of strict Lutheran and Calvinist orthodoxy in the seventeenth and eighteenth centuries, an *enlightened-modern paradigm* of theology had widely prevailed. In the nineteenth century it was to receive its classic expression with Schleiermacher, and its position of leadership with liberal theology. This theology, which conformed only too well to modernity, finally was completely swept up into the optimistic cultural Protestantism that came a cropper only with the catastrophe of the First World War. The leading theologians of Germany had greeted this war in a solemn declaration of moral support and thereby thoroughly compromised liberal theology.

Thus it was that the Swiss pastor and then German professor *Karl Barth,* who in the general political, economic, cultural, and spiritual crisis after World War I had opposed the dominant bourgeois-liberal theology (whose great exponent was now Adolf von Harnack), helped to pave the way for a new paradigm of theology. Barth's "theology of crisis," later called "dialectical theology," demanded, in the face of the collapse of society and culture, of institutions, traditions, and authorities, a paradigmatic shift: away from subjective experience and pious feelings, toward the Bible; away from history, toward God's revelation; away from religious discourse on the concept of God, toward proclamation of God's word; away from religion and religiosity, toward Christian faith; away from the religious needs of the individual, toward God, who is the "totally Other," manifest only in Jesus Christ.

In the name of this "totally Other" God, in the name of God's godliness, Karl Barth protested decisively against every sort of "natural theology": whether it was now appearing in the form of liberal Neo-Protestantism, which in the wake of Schleiermacher was wholly oriented to the pious religious individual instead of to God and to his revelation, or in the form of Roman Catholicism, which in the wake of Scholasticism and Vatican I coordinated God and man, establishing an interplay between humanity and God, nature and grace, reason and faith, philosophy and theology. To that extent "dialectical theology" readopted the great *intentions of the Reformers* and no longer viewed man in the harmonic nature-supernature scheme, but in sharp confrontation as "humanity in contradiction" (E. Brunner). Granted, these crisis theologians did not exactly speak in Lutheran fashion of reason as a seductive "whore" or of philosophy as the "Aristotle's clownery," of the nature of man as "completely corrupt," and of the world as "the devil's." But basically as early as the Reformation the Protestant dichotomy had superseded the Thomistic synthesis, as diagrammed on the next page.

Thus Barth's theology was a programmatic protest against both the medieval Roman Catholic and the enlightened-modern-liberal paradigm of theology and the Church. Both liberal Neo-Protestantism and Roman Catholicism had ultimately come to terms in an uncritical, conformist manner with the dominant political systems: not only with the Empire of Wilhelm II but with National Socialism. Protestant "German Christians" saw in Nazism something like a revelation, and in the Führer a new Luther—or even Christ—linking

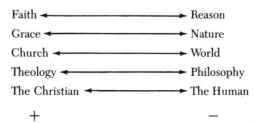

Faith ⟵⟶ Reason
Grace ⟵⟶ Nature
Church ⟵⟶ World
Theology ⟵⟶ Philosophy
The Christian ⟵⟶ The Human

+   −

Christianity and Germanness. Prominent representatives of standard Catholic theology such as the dogmatic theologian Michael Schmaus or the church historian Joseph Lortz, for their part, found that National Socialism was striving for on a natural plane what Christianity strove for on a supernatural plane (order, unity, authority, one empire, one "leader").

In this context Karl Barth's "theology of crisis" initiated the *paradigm change from the modern to a postmodern paradigm,* which at the time, of course, was recognizable only in dim outline. Still it is astonishing how even back then, after the First World War, Karl Barth declared himself decisively against the nationalism and imperialism that represented the legacy of the modern epoch. He spoke out for a politics of peace and social justice, for a Christian "socialism," for a critical-prophetic stance on the part of the Church toward all political systems. But in all this there was also a new theological commitment: in 1934 he inspired the Barmen Synod with its clear confession of Jesus Christ as the "one Word of God," alongside which no "other events and powers, figures and truths [might be acknowledged] as God's revelation."

Karl Barth's grand intentions must be preserved today, but at the same time they have to be translated into the language of a new age: In the human testimonies of the Bible what is at stake is God's Word, which seeks to challenge us to faith (and not only to historical research). When it preaches, the Church has to announce in its human words this Word of God, to which men and women may commit themselves in trust: The biblical message, the crucial criterion of all talk about God, is concentrated on Jesus Christ, in whom for believers God himself has spoken and acted.

When I began to study Karl Barth's theology, Barth (who had been expelled from his chair at Bonn in 1935) had already been teaching from his *Church Dogmatics* at the University of Basel for almost two decades and was publishing volume after volume of the monumental work, which he was destined never to finish. The prophetic-expressionistic theology of his *Letter to the Romans* had meantime become—to use a word beloved in America and unavoidable here—the "Neo-Orthodox" system of the dogmatic theologian, who was trying to lay bare the mystery of divine predestination on hundreds of pages of Christology, and could write enormous chapters on angels and demons. God's creation, which in the "dialectical" phase of the beginning was taken seriously only as a kind of funnel for God's grace, was treated in four thick volumes of *Church Dogmatics,* which obviously had to have consequences for the knowledge of God (by the pagans!) from creation. Still Barth fought shy of this insight even in his teaching on creation. Only in his work on reconciliation, in the last volume of *Church Dogmatics* published in its complete form did Barth—with many reservations—finally concede that alongside "the one light of Jesus Christ" there were also "other lights," alongside the "one Word" there were also "still other words." A new evaluation of natural theology was emerging here, and indirectly (and reticently) of the world religions as well, which Barth had earlier simply dismissed as forms of unbelief, idolatry, and works righteousness.

And so the closed system of *Church Dogmatics,* which, driven by the necessity of a paradigm change had involuntarily moved away from liberal theology to a Neo-Orthodoxy, was exploded, at least in principle. And the bottom was pulled out from beneath Barth's "revelation positivism," as Dietrich Bonhoeffer had criticized it in his letters from a Nazi prison cell. If Barth were a young man again today, he would certainly not be a Barthian, repeating his old ideas. Toward the end of his life—living more under the sign of God's humanness than solely his godliness—he had become reconciled with his old adversary Emil Brunner, who in years before provoked Barth's sharp "No" with his theory of a "point of connection" in man for God's grace, prompting a break between the two men. This Barth would likely have also become reconciled now with his great antagonist, Rudolf Bultmann, who for all his affirmation of Barth's basic theological intentions (the divinity of God, God's Word, *kerygma,* faith . . .) still refused simply to abandon the important concerns of liberal theology and insisted on clinging to the historico-critical method in exegesis, the necessity of demythologization, and an interpretation of Scripture oriented to human existence—in the postmodern, not premodern style.

4. Bridging the Gap Between Exegesis and Dogmatic Theology

In my student years historico-critical exegesis could not be learned within the confines of the Neo-Scholastic program at the Gregorian University, but it *was* taught at the Papal Biblical Institute and later too in Paris at the Institut Catholique and at the Sorbonne (by Oscar Cullmann). Moving to a German university (1959) forced me as a dogmatic theologian to become intensively involved with historical criticism of the Bible. At the end of the fifties and the beginning of the sixties German theology, in any case, was dominated less by the dogmatics of Karl Barth than by the hermeneutics and exegesis of *Rudolf Bultmann*—and his students.

Right from the start I was deeply impressed by the way Bultmann, in uncorruptible honesty and drawing upon a vast expanse of exegetical, historical, and philosophical knowledge—following the Reformers, as far as content was concerned, but Heidegger's existential analysis for his methodology

— tried to make the word of the Bible comprehensible to a modern person so that he could hear it again as God's speaking to us. But right from the start it also struck me as disquieting how Bultmann (fettered to the early Heidegger) had espoused an existential reduction. I was disturbed by

— the way he—for all the justified criticism of mythologems such as the Virgin Birth, the Descent into Hell and the Ascension into Heaven—neglected the Jesus of history with his hypercritical approach;

— the way he turned his focus away from the cosmos, nature, and the environment in favor of human existence;

— the way he reduced real world history to human historicity, the authentic future to human futurity, and thus neglected concrete society and the political dimension in his theology of Being-in-the-world, although in the Nazi period he bravely did his share, together with Barth.

In Tübingen Bultmann's exegesis, as represented by *Ernst Käsemann*, whose posture toward his teacher Bultmann was as loyal

as it was critical, was a genuine challenge for a young Catholic systematic theologian who, with his best exegetical advice coming from Karl
Hermann Schelke, had to find his standpoint between Barth and
Bultmann (from 1960 on). The Bultmann school has Käsemann chiefly
to thank for the rediscovery of the historical Jesus and the problems of
ecclesiology, as well as a sharper focus on the issue of hermeneutics.
Since that time it has become clear to me that the Gospel and the
New Testament have to be sharply distinguished. Admittedly, I did
not become fully aware of all that this fundamental distinction im-
plied in criticism of the substance of the New Testament, until as a
dogmatic theologian—unlike the usual approach, even to this day, in
Catholic and Protestant dogmatics—I not only studied intensively the
results of historico-critical exegesis but also integrated them into dogmatic theology. It was a long way, wearisome and full of conflict.

In this manner it became increasingly clear how much systematic
theology needs exegesis not only as an auxiliary discipline but as the
"basic theological discipline" (J. Blank). This conclusion, de facto rejected by most dogmatic theologians, was one that I fundamentally
had to accept and had to translate into practice, even though it
needed critical completion from the hermeneutical and methodological point of view. For it follows from the primacy of the Scriptures,
which according to the Second Vatican Council—in its attempt to
carry out both the paradigm change of the Reformation and that of
modernity—are to be the "soul," the "principle of life" of Catholic
theology. The primary position of the *original* (authentic) tradition,
laid down in the New Testament, about Jesus the Christ (the *norma
normans)* over against all *subsequent* church tradition (the *norma
normata* of the Fathers, councils, and popes) must have far-reaching
consequences for determining the relationship between exegesis and
dogmatics. The value of dogmatics (I prefer the name "systematic
theology," which obviously includes fundamental theology and ethics) is in no way offended, rather it is bolstered from beneath it.

Of course, the argument that exegesis is the basic theological
discipline must not be formulated with a one-sided bias toward dogmatics (and ethics and praxis). In the process of reviewing, particularly, the history of dogma, theology, and the Church, which no more
than the New Testament should be used simply as a "quarry," this
thesis must be spelled out as a challenge to exegesis itself. The "basis"
of theology is, after all, not the whole thing. Hence, as a systematic
theologian—and I have already done this several times—one can

formulate a more comprehensive thesis in answer to the exegete's challenge, as follows: *Historico-critically grounded exegesis calls for a historico-critically responsible dogmatic theology.*

In fact, the gap between exegesis and systematic theology is the misery afflicting present-day dogmatics. A responsible dogmatic theology inspired by Christian origins can be carried on today—as Gerhard Ebeling rightly insists—only on the foundation of the facts of the Bible as historico-critically mediated by exegesis. It cannot be said often enough: An unhistorical dogmatic theology is as outdated as an unhistorical exegesis, however modern it may pretend to be. A dogmatic theology that takes only inadequate (selective) notice of the findings of exegesis is itself inadequate. A dogmatic theology that, instead of working critically, sticks to a Catholic, Orthodox, or Protestant manner is not scholarly: The scholarly ethos of truth and methodical discipline, critical discussion of results and critical supervision of the problems and methods, are just as imperative for dogmatic theology as for exegesis. Like modern exegesis, so modern dogmatic theology must also follow a strictly historical approach and stand by it uncompromisingly. Its truth too must always be anchored in history.

Now, as everyone knows, any halfway serious dogmatic theology these days claims to be in some way scholarly, critical, and historical. And any serious dogmatic theology is therefore interested in some way or another in historico-critical responsibility. The crucial point, however, is *how* one concretely perceives this historico-critical responsibility, how one applies the results of exegesis. The crucial question is: *Are you ready to interpret the dogmas of your own church* (and every church has its own) *in the light of critical exegesis* and not the other way around? Or will you perhaps suddenly invoke "limits" to the historico-critical method, when you come into conflict with established church doctrine (Catholic, Orthodox, or Protestant)?

There is no mistaking the fact that an unhistorical, compromising biblicism and dogmatism prevail in Protestant theology—with regard to, say, original sin, hell and the devil, but also Christology and the Trinity—even more than Protestants, with their self-conscious progressiveness, readily admit. Bultmann is praised, but in fact ignored just as much as Harnack. His existential interpretation is celebrated while his demythologization is suppressed. In Catholic theology again people are reluctant to confess that certain statements by the Council of Trent, respecting the sacraments, for instance, or of Vatican I on the infallibility of the pope and the councils, can hardly be justified on the strength of the New Testament and the history of the ancient Church. In fear of the revived Roman Inquisition (J. Ratzinger) theologians risk proposing what are at best curious illusory solutions ("moderate" or "fallible" infallibility). We live in a "wintertime Church," as Karl Rahner himself said shortly before his death.

Precisely in the places where theologians do not a priori work in a haughty dogmatic fashion, one can often observe a typical procedural leap: A Catholic or Protestant dogmatic theologian begins to climb the mountain step by step in an exegetically responsible way, but then he comes to a point where the path of theological knowledge seems to stop. So he is suddenly flown up from above to the "summit," and now speaks about the triune God and his mysteries, as if he had in the meantime seen heaven, so to speak, from within. Operating in this way the theologians no longer exactly ignore the results of historical criticism, but they cover them over with speculation, instead of accepting the challenge of exegesis and the history of dogma and modifying their theology—even where the lofty dogmas mentioned are concerned.

Thus it is by no means a matter of course even today when a systematic theologian decides not for Neo-Scholasticist conservatism or speculative harmonization, but instead for logically consistent historico-critical responsibility. What is at stake here is the first constant of all theologizing, which I try to follow in all my theological efforts.

5. The Christian Message as the Basic Norm of Theology

I have phrased the first constant of theology, which holds for a new ecumenical paradigm as well, in the following way: The basic norm of a critical ecumenical theology is the Christian message—which arises out of Jewish tradition—the *Gospel of Jesus Christ.* This primal and fundamental Christian testimony, as expressed in the Old and New Testament, is wholly focused on the living Jesus of history, who is also the norm and criterion for my quite personal Christian faith. The oldest Christian profession of faith reads simply, *"Iesous Kyrios"* "Jesus is Lord." This means, not the emperor and not the pope, not the Church and not the state, not the Party and not the Leader, not money and not power, no, this person Jesus of Nazareth, insofar as he stands for God himself in his preaching and his conduct, his struggling, suffering, dying, and new life—God's Image, Word, Son, Christ.

Given our contemporary awareness of the problem, however, this faith in Jesus Christ has to be justified by theology through historico-critical research on Jesus and protected against misreadings from outside and inside the Church. The historical in-depth exploration of the Jesus of history is possible, thanks to the New Testament sources, and necessary because of the progress we have made in our consciousness of the problem. For Christianity is not based on myths, legends, or fairy tales, and not just on a doctrine (it is no "book religion"), but primarily on a historical personality: Jesus of Nazareth, who is believed as God's Christ. As we know, the testimonies in the New Testament—kerygmatic accounts—do not permit us to reconstruct the biographical or psychological development of Jesus—which also isn't even necessary. But they do make possible something that is urgently demanded today for both theological and pastoral reasons: to get a fresh view of the original outlines of Jesus' message, his way of life, his fate, and hence of his person, all of which has been so often painted over and concealed. *Not a "reconstruction," but a "rediscovery" of the Jesus of history:* This should make it possible—and here I agree with the Catholic dogmatic theologian Edward Schillebeeckx—for the contemporary man or woman to follow the *itinerarium mentis* of the first disciples from the baptism of Jesus to his death, in order to understand why after his death they professed their faith in him as the living Christ, as the Image, Word, and Son of God. Only from the perspective of his preaching and way of life will his execution too become comprehensible, and the cross and resurrection will not be formalized into an abstract "salvation event."

Only the theology that considers the problems posed by history itself and answers them as far as possible is a theology up to the demands of today's awareness of the problem, at least as we find it among people (West or East) with a Western education, and is in this sense a scholarly theology that is truly up to date. That is why we have no choice but to apply the historico-critical method so as to discover what can be said with scholarly certainty or the greatest possible probability about the Jesus of history.

6. Today's World of Experience as the Horizon of Theology

A theology may go on curling up defensively, but like it or not, it is always confronting the world. Of course, it is a contemporary and timely theology only if it takes a stance vis-à-vis the present-day world and opens itself to its distress and hopes. I have said that the *second constant* of theology, which also holds for a new paradigm, is as follows: The horizon of a critical ecumenical theology is our *present-day world of experience* in all its ambivalence, contingency, and variability. Our contemporary reality, ambivalent as it is, is constituted, however, not just by current but also by historical experiences. And the only theology that can be a theology for today is the one that engages itself critically and constructively in the experiences of modern humanity, which finds itself in the transition from modernity to postmodernity.

Lengthy explanations are scarcely needed to show that after the paradigm change of the Reformation in the seventeenth and eighteenth centuries a new paradigm change to modernity has emerged: the *modern paradigm*, as shaped by modern philosophy and science and by the new understanding of the state and society. This "modern" (in the strict sense) total constellation was oriented—in contrast to the Reformation and in connection with many trends of the Renaissance, although the latter with their backwards orientation at first could not prevail against the Reformation and Counter-Reformation —to the *primacy of reason* as opposed to faith, of *philosophy* (with its shift toward the human) as opposed to theology, of *nature* (natural science, natural philosophy, nature religion) as opposed to grace, of the increasingly more secularized *world* as opposed to the Church. In short the universal human element was stressed as opposed to the peculiarly Christian element. To that extent modernity, viewed schematically, appears as a counter-constellation to the paradigm of the Reformation.

7. From the Modern-Enlightened to the Postmodern Paradigm

Thus in the modern period religion was increasingly privatized and ignored, repressed and—on account of the reactionary attitude of

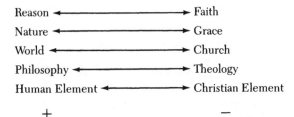

Reason ←————————→ Faith
Nature ←————————→ Grace
World ←————————→ Church
Philosophy ←————————→ Theology
Human Element ←————————→ Christian Element

+   −

the churches—actually persecuted. In any case theology must not let itself be diverted by this countercurrent of opposition and stick doggedly for its part to apologetics. The end of denominational thinking in the seventeenth and eighteenth centuries and the rise of modern thought with the Enlightenment, German idealism, and Romanticism implies for theology an epochal break that is by no means to be understood solely in a negative sense. In this period too there was great theology, and Karl Barth himself continually showed his respect for the classical representative of modern theology, Friedrich Schleiermacher. An abundance of the most varied experiences was channeled into the theology of modernity up until the time of the First World War, and they radically altered its understanding of man, society, the cosmos, and God. These experiences can and must not be undone in postmodernity. Theology has been changed—to indicate a few influences—by permanent findings of modern *natural science,* modern *philosophy,* modern *democracy,* modern *criticism of religion,* the modern *humanities and social sciences,* modern *exegesis and history,* etc.

Since the total cultural upheaval in connection with the two World Wars writers have been continually diagnosing the *"end of modern times"* (Romano Guardini) and the new "spiritual situation of the age" (Karl Jaspers), and unless all the signs are deceptive, we are as a matter of fact in the middle of the transition from the modern to a *postmodern paradigm,* which can likewise be sketched only briefly here. We cannot help seeing that in our epoch

— the world political constellation—as compared with 1918 or even 1945—has completely changed, and European imperialism and colonialism have been replaced by a polycentric world ecumene;

— modern liberation movements, which were already announcing their arrival in the nineteenth century and grew stronger during the wars, have made their appearance on a broader scale since the end of the Second World War;

— a battle is being waged not only against imperialism and colonialism, but also against racism, sexism, and unjust social structures, so that full justice may be done to women, people of color, and the Third World;

— the powers of modernity—science, technology, and industrialism—have become profoundly questionable and must be subjected anew to ethical responsibility and control for the sake of the humanity of the human race and the habitability of the earth;

— many alternative movements—from the environmental movement to the peace movement—seem in many respects to announce a post-materialist world view;

— thus the great god of modernity, called "Progress," has been unmasked by many as a false god, and the cry for the true God has again grown loud, and not only in Christianity . . .

All in all this is an enormous challenge for every theology, especially for the sort that has not yet even integrated the desiderata of modernity and now is supposed to meet the demands of the new postmodern paradigm. In this process the critical desiderata of modernity may not be simply skipped over. All too gladly (and not very honestly) admirers of the medieval-Counter-Reformation-antimodernist paradigm extend a hand to the representatives of the postmodern paradigm. No, the "Enlightenment" may not be skipped over or canceled. It has to be completed: through an Enlightenment that is enlightened about its own capacities and limits, an Enlightenment that no longer ignores, represses, or even crushes religion, but critically integrates it in a new way. Unless the signs are deceiving, we stand in the middle of a process of *rediscovering religion in the First, Second, and Third World.* Religion is evidently proving itself to be more resistant than cultural diagnosticians and critics of religion of every shade are willing to believe. And theology? I can only hint at the opportunity that theology has been given by this situation in intellectual history.

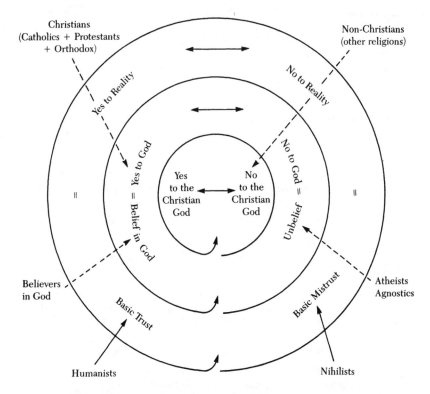

Christians
(Catholics + Protestants
+ Orthodox)

Non-Christians
(other religions)

Yes to Reality

No to Reality

Yes to God
= Belief in God

No to God =
Unbelief

Yes
to the
Christian
God

No
to the
Christian
God

‖

‖

Believers
in God

Atheists
Agnostics

Basic Trust

Basic Mistrust

Humanists

Nihilists

8. Theology in the Postmodern Paradigm

Only a theology placed against the background of contemporary experience, only a strictly scholarly and, precisely for this reason, a cosmopolitan and up-to-date theology—only this sort of theology, it seems to me, can justify its place in the university amid all the other disciplines and sciences. Only this sort of theology is a truly ecumenical theology, which has laid aside the still widespread denominational ghetto mentality and is capable of blending the greatest possible tolerance towards those outside the Church, toward what is universally religious, toward the simply human, with the task of elaborating what is specifically Christian.

Where can theology begin? What are its epistemological foundations? In other words, given the ambivalence, contingency, and variability of our world of experience today, mustn't theology—and here, toward the end of our reflections, we return to our beginning—face the question of the *supposedly evident substructure of our knowledge?* This question is directed not only at Neo-Scholasticism and the medieval paradigm, but also to Descartes and the paradigm of modernity: In taking the path of the methodical doubt weren't we on a really narrow trail, namely that of intellectual, mental certainty? If one were really doubting radically, shouldn't one have had to doubt precisely about this certainty? Therefore wouldn't we have to start off at a much deeper point and ask not only about the truth of our rational thought, but—a radical questioning that even "critical rationalism" (Hans Albert) steadily evades—about the very rationality of reason? Not only about the reality of God and the world, but about the reality of our own existence, which we experience in doubting and thinking? Thus can the contemporary person still take the Cartesian-intellectual route to basic certainty?

People often do not realize that in all their thinking and doing they for all practical purposes constantly presuppose the rationality of reason and so rely upon the ambivalent reality of the world and humanity. That means, in all our doubting and thinking, in our intuitions and deductions there is an a priori, a *prior act of trust,* that is in charge. This is something, of course, that we generally take for granted and that everyone—Christian or non-Christian, theist or atheist—can venture to do in a thoroughly rational way, but that he or she can also refuse to do.

This basic insight, which first occurred to me in my student years in Rome, which I presented in my maiden lecture at Tübingen (1960), and finally developed on a broad scale in *Does God Exist?* (1978), forms, as I see it, the fundamental theological approach for overcoming both the standard medieval-Neo-Scholastic harmony ("faith over reason") and the dichotomies of Reformed Protestantism ("faith versus reason") and enlightened modernity ("reason vs. faith"). Such traditional ways of framing the question become radically outmoded, if one reflects

— that given the utterly uncertain nature of reality we are dealing here with a fundamental choice of position, a positive or negative key decision, which determines, supports, and colors the individual's stance toward reality as a whole: the basic attitude toward oneself, toward other people, society, and the world;

— that the individual, in an overwhelming mistrust of life, reason, and reality as a whole, can say No, in principle or in fact (even though in practice it is hardly possible to stick to it consistently), to the uncertain reality of oneself and the world, a No by which he closes himself off to reality (the option of nihilism—in principle or in fact);

— that the individual, in a fundamental act of trust in life, reason, and reality as a whole, can say Yes in principle or in fact (and in practice it is possible, despite all the difficulties and tribulations, it is possible to stick to it consistently) to the uncertain reality of oneself and the world, a Yes by which one opens oneself to reality (the option of basic trust—in principle or in fact);

— that the very act of having this basic trust reveals an original rationality, an inner reasonableness: a basic trust that in this so broken world can be experienced as a gift. But trust, if it is a gift, remains at the same time a continual task, a rationally responsible—hence thoroughly sensible—act of daring, which, however, itself remains in the final analysis a supra-rational daring.

This is the way between an irrational "uncritical dogmatism" and an ultimately likewise irrationally based "critical rationalism": the *way of critical rationality*. But with an eye to the classical solutions from the history of theology, the following lines of demarcation have become clear:

(1) As opposed to the standard medieval-Neo-Scholastic thinking it can be shown that *faith is not simply higher than reason.*

- For even on the supposedly "natural" level of reason and evidence what is at stake is an absolutely evident—not a "simply" evident—basic trust (or mistrust), a trustingly accepted or nihilistically rejected "grace."

- Even the fact that God exists, is accepted not strictly on the grounds of proof or evidence from pure reason, as "natural theology" claims, but on the ground of a trust—itself grounded in reality.

(2) As opposed to the Protestant Barthian dichotomy it must be stressed that *Faith is not against reason.*

What takes place on the level of reason—in everyday thinking, in occupations and the sciences, in philosophy, in the religions—is not simply irrelevant for faith or opposed to it in advance, but is determined by the dialectic of affirmation and negation, basic trust and basic mistrust, justification and rejection, in which every person—Christian and non-Christian—finds himself. Even faith in God is not exclusively possible because of the revelatory testimony of the Bible, as Barthian theology asserts. Rather—as in the case of non-Christians who believe in God—it is also possible on the strength of a trust (itself grounded in reality), which thus becomes a trust in God, a belief in God (thanks to God's revelation and grace).

(3) As opposed to the modern-enlightened dichotomy we can work our way through to the fact that *reason is not against faith.*

- For even the rational functioning of reason presupposes a trust in reason that cannot be explained in a purely rational way.

- And faith in God is not an irrational, blind, daring leap, but a trust that is responsible in the eyes of reason and grounded in reality itself.

Working from this key ecumenical approach I was able to develop what faith in God—and in particular Christian faith in God—means today; that is, to reflect *On* [What] *Being a Christian* (1974) can mean in the *postmodern paradigm,* and how, from the perspective developed out of those reflections, *Christianity and the World Religions* (1984) are to be understood. But before I break off the introduction to "my" theology (an introduction less oriented toward contents than historical-hermeneutical), I wish only to note briefly in conclusion what concrete standards I have set for it in the framework of this contemporary paradigm. Let others judge how well I have met them.

9. Ethos and Style of Critical Ecumenical Theology

First of all, in what concerns the *ethos* of all theologizing, I find the following criteria important. (It is worthwhile to make a case for them once again, since they are the *"cantus firmus"* of this book.) A theology in the new postmodern paradigm needs to be

(1) Not an opportunistic-conformist, but a *truthful,* theology: a thoughtful account of faith that seeks and says the Christian truth in truthfulness.

And this is altogether to serve the *unity* of the Church of Jesus Christ. For there is no truthful Church without a truthful theology.

(2) Not an authoritarian, but a *free* theology: a theology that meets its responsibilities without hindrance from administrative measures and sanctions from the Church's leadership, that expresses and publishes its reasoned convictions within the guidelines of its knowledge and conscience.

And this is altogether to serve the *authority* of the Church, for there is no free Church without a free theology.

(3) Not a traditionalistic but a *critical* theology: a theology that knows itself to be freely and truthfully obliged to the scholarly ethos of truth, to methodological discipline, and to the critical scrutiny of all its problems, methods, and findings.

And this is altogether to serve the *edification* of the Church, its building up in this society, for there is no critical Church in this society without a critical theology.

(4) Not a denominational, but an *ecumenical* theology: a theology that no longer sees in every other theology the opponent, but the partner, and that is intent not on separation but on understanding, and this in two directions: *inwards,* for the domain of the ecumene between the churches, among Christians; and *outwards,* for the domain of world ecumene outside the Church, outside of Christianity, with its different regions, religions, ideologies, and disciplines. This kind of ecumenism corresponds to the transcultural or universalist aspects of paradigm analysis in theology and in other fields.

And this is altogether to serve the *mission* of the Church in this society. For there is no ecumenical Church without an ecumenical theology.

This is a suitable place to stress what I have already formulated in connection with the publication of *Does God Exist?* (1978): A theology in the new paradigm also demands a different style for all theologizing. The following principles should be valid for such a theology:

(1) No esoteric teaching for believers alone, but lucidity for nonbelievers.

(2) No prizes awarded for "simple" faith or defending a "churchly" system, but uncompromising efforts to reach the truth, following strict scholarly principles.

(3) Ideological opponents are neither to be ignored nor labeled as heretics nor ideologically co-opted, but to be interpreted with the greatest possible breadth and tolerance, *in optimam partem*, and at the same time exposed to fair, objective discussion.

(4) We must not just demand the interdisciplinary spirit, but put it into practice: dialogue with related fields and concentration on one's own object belong together.

(5) No hostile opposition, but no chummy neighborliness either, rather a critical-dialogic co-existence, especially of theology and philosophy, of theology and science, of theology and literature: Religion and rationality, but also religion and poetry belong together,

(6) The problems of the past should not have priority, but the broad and many-layered problems of men and women and human society today.

(7) The *norma normans* of any Christian theology cannot, once again, be any churchly or theological tradition or institution, but only the Gospel, the original Christian message itself: a theology everywhere oriented to the historico-critically analyzed facts of the Bible.

(8) We should speak neither in biblical archaisms and Hellenistic-Scholastic dogmatic pronouncements, nor in fashionable philosophical-theological jargon, but in language intelligible to today's men and women; and no effort should be spared to achieve this.

(9) Believable theory and livable practice, dogmatics and ethics, personal piety and institutional reform are not to be separated, but to be seen in their absolute interconnectedness.

(10) No denominational ghetto mentality, but ecumenical breadth, which takes into consideration both the world religions and the modern ideologies: the greatest possible tolerance toward whatever is outside the church, toward what is universally religious, toward what is human pure and simple, and, on the other hand, elaboration of the specifically Christian belong together.

If I had after all to give the theology of the new paradigm a name, I would call it, in abbreviated form—without tying myself down to the term—a *critical ecumenical theology*. For me quite personally—let me repeat it here—this means a theology that tries, in a new age, to be the following things at once:

(1) "Catholic," constantly laboring on behalf of the "whole," the "universal" Church—*and* at the same time "Protestant," strictly intent on Scripture, on the Gospel.

(2) "traditional," always responsible in the face of history—*and* at the same time "contemporary," passionately addressing the issues of the present;

(3) "Christocentric," decisively and distinctively Christian—*and* still "ecumenical," oriented toward the "ecumene," the whole "inhabited globe," all Christian churches, all religions, all regions;

(4) theoretical-scholarly, occupied with teaching and truth—*and* at the same time practical-pastoral, laboring on behalf of life, renewal, and reform.

But enough self-description. The great thinker Blaise Pascal admonished authors who speak about "my book, my commentary, my history," etc., like houseowners. They would do better, he thought, to speak of "our book, our commentary, our history," since such things usually contain more of other people's goods than their own.

C.

A NEW DEPARTURE
TOWARD A THEOLOGY
OF THE WORLD
RELIGIONS

I

On Paradigm Change in the World Religions

Preliminary Reflections on an Analysis of the Religious Situation of the Age

Peace among the religions is the prerequisite for peace among the nations. What we need today is a globally oriented analysis of the religious situation of the age, under the heading of the question: At the end of the second Christian millennium what is the situation of the religions in today's world, since none of the great religions can exist for itself alone? Where do we find antagonisms and parallels, divergencies and convergencies, where, in other words, do we see openings for dialogue and for increased understanding?

Needless to say, this sort of global analysis faces tremendous difficulties if it is to be something more than a compilation of data, a lexicographical discourse on individual continents and countries, a purely historical or phenomenological juxtaposition of individual religions and denominations. There is no lack of information (though of course it cannot all be gotten from books). On the contrary we are suffering from an information overload that also affects specific regions and their religions. Our main problem is rather the critical synopsis of all the major religions, if we wish to have a global perspective on the religious situation of the age. And here some reflection on paradigm changes in the world religions can be extremely helpful, because they link *periodization* and *structuring*.

To be sure, such reflections still leave us at the beginning of our task. One significant step forward was the symposium (organized in January 1984 at the University of Hawaii) on paradigm change in two religions that seem to be most alien to each other, Buddhism and Christianity. This gathering met with an unusually vibrant echo, and there is no doubt about its long-term effects. So let me present some basic hermeneutic considerations that come to mind in connection with the symposium and the follow-up work done since then. For reasons of space it will be necessary to concentrate on the two religions dealt with at the symposium, Christianity and Buddhism.

1. The Distinction Between Religion and Paradigm

Each of the great world religions has gone through its paradigm changes—the religions of the Semitic-prophetic tradition (Judaism, Christianity, and Islam) as well as those of Hindu (Hinduism, Buddhism) and Chinese (Confucianism, Taoism) origin. But if we wish to avoid total confusion, the term "paradigm"—which is as broad as it is elastic and hence very handy—must be used in a definite and precise fashion. And then "religion" and "paradigm" can on no account be identified, nor can religion be reduced to a single paradigm. Rather both terms have first to be clearly separated before they can be connected with each other.

The importance of this distinction can be made clear in a thoroughly practical fashion with the issue of *conversion:* If, for example, a Catholic, disgusted by the authoritarian Roman system, becomes a Protestant; or if a Protestant, attracted by Catholic unity and universality, becomes a Catholic, then in both cases no change of religion takes place (both persons remain Christians), but there is a *paradigm change*—as an individually performed change of denomination. Likewise not religion but a paradigm (school, sect, orientation) is changed when adherents of Theravāda convert to Amida Buddhism or vice versa. There should be no dispute about the fact that both remain Buddhists.

But conversely if a Christian (Catholic, Orthodox, or Protestant) in search of a less dogmatic, moralistic, and dualistic religion, becomes a Buddhist; or if a Buddhist (of whatever sort), in search of a more historically, ethically, and personalistically structured religion, becomes a Christian, then under normal circumstances what takes place is not only a change of paradigm, but a *change of religion.* In this conceptual clarification we need not enter into problem, especially prominent in the Asian tradition, of "religious dual citizenship." If being a Christian is understood as the following of Christ, and being a Buddhist as following the eightfold path of the Buddha, then in any event it should hardly be possible to presuppose an identity between the two religions, whatever the individual in his heart and mind thinks he can do to reconcile them.

Now, needless to say, making distinctions and connections between "religion" and "paradigm" is so difficult because both terms overlap, indeed they can reciprocally embrace one another without however being wholly congruent. One could distinguish religion and paradigm as content and form, as image and frame, as text and context. But it quickly becomes clear that more precise differentiations have to be made.

With *paradigm* we mean (following the definition taken over from Thomas S. Kuhn and constantly used in this book) of a *total constellation:* the conscious-unconscious "total constellation of convictions, values, and patterns of behavior" that obviously shape religion but not just religion. Whether we are talking about the original Jewish-Christian or the ancient Church-Hellenistic or finally the medieval-Roman Catholic paradigm, or about the Reformation-Protestant or modern-enlightened and finally the postmodern paradigm, the fact is that these paradigms—and evidently we are not concerned here with any sort of micro- or mesoparadigms, but with macroparadigms—carry far beyond religion and have a determining influence on economics, law and politics, science, art, and culture, all of society. Hence they are paradigms not only of religion but of society as a whole. And a similar point could be made about Buddhism: about primitive Indian Buddhism, the old Buddhist Lesser Vehicle (Theravāda); about the subsequent Great Vehicle (Mahāyāna); and finally also about the Tantric Diamond Vehicle (Vajrayāna). As prevailing, wide-ranging, and deeply rooted total constellations of conscious-unconscious convictions, values, and patterns of behavior, these paradigms are thus ("extensively") "more" than simply religion, more comprehensive than religion.

Still, insofar as *religion* is a particularly large factor within this total constellation and represents a very specific (transcendentally grounded and with immanent consequences) theoretical-practical system of coordinates, it is ("intensively") "more" than a paradigm, more concentrated than a paradigm. For with a religion—hard as religion (like art) is to "define"—we are always dealing with an "encounter with the *Holy*"(R. Otto), at once a *message of salvation* and a *way of salvation,* something that can maintain itself through all possible paradigms. Religion—and here I mean above all the "higher" religions—is not only a conscious-unconscious basic model of the world, society, religion, and the Church; it is in the context of such models, a consciously believing view of life—be it lived in a more traditional, superficial, and passive way, or deeply felt, committed, and dynamic—an attitude toward life, a way of life oriented to an ultimate true reality that transcends, wraps round, and permeates with its power humanity and the world (whether called God, the Absolute, or Nirvāna). Religion, therefore, does not simply pass on more or less self-evident, universal convictions, values, and behavior patterns of an epoch. In religion too—though naturally this process is deeply interwoven with those widespread convictions, values, and behavior patterns—a comprehensive meaning of life is conveyed, the highest ideals and unconditional norms are proclaimed and guaranteed, and a final spiritual homeland and community is offered to believers. And to this extent every religion (differently from, say, a philosophy) endures as a concrete community on the strength of a concrete tradition and thus in the course of epochs passes through different constellations, models, and paradigms.

All this means that religion is not the same thing as a paradigm, but religion is, lives, and evolves (diachronically: through periodization) *in* (various epochal) paradigms. That makes it possible for us in a given epoch (synchronically: by structuring) to distinguish thoroughly (though not to separate) between the general *paradigm of society* (the social paradigm) and the particular *paradigm of religion* (the Church, theology: the religious paradigm). With all these paradigms at work in the given epoch, obviously there can be no talk of the absolute dominance, only of the *relative prevalence* of a specific historical constellation, which in no way excludes countermovements and counterfigures, side effects and interference factors of every kind. But when we speak here about the *epochal* (encompassing several centuries) macroparadigms (of society, religion, the Church, and theology, with all the meso- and microparadigms contained in them), then naturally the complex question of periodic thresholds arises. It seems that the demarcation of the various epochs or periods, their historical "periodization" creates tremendous difficulties.

2. *The Question of Epochal Thresholds*

No doubt, acts of historical periodization, defining the thresholds of epochs, are from the very first *our own assessments* and therefore relative. The division of time can never be undertaken from a standpoint outside of time, only from within time itself. And if today even physicists can no longer simply describe objective reality as it exists independently of the observer, but only a science of our *knowledge* of matter, this is even more true of the historians: History is a science of our *knowledge* of the past. It is determined by its point of view, perspectivistic, and conditioned by the interests of the historians. It is in no way simply a science, as Ranke thought, that reports *"wie es eigentlich gewesen"* (how things actually were), but at the same time is always interpreting. There is no recital of facts, therefore, without interpretation, and so no periodization without making decisions. Granted, these are decisions and assessments that can no more be simply arbitrary than can the models used by physicists—if they are not to collide with reality itself. Periodizations are also not whimsical. They have to do as much justice as possible to the "facts," and not block their own view of reality.

Yet, it goes without saying that depending on one's standpoint, criteria, and interests one can make Christian antiquity end and the Middle Ages begin in this or that century. Only rather long reflection makes it clear that, say, Augustine and Thomas Aquinas are best seen as the beginning and high point in the context of one and the same Latin-medieval paradigm of theology. Depending on one's standpoint, criteria, and interests, one can also make the modern period in Europe begin with the *"Renaissance"* (a later term that for some scholars just cannot be unequivocably defined), although it took its orientation from antiquity and not from autonomous reason and progress. Or one could have modernity start with the *Reformation* in the sixteenth century or, finally, with the new philosophy, science, conceptions of the state, and the commencement of secularization in the seventeenth and eighteenth centuries. Nevertheless, in surveying Christianity, one would miss reality completely should one ignore the decisive temporal shift of the Protestant Reformation (which despite everything was bound to the Renaissance through humanism). And to that extent I think it right firstly to emphasize the Reformation-Protestant paradigm over against the medieval paradigm, and to make the actual "modern period" begin with the seventeenth and eighteenth centuries. Not Luther, the anti-Copernican, antidemocratic man who in some ways was still looking back to the Middle Ages, but Descartes, Galileo, Newton, Hume, Rousseau, Voltaire, and Kant are typically "modern" individuals.

If the contemporary becomes the old only because of the new, then we should note well that every age has its *precursors and preliminary signs*. As far back as Wyclif and Hus people were speaking up for ideas of reform, but only with Martin Luther did the age of the Reformation begin. Back in the nineteenth century Kierkegaard and Dostoyevsky were advancing existentialist notions, but not until the crisis of the First World War did the period of existential philosophy and theology begin. Ever since Hegel we have known that epochs do not follow one another in continual succession but with gaps between. Not cumulative linearity but dialectic is their law. Still we should not forget that the crisis of the old paradigm is not by a long stretch always the beginning of the new one. Otherwise the Reformation would have had to begin a hundred years before Luther. This means that

— not until the ancestors of a movement come out of the private and into the public sphere,

— not until the members of the opposition become representative,

— not until inspirations and examples shape norms, and the new has not merely dawned, but fully risen, only then can one speak of a shift in world time, of an epochal paradigm change.

The first evidences, then, do not decide the issue, but the transformation of the new into the normative. And after looking chiefly at the macroparadigms here, the problem of periodization is complicated by the fact that the new developments in the different domains start off *differently*, and the periodization cannot be synchronized in all sectors and disciplines. Romanesque and Gothic art begin in different countries at different times, and baroque music was still being composed when the day of baroque painting had long passed. Terms like "modern" are used in art and the philosophy of history for completely different epochs. There is a difference between the domains of experience and linguistic usage (Wittgenstein's "life worlds" and "language games"), between developments and temporal patterns in history and semantics.

So there is nothing left for us to do but to make decisions based on the subject itself. And since the subject here is religion, periodizations should be made as far as possible—against the background of world history, of course—in terms of the history of religion, of the Church, and of theology. In determining the location of epochal thresholds there should be no striving for originality in (un)academic self-promotion. Rather the point of departure should be the broadest possible consensus of historians, who as a rule, in fact, connect the Reformation with an epochal threshold. In the periodization that I suggested (cf. the schema on p. 128) and the paradigms established from that perspective I took this broadest consensus as my point of departure. It is less important here when exactly the beginning of a paradigm change is dated (the shift seldom takes place in so dramatic a fashion as with Luther), but when the paradigm in question has matured, made its breakthrough, and prevailed. Admittedly, it is remarkable in the area of religion how some paradigms can go on existing apparently as they please. And it is worthwhile to ponder the phenomenon of the persistence, the "survival" of seemingly outdated paradigms in the major religions. An articulated theory of paradigms helps us in this way both to periodize the past and to structure the present.

3. The Survival of "Outdated" Paradigms in Art and Religion

The case of Galileo showed that even in *science* it sometimes takes almost a hundred years until an old paradigm (here the Ptolemaic) is replaced by a new one (the Copernican). But once the old one is replaced, it is definitively disposed of. It can neither simply endure nor celebrate its resurrection. Romantic restoration movements are out of the question in astronomy, physics, chemistry, and biology, and no student of these disciplines has to take seriously the older paradigms that have been dropped. In textbooks they appear at most in introductions or footnotes for didactic purposes. And why can the old paradigms in science be simply liquidated? Because in the "exact" sciences hypotheses, with the help of mathematics and experimentation, are empirically verified or falsified, and the decisions in favor of the new paradigm can in the long run be "compelled" through the use of evidence. In the natural sciences—think only, for example, of the calculation of planetary orbits—success can be shown in the balance sheet with numbers. In *art* the situation is altogether different: Mathematics and experimentation can decide nothing definitively here, much less replace a paradigm. Although every art work is the creation of a specific artistic epoch, works of art from earlier epochs in no way lose all their value on account of a paradigm change. The works of the Italian Renaissance painter Botticelli or Raphael, for example, are not liquidated, because painters (after Michelangelo) have begun to work in the "baroque" style—à la Rubens or Rembrandt, say. It is true that older artists, under heavy pressure from the new style, can temporarily lose value and have their price sink. For every new epoch ultimately gains its feeling of self-worth by first unduly devaluing its predecessor. And yet the old works in principle maintain their validity. All genuine art has a transtemporal, permanent value. And an old style can, in times of doubt about the new, even enjoy a resurrection. Thus the Pre-Raphaelites in England or the Nazarenes in Germany both sought to revive (religious) art in the nineteenth century by taking the painters of the early Italian Renaissance such as Raphael and Dürer as their model. Still, "Nazarene" was already then a mocking title for these artists (some of whom had converted to restoration Catholicism), who despite their lofty intentions were, after all, epigones, whose art proved to be a brief episode that ended in kitsch.

This means that greatly as one may treasure the "old masters" in art, if a modern painter goes on painting or begins to paint all over again in the old style, his art will be considered "antiquated," backward, and outmoded. Of course, in times of romantic restoration, such art can—in its bondage to the *Zeitgeist* (the Nazarenes wanted a new German religious-patriotic art)—enjoy success for a while and even sell as a novelty. In the age of historicism there was a whole series of such "new styles," but they were all merely "historical styles" (Neo-Romanticism, Neo-Gothic, Neo-Byzantinism). All their re-shaping could not in the long run conceal the calamitous fact that their old forms had in modern times lost their old content, and no new life could be breathed into them. The classicist sculptures of a Canova or Thorwaldsen in their very flawlessness showed their inner emptiness, showed themselves for what they were—a dead pose. With the fading of the restoration *Zeitgeist*, then, these "new styles" breathed out their borrowed life. Simply put, in a new total constellation "old works" can indeed maintain their value for artistic *enjoyment*, but an "old style" cannot endure in artistic *production.* In art a crisis of the age sooner or later leads to a crisis of style, and this in turn to a change of style, which, however, does not exclude the adoption of elements of the old style in the new one.

But what about the dying off of paradigms in *religion?* Even less than in questions of aesthetics can anything in matters of faith, morals, and ritual be decided mathematically-experimentally (although in the age of positivism the wrongheaded demand for "empirical verification" often led to the setting up of meta-empirical truths). Now, obviously, religions can also die, as countless examples from the history of religions show. But reflection on the scheme of paradigms worked out for Christianity (p. 128) in the contemporary context points us toward a surprising insight (which can easily be given graphic representation): In the domain of the "high religions" old paradigms do not by any means necessarily disappear. Instead they can survive alongside new paradigms—in some circumstances for centuries. Indeed, if we leave out of the picture the narrowly limited Jewish-Christian paradigm, which because of its apocalyptic tendencies displayed a special eschatological character and which perhaps has found in Islam a different sort of continuation, then all the Christian macroparadigms—from the Byzantine-Hellenistic through the medieval-Roman Catholic all the way to the Reformation and modern-Enlightened—have given visible proof of their continued survival. And they also offer to millions of people, even today, a permanent spiritual home, tradition, and community.

But then, with all the capacity of the new religious paradigms to perceive and "process" crises, what is the source of the high *capacity of the old religious paradigms to endure and survive?* This ability obviously far surpasses that of art, where the replacement of one style by another has enormously speeded up (Romanesque flourished for two hundred years, Gothic for three hundred, Renaissance for two hundred, Baroque for one hundred fifty, classicism for sixty, while the newer "-ism styles" often lasted only one or two decades). This question as to the capacity of religious paradigms to endure and survive urgently needs further investigation, and so let me just offer a few suggestions for further reflection, which concern religion in both the objective and the subjective sense.

As far as *objective religion* goes—the various doctrines and myths, rites and symbols, institutions and constitutions—one is immediately struck by the more massive (compared with art) institutionalization of religion: In art, too, critics have tried to develop standards and norms theoretically (a normative aesthetic) and to implement them practically (in commissions, in the academies, museums, and exhibits)—at least up until Impressionism and its code of *"L'art pour l'art."* But only in the realm of religion are the standards and norms, and especially the particular doctrinal laws—dogmas and moral commandments—given a direct, transcendental foundation, guaranteed with the highest, divine authority, and secured with sanctions in time and eternity. Representatives of institutionalized religions have always exploited this, in order to cover not only the main object of religion but also all possible trivialities, often mere oddities, and above all their own power, with the aura of divine eternity and immutability. How many sorts of all too earthly institutions (Roman agencies) and legal positions, liturgical objects and folkloric rituals, have been declared to be "holy," untouchable, and thus immunized against any sort of criticism and reform. Even the tiniest details in matters concerning faith, morals, and the Church have been regulated by law, and deviations from it avenged by churchly punishments, by excommunication, being put on the Index, removal from office in this world, and the threat of the devil and hell for eternity, so that the traditional medieval paradigm (i.e., "the believers") could still be "protected" against the consequences of a fully transformed awareness of time as late as the middle of the twentieth century. In this way not only could the Christian message itself, the core of Christianity be preserved, but along with it mysteries and customs (often of pagan origin), superstition, the mania for miracles and the cult of relics, problematic symbols and rites that, as we know, can still be performed when they have completely lost their original meaning, when they have become incomprehensible or have been allegorically reinterpreted (consider the use of incense, certain signs, gestures, and garments in the liturgy).

But as far as *subjective religion* goes—piety and religious experience—there is a further point to look into: The more banal a truth (truism, platitude, etc.), the greater the security. Conversely, the more significant a truth (as, for instance, aesthetic and *a fortiori* moral and religious truth, in comparison with mathematical truth), the weaker the security. But then all the greater my personal commitment, in order to achieve certainty (which is not to be confused with the perfect "coverage" of security). Concretely speaking, the absolutely secure *banal* truth $2 \times 2 = 4$ demands a great deal less personal commitment than the *deep* truth—externally insecure for me, threatened by doubts—that "despite everything my life has a meaning." This means that the "deeper" a truth is for me, the more I have to make an effort to open myself to it, to give all my inner attention to it. And the "deeper" a truth is, all the more do I feel myself called into question by the pointed questions it puts to me, and all the more, as a result, do I struggle with intellect, will, and emotions against all changes and feelings of insecurity. One need only assault a person in his "deepest" religious or quasi-religious convictions to see at once how nervously and passionately he reacts. Nobody wants his "Holy of Holies" to be taken away from him. This natural religious conservatism is set in motion quite deliberately by both political and religious rulers in order to preserve the status quo: which only serves as further proof how many "questions of belief" are at bottom "questions of power."

Because religion, both objectively and subjectively, deals by definition with the eternal in time and with the divine in man, it is all too easy here for *everything* temporal and human, for the all-too-human to participate in the eternal-divine and its unchangeability. That explains why apparently outdated paradigms in the world religions can survive for centuries. Still the question arises: Are these paradigms then really "outdated"? Or, in other words, does every paradigm change also immediately mean progress?

4. Does Paradigm Change Mean Progress?

In the religious domain, as we saw, we have an extremely slow (in relation to science and even to art), wide-ranging, many-layered process of transformation that is generally reflected on only after the fact. If a "Big Bang theory" that has the new shape of a religion suddenly emerging from the void contradicts historical reality, then so does the theory of organic evolution, where the new shape is simply understood as the product of an innocuous continual development. This is an approach where all the doctrinal and defensive developments of religion are declared to be welcome blossoms on the same tree, where all contradictions are overlooked, all breaks are papered over, all losses buried in silence, and all revolutions disguised as evolution. No, human beings are not plants, and the history of humanity often does not develop organically. Even the development of dogma is in fact often the entanglement of dogma.

In *art* a paradigm change does mean a further development, but not simply a higher development, not simply movement from the primitive to the perfect. Spanish painting, for example, whose genesis came later than Italian quattrocento painting is not "higher" than its predecessor. El Greco is not qualitatively "better" than Leonardo. Every work of art is complete in itself and demands to be measured against the aesthetics of its own time. Every epoch in the history of art deserves the interest of posterity.

In *religion,* too, a paradigm change does not simply mean progress and only progress. In religion, too, much is gained in the paradigm change, but much that was true and good in the earlier paradigm is lost, forgotten, or repressed. Even in the theological classics, where, as in classical art, a harmony was reached between inner content and outer form, we cannot simply make a qualitative distinction in the sense of a higher development. Scholasticism, for instance, which assimilated so many impulses of previous theology and philosophy, is not "higher" than the work of the Fathers. Thomas is not more "perfect" than Augustine or Origen. Every significant theology, which has arisen in its specific form out of a given temporal situation, is "unique," is a response to a challenge, is in its own way "great," and in any case must first be judged in accordance with the standards of its own epoch. Every epoch in the history of the Church and theology has its intrinsic value, so that neither should one age be declared "dark" (the Middle Ages) nor another "exemplary" (antiquity).

In the final analysis, then, is everything in both art and religion— by contrast with science—"stationary" and hence, as far as value goes, simply "equal"? No, as the reflection on "historical styles" already suggests, in religion too every religious paradigm absolutely does not have to be appropriate to every age, as if there could be no backward theology, no reactionary Church, no dysfunctional religion, as if criticism of a religious paradigm were a priori unjustified. Naturally, the crisis of a religious paradigm can be disguised: Just as, at least in the Baroque, artists conjured up the illusion of a still pre-Copernican medieval heaven on the ceiling of their triumphalist churches, while at the same time the theologians in their huge folio volumes managed to evoke the fair semblance of an unruffled, at best externally adapted Scholasticism. The really "modern thinkers" had been placed one and all on the Index of Forbidden Books and could not, must not, be considered. Neo-Thomist textbooks in the nineteenth and twentieth centuries were ultimately related to the classic summas of Thomas somewhat as the classicist temple of the Madeleine in Paris was related to the Parthenon. So long as a society as a whole is behind the time, the backwardness of its religion is relatively less conspicuous. So long as, for example, modern Greece (not without the Church's complicity) was a socially backward country, the old Hellenistic paradigm of the Church and theology remained—relatively—appropriate to the situation. So long as Italy and Spain (under Roman custody) closed themselves off to modern science, technology, industry, and democracy, the medieval-Counter-Reformation (and ultimately antimodernist) paradigm remained—relatively—efficient.[1]

As soon, however, as the history of the Church and theology begins, so to speak, to hobble behind world history, as soon as after individual (for the most part "unchurchly") precursors, society as a whole arrives at an epochal threshold and moves into a new paradigm, as soon as the persistence on the part of the Church and theology in the old paradigm leads to a separation from the general social and religious paradigm, then the situation becomes life-threatening for religion. This was seen not only in the French Revolution and the Italian Risorgimento, but in the Russian Revolution too and the Spanish Civil War. In the new historical situation the religious paradigm no longer corresponds to the social paradigm at all. It survives, but becomes *backward, anachronistic,* doctrinaire and authoritarian, its condition marked by narrowing, fixation, intimidation, and repression, which cause harm to both religion *and* society. In this sense the passing through the Reformation and the modern-paradigm changes effected by Vatican II meant a historical shift and a liberation for the Catholic countries of southern Europe and Latin America. Without Vatican II there would have been no liberation theology, no base-community movement, no progressive episcopacy. This was an epochal shift and liberation that Greek (or Russian) Orthodoxy has yet to make—unless it wishes definitively to sink down, in the large cities and in the countryside, into mere religious folklore, meaningless for both private life and the world at large, to slip to the level of a mere outdated paradigm. As I have discussed elsewhere, Islam and other world religions as well are facing similar problems of paradigm change.

Thus rejecting the notion of automatic progress in no way means that a paradigm ought not to be scrutinized as to whether or not it is suitable to our time. The realization that all epochs are unique and unrepeatable should suffice to forbid any attempt at an antiquated transmission or reactionary restoration of an earlier paradigm. On the contrary, quite in keeping with the criteria developed here and continually expressed by the key words "horizon" and "center"—our *"cantus firmus"*—a paradigm of the Church and theology, at least in Christianity, has to face some questions:

(1) Is this paradigm—measured against the paradigm of society as such—still *up to date?* And at the same time:

(2) Is this paradigm of religion—measured against the Gospel of Jesus Christ as the norm—really *in keeping with the Scriptures?*

In stressing both the dimension of secular time and the primal core of Christianity we should note only that the ("Catholic") schema of progress (continual ascent to greater truth) is not replaced by a ("Protestant") schema of decadence (ever sharper decline from the golden age of Christian origins). No, a genuinely *dialectic* historical theory of paradigm change encourages neither a self-righteous Catholic triumphalism nor a self-tormenting Protestant melancholy. Without forcing all the tribulations and confusion of history into schemata, this sort of dialectical theory of history takes seriously both the *continuity* and the *discontinuity* in the historical process and implies a "sublation" (*aufheben,* in the threefold Hegelian sense) of both the scheme of progress and that of decadence.

Such an understanding of paradigm change in Christianity ought to check the danger of *mutual excommunication by the churches:* the danger, that is, of a paradigm, which has come out of a historical upheaval, being rejected in advance as heretical—with matching hostile reactions on the other side. We know that the Byzantines in the Middle Ages rejected as heretical the paradigm that came into being in the West as the result of a completely new historical situation—tribal migrations, the increasing importance of the bishop of Rome, the theology of Augustine, and finally the German Empire; while conversely Rome excommunicated the "backward" Orthodox. We know that in the sixteenth century Rome rejected the Reformation paradigm, which was created by fresh reflection on the original Gospel (especially its understanding of justification) with the practical reforms that followed from that (use of the vernacular in the liturgy, the chalice for lay people, married priests), calling it all uncatholic, while by the same token Luther declared the pope the Antichrist and Rome the Whore of Babylon.

Positively stated, historico-critically responsible thinking in paradigms will *help reciprocal communication*. This kind of thinking, if it is supported by the ethos of truthfulness, and resists the temptation of historians to offer their services to the powerful, and does not shy away from the risk of uncorruptible judgment, will make it possible to do justice to the various stages of development and forms of religion without placing them all on the same level, but also without absolutizing any one of them (always one's own) and downgrading the others. And I mean this quite concretely. For on the one hand there can be no religion without a paradigm, without a total constellation (not shaped only by religion) of convictions, values, and patterns of behavior. There is neither a Christianity nor a Buddhism "in itself." On the other hand, however, no given total constellation ought to be simply identified with a given religion, nor should a given configuration of this religion be declared the "one, holy" form.

This brings us right back to the problem of the world religions, and we can—after clarifying, for the sake of simplicity, some initially complicated arguments—return in the last part of our reflections to Buddhism (for a fleshed-out version of the following considerations I refer to the chapter on Buddhism in *Christianity and the World Religions*).

5. Constants and Variables in Buddhism

Paradigm analysis, applied to Buddhism helps us

— to avoid dismissing in advance any of the great historical forms of Buddhism, such as "faith Buddhism" or Tantric Buddhism, as unbuddhist. Instead we can understand each of them in their own historical context, with their genesis and inner meaning, and acknowledge that every developmental stage of Buddhism has its own inner logic and its own right to exist *as Buddhism*. This allows us

— to avoid playing any of the different Buddhist paradigms off one another, instead carrying on a dialogue with all important forms of Buddhism (from primitive Buddhism through the three "Vehicles" to Zen and Shin);

— to refer to differences and similarities between Buddhist and Christian paradigms (for instance, with respect to "medieval" thinking on earning merit);

— but finally to measure critically every new form of Buddhism (and of Christianity) against its source (Gautama, the Buddha, or Jesus, the Christ)

With such a powerful and many-branched two-and-a-half-thousand-year-old structure like Buddhism even experts have a hard time seeing the forest for the trees; that is, seeing the *unity* for all the *differences*. Thus, for example, the Tantric Buddhism of Tibet is viewed by some as a "re-Hinduization" and a backsliding from pure Buddhism, while others discredit the Japanese "Pure Land Buddhism" as basically unbuddhist "Amidism." Both these criticisms, of course, run contrary to the believers in question, who despite the many differences from other Buddhists feel themselves to be thoroughly authentic Buddhists. They just live their Buddhism in an utterly different total constellation, in a different paradigm.

This is familiar to Christians from their own history: As in Buddhism, so in Christianity many Christians have a hard time seeing any real common ground in the Byzantine imperial Church, the medieval papal Church, and the Protestant princely and provincial churches, which all excommunicated one another. It is likewise difficult to see what legitimates them as successors to the first Jerusalem community. And yet upon closer inspection, in Christianity as in Buddhism, despite all the striking *variables,* some fundamental and durable *constants* can be sighted: the same stars *(stellae)* by which we orient ourselves, although of course they keep forming new epochal constellations.

Now it is certainly no definition, but rather a formula for professing his faith, when the Buddhist says, "I take my refuge in the Buddha, in the *dharma* (teaching), in the *sangha* (community of monks)." This is not unlike the way the Christian "takes refuge," "believes" in Christ, the Gospel (his message), and the Church (the community of believers). In both cases we are dealing with *constants,* permanent determining factors that have basically shaped these religions through all the centuries across all the countries and continents and through all the paradigm changes.

And yet a paradigm change took place from primitive Buddhism (entirely a monastic affair) to Theravāda Buddhism (a religion for the masses). And many centuries later there was a further "turning of the wheel of teaching," and a second all-transforming paradigm change occurred within the Buddhist movement, the shift to the Mahāyāna Buddhism of the Great Vehicle, which presented a far freer interpretation of the original teaching, something that was in fact on many points a decidedly lay religion. Despite all this *the central key constants of specific Buddhist doctrine, practice, and institutional life* were preserved even in the Great Vehicle:

— There was still the "refuge in the Buddha," the great, supremely masterful teacher and pioneer of salvation, to whom (though it was only a mythological fiction) were attributed doctrinal texts written in the first to fifth century A.D., something that continues to be characteristic of later Buddhism;

— There was still the "refuge in the *dharma,*" in the teaching of the "Four Noble Truths," about suffering and how to overcome it, about the transitoriness and nothingness of the world and the ego, about wiping out ignorance, greed, and hatred through enlightenment and wisdom: a teaching that was not only to be repeated, but in the face of new human needs and capacities was to be reformulated, that was "incomplete" and had to be brought to the "perfection of knowledge;

— There was still the "refuge in the *sangha,*" in the community of monks, but the traditional rule of their order could now also be lived in a multiplicity of different teachings and much freer forms (even including marriage), which leveled the difference between monks and lay people.

Nevertheless these same fundamental Buddhist data, these same fundamental ideas, attitudes, and practices appear now in a different context, a different frame of reference, the same basic constants in a *new constellation of variables:*

— The way to definitive salvation is now to be opened up to many individuals, instead of to a few monks. Instead of the monastic ideal of the *arhat,* the Theravāda saint withdrawn from the world, we now have the ideal of the humanitarian saint, the *bodhisattva:* the monastic religion is now increasingly becoming a religion for the laity.

— Instead of seeing the nature of all existence only in its fleetingness, painfulness, and lack of substance, the latter is now radicalized as emptiness: lack of essence as the true essence of the universe or—taking a more positive view under Taoist influence—as the cosmic Buddha-nature, common to nature and man.

— Instead of salvation through renunciation and turning away from the world there is now the possibility of enlightenment, of liberation, of wisdom amid life here and now: *nirvāna* in *samsāra.*

It should be obvious that with this paradigm change, slow, wide-ranging, and many-layered as it was, we are facing an epochal, indeed a *revolutionary change*—a change that, despite all the essential differences can be compared with the change from the Hellenistic-Byzantine to the medieval-Roman Catholic paradigm. Here too, certainly, the sun and stars remain, but the constellation has totally changed. A change that embraces not only doctrine, but also ethos and ritual, indeed the whole concrete life of religion, as it is inscribed—deeply or less deeply, positively or negatively—in the hearts of men and women as a supremely contemporary matter that openly or hiddenly shapes everyday existence.

But—and here at the end of the chapter we return to the beginning—Christianity and Buddhism are not only two different paradigms, whose variables and constants can be described historico-critically, from the objective distance of the historian. They are two different religions with their own peculiar claim to truth that makes existential demands and calls the individual to commitment. In other words, for all our paradigm analysis, when we look at the various religions we cannot bracket the *question of truth.* It should and must have a central position at the end of this book. The question, then, is this: Is there actually one true religion, or are there several true religions?

II

Is There One True Religion?

*An Essay in Establishing
Ecumenical Criteria*

It is easy to insist that no critical ecumenical theology today is thinkable apart from the dimension of the world religions, but this desire is hard to realize. After concentrating in the sixties and seventies on the internal Christian ecumene, while always trying to keep the world religions in view, I myself found I had some radical new learning to do. It is a wearisome job to make oneself knowledgeable about the various religions with their complex history.

To be sure, I became increasingly aware that discussion with the other world religions is actually essential to survival, necessary for the sake of peace in the world. Are not the most fanatical and cruel political struggles colored, inspired, and legitimized by religion? How much would the affected peoples have been spared, if the religions had been quicker to recognize their responsibility for peace, love of neighbor, and nonviolence, for reconciliation and forgiveness, if they, instead of helping to foment conflicts, had resolved them? Thus any ecumenical theology today has to acknowledge its *share of responsibility for world peace.* There can be no peace between the world religions. And there can be no peace between the world religions without peace between the Christian churches. The Church's ecumene is an integral part of the world ecumene: ecumenism *ad intra,* concentrated on Christendom, and ecumenism *ad extra,* oriented to the whole inhabited earth, are interdependent.

But the confrontation between the world religions goes beyond the issue of peace. It calls decisively for a clarification of the *question of truth.* Much as the material analysis of the various religions, much as comparison of religions can make convergencies and divergencies apparent, the question of the truth must still be raised continually and inexorably.[1] Is there one true religion or are there several? Is there a system of criteria for justifying the claims to truth of the individual religions? What does a critical ecumenical theology say nowadays about the problem of the "true religion"? The following remarks are aimed at this basic question of interreligious ecumenical dialogue.[2]

No question in the history of the churches and the religions have led to so many disputes, bloody conflicts, and indeed "wars of religion" as the question of truth. Blind zeal for truth has brought on unrestrained injury, burnings at the stake, destruction, and murder at all times and in all churches and religions. Conversely, fatigued forgetfulness of truth has as its consequence disorientation and anomie, so that many people no longer believe in anything at all. After a history of bloody conflicts the Christian churches have learned to blunt the edge of the dispute over truth and to arrive at common answers in the ecumenical spirit. These answers, of course, should at long, long last be followed by practical consequences. The same pattern has yet to be seen in the relations of Christianity to the other religions. Still, some people ask: Is there any theologically responsible way that allows Christians to accept the truth of the other religions without giving up the truth of their own religion and, with that, their own identity?

1. One or Several: A Pragmatic Solution?

Nevertheless others ask, conversely: Is this still a question at all for us, the descendants of the Enlightenment? Aren't we fighting rearguard actions in intellectual history because we are still afraid of the diffusion of our own identity? Hasn't a pragmatic solution been found long since? "Of these three religions only one can be the true one," Sultan Saladin had claimed in Lessing's famous "dramatic poem" *Nathan the Wise,* and turning to Nathan, he added, "A man like you does not remain standing where the accident of birth has flung him: or if he remains, he remains because of discernment, reasons, the choice of what is better" (act 3, scene 5).

But what is discernment based on? What are the reasons for choosing what is better? Lessing's solution is contained, as we all know, in the parable of the three rings: If—and this is the assumption —the theoretical clarification of the question of truth fails, if "the right ring cannot be proved true," what rule holds then? The answer: only practical experience. Let everyone "strive . . . in accordance with his uncorrupted, unprejudiced love!" That is, let the power of the genuine ring prove itself "with meekness, with cordial peaceableness, with benefaction, with most heartfelt acquiescence in God." Thus proof comes only through devout humanity in life itself. For our problem this means that every religion is genuine, is true, insofar as it practically and factually gives proof of the "miraculous power" to make a person welcome "in the eyes of God and man." Doesn't this point of view, as clear as it is simple, spare us the trouble of posing the fatal question of truth?

In this century it was above all the Americans Charles Sanders Peirce, William James, and John Dewey who proposed a pragmatic solution to the quest for truth. In looking at the truth of religion, pragmatism simply asks how a religion, on the whole, "works," what practical consequences it has, what its actual value is for the shaping of one's personal existence and life together in society—in history, here and now.

No one could deny that such a concept of the function and utility of religion contains much that is right. In religion don't theory and practice overflow into one another? Doesn't there have to be practical proof of what a religion "is good for," in keeping with the words of Scripture, "By their fruits you shall know them"?

The question is only, Can truth be simply equated with practical usability? Can the truth of a religion be reduced to usefulness, helpfulness, and the satisfaction of needs? Can it be sacrificed in case of emergency to tactical necessity, or even surrendered to commercial or political exploitation? And might not a religion that is seldom practiced still be true? Might not a program that is forever being violated nevertheless make sense? Might not a message that finds little or no faith still be a good one?

In any case we need to reflect here whether there is not a deeper understanding of pragmatism than its utilitarian variety reveals, a pragmatism that is not a mere reduction of religion to practical reality, but its reconnection to the practice of a truly good life. Still in any case the questions arise: By what criteria should such complex phenomena as the major religions be judged? Should we characterize the effects over millennia of Buddhism in Asia or Catholicism in Europe as good or bad? Don't all contemporary religions have their credit and debit sides? And doesn't such a way of looking at things continually seduce the observer into comparing the high ideals of one's own religion with the more lowly reality of the others; for example, comparing real Hinduism or real Islam with ideal Christianity?

Thus the question, "What is the true religion?" must be returned to those who asked it. Back in the very beginning of his classic treatment of *The Varieties of Religious Experience* (1902) James argued that a usable criterion for judging authentic religion was not only the "ethical test" but—along with immediate certainty—the "philosophically demonstrable reasonableness." But what does "philosophically demonstrable reasonableness" mean in this context? Evidently, for all one's orientation to praxis there is no getting around the question of truth. In order to prepare a constructive answer here, I would like to undertake in the second part an examination of four basic positions.

2. Four Basic Positions

a) *No religion is true.* Or, *all religions are equally untrue.* I have no intention of repressing the atheistic position here—though with its various critiques of religion it is certainly not my topic. Still it implies a permanent challenge for all religions. Normally, the lamentable condition of any religion itself provides reason enough for suspecting that its teachings and rites are aimed into the void, that religion is nothing but projection, illusion, empty promises; in short, that there is nothing to the truth of this religion, indeed to the truth of all religion . . .

Now I cannot and do not wish to prove that religion is actually aimed at a reality, indeed the first-and-last, realest reality. But for their part the atheistic opponents of religion have no proof that religion is simply a venture into nothingness. Like God, this nothingness is nowhere to be found. Pure, theoretical reason, bound up as it is with this world, cannot reach far enough to answer this question. On that point Kant was right once and for all. Putting it positively, in the famous, crucial question of the truth of religion, we are dealing with no more and no less than the *great question of trust* of our life: in the face of all the obvious absurdity of this world to say *Yes* nevertheless, in a tested, illusion-free, realistic act of trust, Yes to the primal Ground, Mainstay, and Meaning of the world and humanity that is accepted in the major religions. This is a thoroughly rational Yes, insofar as it has to show for itself, if not strict proofs, at least good reasons.

Anyone who says *No* will have to take responsibility for that in the eyes of history. It is the primal, ancient religious history of humanity, which can be traced back at least as far as the burial rites of Neanderthal man, that the arguments of atheism (which are closely connected to specifically Western culture and intellectual history—Nietzsche's "God is dead" presupposes 2,500 years of Western metaphysics) greatly relativize. It makes no difference whether one considers the human race (diachronically) in its many thousand years of history or (synchronically) in its global extension: One will never find a tribe that lacked faith in some sort of transcendence. From the global perspective, atheism among the masses is a typically Western "achievement," even though it has spread to the East. It is thus the affair of a cultural minority in this century.

b) *Only one single religion is true.* Or, *all other religions are untrue.* The *traditional Catholic position*—prepared in the early Christian centuries by Origen, Cyprian, and Augustine, and defined as far back as the Fourth Lateran Council (1215)—is widely known: *"Extra Ecclesiam nulla salus!"* Outside the Church there is no salvation. Fifty years before the discovery of America the ecumenical council of Florence (1442) unequivocally stated, "The holy Roman Church . . . firmly believes, confesses, and proclaims that no one outside the Catholic Church, neither heathen nor Jew nor unbeliever nor schismatic will have a share in eternal life, but rather is condemned to the eternal fire prepared for the devil and his angels, unless he joins it [the Catholic Church] before his death."[3] Doesn't that settle once and for all the claim of the other religions to truth and salvation? That is how it was, it seemed, at least from the fifth to the sixteenth centuries.

As early as the age of the discovery of new continents Catholic theology tried to come to a *new understanding* of that uncompromising "Outside the Church" doctrine, which meant for the most part to reinterpret it and, finally, to turn it inside out. It was never openly corrected because it was "infallible." Of course, as early as the Council of Trent theologians like Bellarmine and Suárez recognized an unconscious "longing" *(desiderium)* for baptism and the Church as sufficient for salvation. And in the seventeenth century Rome condemned the principle cited by the rigorous French Jansenists, *"Extra Ecclesiam nulla gratia"* (Outside of the Church there is no grace).[4] In 1952 the Roman "Holy Office" (Congregation of the Faith) felt itself obliged, paradoxically enough, to excommunicate a campus chaplain, Fr. Leonard Feeney, who with the old Church Fathers and the Council of Florence asserted that all people outside the visible Catholic Church were damned. Once again without making any formal correction the Second Vatican Council finally declared, invoking God's all-embracing salvific will and plan of salvation in its Constitution on the Church (1964): "Those individuals, who for no fault of their own do not know the Gospel of Christ and his Church, yet still search for God with an upright heart and try to fulfill his will, as recognized in the commands of conscience, in deeds prompted by the working of his grace, can attain eternal salvation" (article 16). And in the Declaration on the Non-Christian Religions the appreciative description of the other religions culminates in the sentence, "The Catholic religion rejects nothing of all that which is true and holy in these religions" (article 2).

This means, the traditional Catholic position is today no longer the official Catholic position. Even the non-Christian religions can be —since people are, after all, bound to the historical and socially constructed forms of religion—ways to salvation. Perhaps not normal, "orderly" ways, but nonetheless perhaps historically "extraordinary" ways. As a matter of fact contemporary Catholic theology distinguishes, thanks to this about-face, between the Christian way of salvation—the "ordinary" way—and the non-Christian way of salvation—the "extraordinary" way (sometimes, too, between "the way" and the various "paths").

However one may judge this theological solution and terminology, the important thing is that for the first time in its history the Catholic Church has formally expressed itself *against* a narrow-minded, arrogant *absolutism*, which posits its own truth "absolutely"; that is, "loosed from" the truth of the others. It has backed off the standpoint of exclusivity that condemns the non-Christian religions and their truth *en bloc* and opens the door wide to every kind of apologetics, inability to learn, and dogged insistence on being in the right. It has moved away from the dogmatism that fancies it has the whole truth a priori in its possession, and holds out for the other positions only condemnations or demands for conversion. No, contempt for other religions is now to be followed by respect for them, neglect is to give way to understanding, proselytizing by study and dialogue. Thus the Catholic Church took a step as much as twenty years ago that many *Protestant theologians* still hesitate to take today. Still on the path laid out by the younger Barth and dialectical theology—and often without careful knowledge and analysis of the world religions—they can only go about dogmatically with that Protestant claim to truth: by which "religion" is nothing but "natural theology" and so a "power trip," a sinful revolt against God, unbelief pure and simple. For its part, they say, Christianity is no religion at all, because the Gospel is the end of all religion. I think that, to my taste, such "dialectical theology" would have to be more dialectical.

No, the world religions must neither be dogmatically condemned nor, as other theologians have done, simply ignored. A noble-minded *Ignoramus* ("we don't know") is all the *more* irresponsible. And if Protestant theology has no answer to the question of the salvation of the majority of the human race, then has it any reason to wonder that people today, as Voltaire in his time, pour out their scorn at the presumptuousness of the "one holy Church" or content themselves with enlightened indifferentism? That is why the ambivalent attitude of the World Council of Churches is completely unsatisfactory: Neither in its "Guidelines for Dialogue with Individuals of Different Religions and Ideologies" (1977/1979) nor at the latest plenary assembly in Vancouver (1983) did it ever manage to answer the question about salvation outside the Christian churches. Conflicting viewpoints on the part of the member churches prevented it.

There is no missing the fact that nowadays the problem is being posed more intensely. After the discovery of the giant continents outside of Europe the world religions were first and foremost external, *quantitative* challenge for Christendom. But they have now become an internal, *qualitative* challenge not just for some enlightened spirits but for the Christian churches themselves. It is no longer just the fate of the world religions that stands in doubt as it did in the "Christian" colonialist epoch. The fate of Christianity itself is at stake in an epoch of postcolonialism and postimperialism.

And the question now is If Christian kerygmatics today, unlike the earlier kind, has come to see the riches, instead of the poverty, of the world religions, what does *it* have to offer? If Christian theology recognizes manifest light everywhere, to what extent will it bring "the Light"? If all religions contain light, why should Christianity in particular be *the* truth? If salvation can already be found outside the Church and Christianity, why should there be a Church and Christianity at all? A simple answer to this question is provided by the third position:

  c) *Every religion is true.* Or, *all religions are equally true.* Anyone who really knows the world religions will hardly claim that they are all alike. That would be to flatten the key differences between the basic types of mystical and prophetic religion, and to suppress all the contradictions between the individual religions. It would be to overlook the fact, as Wilfrid Cantwell Smith in particular has stressed, that even individual religions do not simply remain the same in the course of history, but develop and become more complex—often astonishingly so.

  But don't we have to distinguish *objective* religion (the often contradictory myths and symbols, doctrines, rites, and institutions found in the various religions) from *subjective* religion, piety, the fundamental religious experience of the Universal One and Absolute, which we meet at the primal roots of every religion? Still, recourse to a fundamental religious (mystical) experience, supposedly everywhere the same, does not solve the question of truth. Why? Because religious experience never comes in isolation. Religious experience is a priori interpreted experience, and for that reason it is stamped by the religious tradition in question and by its different expressive forms.

  But there is even more to it than this. Anyone who claims that all religions are in principle equally true, is excluding from the domain of religion—of all things—the human capacity for error and moral mistakes. But why shouldn't the old saying that "To err is human" also hold for religion? Is there a religion that has not been poured into the mold of human forms? Could it be that all religious statements, all myths and symbols, all revelations and professions of faith, and finally all rites and customs, authorities and phenomena in Hinduism, Buddhism, Islam, Judaism, and Christianity are true and valid in the same way, are equally valid in the full sense? No, the reality of the person having an experience in no way guarantees the reality of what he or she experiences. There is a difference between religious and

pseudoreligious experiences, and we cannot place magic or the belief
in witches, alchemy or naive belief in miracles and all sorts of foolish-
ness on the same level as belief in the existence of God (or the reality
of Brahman), in salvation and redemption. There can be no talk about
"religious experiences" being equally true.

Just as everything isn't simply the same, neither is everything
simply equal—not even in one's own religion. "Anything goes," "Everything is possible" just cannot silence the basic questions of human
life about *truth* or ultimate reliability and commitment. Or could it be
that in the religious sphere everything is legitimate because it does
happen ("the power of the factual") and may possibly come along in
picturesque garb (religion dressed as folklore)? If it is the "truth" and
only the truth that, according to the Gospel of John, "makes us free,"
we have to push our questioning further.

Along with exclusivist absolutism we must also avoid the crip-
pling *relativism* that makes all values and standards a matter of equal
indifference. That also holds, by the way, for Lessing. For the discretionary pluralism that was slowly emerging in his time, but is now
modern and intellectually popular, the pluralism that approves without making distinctions between one's own and other religions, has no
more right to invoke Lessing than the indifferentism for which all
religious positions and decisions are the same and spares itself the
trouble of "discerning the spirits."

d) *Only one religion is true.* Or, *all religions have a share in the
truth of the one religion.* If the standpoint of exclusivism, which
recognizes no truth outside its own, is just as unacceptable as the
relativism that relativizes all truth and makes all values and standards
a matter of equal indifference, that approves and upholds one's own
and the other religions without making any distinctions, it would
seem that the standpoint of generous, tolerant *inclusivism* is the real
solution.

We meet this approach above all in *religions of Indian origin:* All
empirical religions represent only different levels, partial aspects of
the inherent, universal truth. The other religions are not untrue, just
provisional. They have a share in the universal truth. By invoking
mystical experience one can claim such a "higher kind of knowledge"
for one's own religion. The result is that every other religion is de
facto reduced to a lower or partial knowledge of the truth, while one's
own religion is elevated to a supersystem. Every other religion is

integrated into one's own as a preliminary stage or partial truth. Any special, peculiar claim it might have is denied. What looks like tolerance proves in practice to be a kind of conquest by embracing, a co-optation by admission of validity, an integration through relativization and loss of identity.

A variety of this inclusivism can be found—paradoxical as that may sound—*in Christianity too.* Karl Rahner's theory of the "anonymous Christian" is in the final anyalysis still dependent on a (Christian) *standpoint of superiority* that sets up one's own religion as the a priori true one. For, according to Rahner's theory, which attempts to solve the dilemma of the "Outside the Church" dogma, all the Jews, Hindus, Muslims, Hindus, and Buddhists are saved not because they are Jews, Muslims, Hindus, and Buddhists, but because in the final analysis they are Christians, "anonymous Christians," to be precise. The embrace here is no less subtle than in Hinduism. The will of those who are after all not Christians and do not want to be Christians, is not respected but interpreted in accordance with the Christian theologian's interests. But around the world one will never find a serious Jew or Muslim, Hindu or Buddhist, who does not feel the arrogance of the claim that he or she is "anonymous" and, what is more, an "anonymous Christian." Quite apart from the utterly perverse use of the word "anonymous"—as if all these people did not know what they themselves were—this sort of speculative pocketing of one's conversation partner brings dialogue to an end before it has even gotten under way. We must not forget that followers of other religions are to be respected as such, and not to be subsumed in a Christian theology.

What, then, is required of a Christian's fundamental attitude toward the world religions?

— Instead of indifferentism, for which everything is all the same, somewhat more *indifference* toward supposed orthodoxy, which makes itself the measure of the salvation or perdition of mankind, and wants to enforce its claim to truth with the tools of power and compulsion;

— instead of relativism, for which there is no absolute, more sense of *relativity* toward all human establishing of absolutes, which hinder productive co-existence between the different religions, and more sense of *relationship,* which lets every religion appear in the fabric of its interconnections;

— instead of syncretism, where everything possible and impossible is mixed and fused together, more will to achieve a *synthesis* in the face of all denominational and religious antagonisms, which are still exacting a daily price in blood and tears, so that *peace* may reign between religions, instead of war, hatred, and strife.

Given all the religiously motivated intolerance, one cannot stop demanding tolerance and religious freedom. But at the same time too there must be no betrayal of freedom for the sake of the truth. The *question of truth* must not be trivialized and sacrificed to the utopia of future world unity and the religion of world unity. As a threat to cultural and religious identity, a religion of world unity would be feared in the Third World, where the history of colonization, and the history of the missions that is part and parcel of it, are still by no means forgotten. On the contrary, as Christians we are challenged to *rethink* the question of truth in the spirit of a freedom rooted in Christianity. For, unlike arbitrariness, freedom is not just freedom *from* all ties and obligations, something purely negative. It is at the same time positive: freedom *for* new *responsibility*—toward our fellow men and women, toward ourselves, toward the Absolute. True freedom, therefore, is freedom for the truth.

3. The Knotty Question of a Criterion for Truth

We could go on with long and complicated discussions on the question of what truth is, and take a position on the various contemporary theories of truth (the theory of correspondence, reflection, consensus, coherence, etc.) But the question of the true religion must remain firmly planted in the foreground. The following initial thesis will serve as a presupposition for everything I shall now have to say about the possible *untruth* in religion: Christians have no *monopoly on the truth,* although they also do not have the right to renounce *their profession of faith in truth* by adopting some sort of discretionary pluralism. Dialogue and witness are not mutually exclusive. Confessing the truth includes the courage to sight untruth and speak up about it.

It would, of course, be a crude prejudice to identify the boundary between truth and untruth in advance with the boundary between one's own and whatever other religion. If we stay sober about this, we shall have to grant that the *boundaries* between *truth and untruth* also pass *through one's own religion.* How often are we not right and wrong at the same time. That is why criticism of another position can be justified only on the basis of vigorous self-criticism. Only then can an integration of the values of others be justified as well. This means that *in religion, too, not everything is equally true and good.* There are also things that are untrue and not good in teachings on faith and morals, in religious rites and customs, institutions and authorities. Needless to say, this also holds for Christianity.

With good reason *criticism by the world religions* of *Christianity* is clear and pointed. Christians have too little awareness of how often, despite its ethic of love and peace, Christianity, in its actual appearance and activity, strikes the adherents of other religions as exclusive, intolerant, and aggressive;

— it strikes other religions not as integral, but—because of its other-worldliness and hostility to the body and secular life—as internally torn;

— it strikes them as almost morbidly exaggerating the consciousness of sin and guilt of human beings, who are supposedly depraved at the core, in order to bring their need for redemption and dependence on grace all the more effectively into play;

— it strikes them as, besides, using its Christology to falsify the figure of Jesus—seen in the other religions almost universally in a positive light—by making him exclusively divine (the Son of God).

Whatever is valid in this criticism, one thing is clear: The question of the truth of any religion aims at more than pure theory. The nature of truth is never established only in systems of true statements about God, man, and the world, never only in a series of propositional truths, as opposed to which all others are false. Truth is always at the same time also a *praxis,* a way of experience, enlightenment, and proven worth, as well as of illumination, redemption, and liberation. If, accordingly, religion promises an ultimate, all-encompassing sense for our living and dying, if it proclaims supreme, indestructible values, sets up unconditionally binding standards for our acting and suffering, and provides a spiritual home, then this means: The dimen-

sions of the *True (verum)* and the *Good (bonum),* of the meaningful
and the valuable, overflow into one another in religion; and the question of the truth (understood more theoretically) or meaningfulness of
religion is at the same time the question of its goodness (understood
more practically) or valuableness. A "true" Christian or Buddhist is
the "good" Christian or Buddhist. To that extent the question "What
is true and what is false religion?" is identical with the other, "What is
good and what is bad religion?"

The basic question, then, about the true religion has to be framed
differently: How are we to manage to distinguish between true and
false, valuable and valueless, in the religions themselves? Here we
may think not only of the Hindu caste system, the Shaktist form of
Tantric Buddhism with its dubious sexual practices, of the "holy wars"
and cruel forms of punishment in Islam, we must also recall phenomena in Christianity such as the Crusades, the burning of witches, the
Inquisition, and persecution of the Jews. Thus we can easily see how
thorny and difficult the question of the *criteria for the truth* is, if they
are not to arise simply from subjective whim or to be sticks for hitting
other people over the head with.

Of course—and this is a point we shall have to return to—no
religion can entirely dispense with applying its *quite specific* (Christian, Jewish, Islamic, Hindu, Buddhist, etc.) *criteria of truth* to the
other religions. But in each religion believers should realize that these
criteria can be relevant, in the first instance, only for themselves; they
cannot be relevant, much less obligatory, for the others. For if the
others, whoever they may be, should likewise insist on their own
criteria for truth, the prospects for genuine dialogue automatically
disappear. Thus, for example, the Bible can fulfill its criteriological
and liberating function only in discussions between the Christian
churches, or at most in discussions between Christians and Jews. But
in conversation with Muslims and still more with Hindus and Buddhists a direct appeal to the Bible as a criterion of truth would be out
of place. What is the alternative then, if in religious dialogue Christians may no longer simply call upon the Bible (or Muslims upon the
Qur'an, or Hindus on the Gita, or Buddhists upon the Sutras) as the
irrefutable authority, so as to be in the right, in the truth vis-à-vis the
others? In all caution let me *attempt* another approach and offer it for
discussion: We shall go through a sort of inward spiral, in three stages
of argument: from the ethical in general to the religious in general
and only from there to Christianity in particular.

4. The Human Element:
General Ethical Criterion

When we compare our religion with the other, but also when we reflect upon the misuse of our own religion, the question arises for all religions of the criteria for the true and the good: of *general* criteria, which can be applied analogously to all religions. This is important, it seems to me, not least of all for questions of international law. Neither the descriptive discipline of religious studies (which has little interest in normative criteria, but itself presupposes definite notions—often without scrutinizing them—of humanity, nature, history, the divine —for instance, tacitly preferring the "mystical"), nor Christian theology (which hitherto has scarcely made serious comparisons of itself with other religions and has for the most part evaded this difficult problem) have done the required criteriological work. But it is precisely this lack of theory that challenges one to offer a suggested solution—no more than that.

The inevitable starting question here must be Can all means be sanctified by religious ends? Thus, in the service of religious devotion is everything allowed—including the misuse of economic power, of sexuality, or aggressiveness? May something be a *religious commandment* that evidently harms, injures, perhaps even destroys human beings? There are examples in abundance in every religion: Can human sacrifices be justified because they are offered to a god? May children be slaughtered for reasons of faith, may widows be burned, heretics tortured to death? Does prostitution become divine worship because it takes place in a temple? Can prayer *and* adultery, ascesis *and* sexual promiscuity, fasting *and* drug consumption be justified in the same way, if they serve as means and paths to "mystical experience"? Are charlatanism and bogus miracles, every possible kind of lying and deception allowed, because they are done for a supposedly "holy" purpose? Is magic, which aims to compel the deity, the same as religion, which implores the deity? Are imperialism, racism, or male chauvinism to be affirmed where they appear with religious underpinnings? Can one even have nothing to object against a mass suicide like the one in Guyana because it was religiously motivated? I would say no.

Institutionalized religion—whichever one—is not a priori "moral" in each and every thing; and some collectively ingrained mores need scrutiny too. That is why, along with the specific criteria, which every religion has for itself, the *general ethical criteria* need to be discussed more than ever today. In this context we cannot, of course, get into the increasingly more complex hermeneutical questions regarding the basic forms of contemporary ethical reasoning (empirical, analytical, or transcendental-anthropological argumentation) and the validation of norms. An orientation to the human element, to what is truly human, means in any case—let me say this to avoid misunderstandings beforehand—no reduction of the religious to the "merely human."

Religion has always shown itself to be most convincing where it succeeded (long before all modern strivings for autonomy) effectively to bring out the human element against the background of the Absolute. One need mention only the Decalogue, the Sermon on the Mount, the Qur'an, the sermons of the Buddha, and the Bhagavadgita.

On the whole, of course, Christianity itself, which so long resisted freedom of religion and conscience, profited from the fact that humanism (though certainly often secularized and hostile to the Church) separated itself out from the Christian faith, criticizing religion and spreading its sphere of influence through the modern process of emancipation. This humanism called upon the (often rather unchristian) churches in a new way to translate into reality what were basically primal Christian values, such as freedom, equality, fraternity and "human dignity." For it was precisely by being religiously and ecclesiastically emancipated in modern autonomy that *the human element* could once again find a home in the domain of Christianity—before all other religions.

Conversely, Christianity, religion as a whole, can—particularly in a time of disorientation, the atrophy of human ties, a widespread permissiveness, and a diffuse cynicism—establish for the conscience of the individual (more so than all psychology, pedagogy, and even positive legislation) why morality is more than a question of personal taste and judgment or social convention: why morality, ethical values, and norms oblige us *unconditionally* and so *universally*. In fact, only the Unconditioned itself can oblige unconditionally, only the Absolute can bind absolutely, only religion can unconditionally and universally create and at the same time concretize an ethic, as it has indeed been doing for thousands of years, sometimes badly, sometimes well.

In any case, there is no mistaking the fact that in the question about the human element in other religions as well a process of reflection has been set in motion. Thus, the question of *human rights,* for instance, is being intensively discussed in Islam, especially since it has become increasingly clear that the *sharī'a,* Muslim law, often flagrantly contradicts the General Declaration of Human Rights of the United Nations (1948). This is particularly the case with respect to legal equality for women (laws on marriage, divorce, inheritance, and work) and for non-Muslims (prohibited from certain professions, etc.), all of which naturally implies probing questions directed at the Qur'an itself. There are grounds for hope that in the question of human rights and general *ethical criteria*—despite all the difficulties —an elementary basic consensus on the "key premises of human life and fellowship" (W. Korff) might take shape, with time, between the world religions, a consensus equal to the demands of a modern, humane consciousness. These are *guiding convictions* of key human values and key demands that certainly first forced themselves upon human consciousness in the course of historical evolution, but then— exactly like the Copernican world picture—achieve lasting, irreversible, unconditional validation, indeed often get codified into law (as "human rights" or "basic rights"), even though they continually need to be given fresh shapes.

In any case we cannot miss the progress that has been made toward more humanity within the various religions—for all the time gaps in awareness. One thinks, for example, of the abolition by Roman Catholicism of the practices of the Inquisition—the stake and the rack —which were customary well into modern times; or of the humane reinterpretation of the doctrine of the "holy war" and reforms in the penal code in the more progressive Islamic countries; or of the abolition of human sacrifice and suttee, which, although they had been rejected from the first by Indian Buddhists and Christians, were practiced in isolated regions of India up until the English occupation. Numerous examples from the Far, Middle, and Near East have convinced me that in the future a strongly growing awareness with respect to human rights that need safeguarding, the emancipation of women, the realization of social justice, and the immorality of war is likely to be observed in all the world religions. The world-wide religious movement on behalf of peace has, in particular, made strong progress. All these religious motivations and movements—something we have become conscious of not least of all in connection with

Poland, Iran, and Afghanistan—point to the presence of a political-social factor that must be taken very seriously. Hence my question: Should it not be possible, *invoking our common humanity*, to formulate a general ethical *criterion* that is based on the *human, the truly human element*, concretely on human dignity and the *basic values* related to it?

A new *reflection on the human* is at work in the world religions. A particularly clear example of this is the declaration of the "World Conference of Religions for Peace," held in Kyoto, Japan, in the year 1970: "When we were together to deal with the overriding theme of peace, we discovered that the things which unite us are more important than the things which separate us. We found that we have in common

— a conviction of the fundamental unity of the human family, of the equality and dignity of all men and women;

— a feeling for the sacrosanctness of the individual and his conscience;

— a feeling for the value of the human community;

— a realization that might is not the same as right, that human power cannot be self-sufficient and is not absolute;

— the faith that love, sympathy, selflessness, and the power of the mind and inner truthfulness have, in the end, greater power than hatred, hostility, and self-interest;

— a feeling of obligation to stand on the side of the poor and oppressed against the rich and the oppressors;

— deep hope in the ultimate victory of good will."

The basic question in our search for criteria thus reads: What is *good* for the individual? The answer: What truly helps him or her to be a human being. Accordingly, the basic ethical norm is Man should live in a human, not an inhuman, fashion; he should realize his humanness in all his relationships. The moral good is what allows human life in its individual and social dimension to succeed and prosper in the long run, what makes possible the optimal development of the person in all his layers and dimensions. Accordingly, human beings should realize this humanity in all its strata (including that of the instincts and emotions) and dimensions (including their connection to society and nature) as individuals and as a community. But that means at the same time that humanness would fail at its core, if the dimension of the "trans-human," the unconditioned, all-embracing, Absolute were denied or faded out. Humanness without this dimension would be a mere torso.

According to the basic norm of genuine humanity, *good* and *evil*, true and false, can be distinguished. We can also distinguish what is basically good and evil, what is true and what is false in *any individual religion*. This criterion might be formulated with regard to religion as follows:

a) *Positive criterion:* Insofar as a religion *serves* the virtue of humanity, insofar as its teachings on faith and morals, its rites and institutions *support* human beings in their human identity, and allows them to gain a meaningful and fruitful existence, it is a *true* and *good* religion.

In other words:

Whatever manifestly protects, heals, and fulfills human beings in their physical and psychic, individual and social humanness (life, integrity, justice, peace), what, in other words, is humane and truly human, can with reason invoke "the divine."

b) *Negative criterion:* Insofar as a religion *spreads inhumanity*, insofar as its teachings on faith and morals, its rites and institutions *hinder* human beings in their human identity, meaningfulness, and valuableness, insofar as it *helps to make them fail to achieve* a meaningful and fruitful existence, it is a *false* and *bad* religion.

In other words:

Whatever manifestly oppresses, injures, and destroys human beings in their physical and psychic, individual and social humanness (life, integrity, freedom, justice, peace), what, in other words, is inhumane, not truly human, cannot with reason invoke "the divine."

For all the doubtful individual cases, there is no lack of manifest examples—as I merely hinted at before—of good *and* evil, true *and* untrue in the previous history of either Hinduism or Buddhism, Judaism, Christianity, or Islam. Wherever religion is the force that lowers the dignity of the individual or of a race, class, caste, or sex, wherever individual persons or whole groups are exposed to physical, psychic, or mental injury or even destruction, then we are dealing with a false and bad religion. We must consider here that it is precisely in the realm of religion that my self-realization and the self-realization of others, along with our common responsibility for society, nature, and the cosmos, are inseparably joined.

Hence all religions must take thought anew for the demands of human nature: This element of the human that has been given to all men and women is a general ethical criterion that holds for every single religion. But the religions must continually remember—and here we go on our spiral inward—their *primal, peculiar "essence,"* as it shines forth in their origins, in their normative scriptures and normative figures. And they will continually be reminded by their critics and reformers and prophets, by their wise men and women, wherever it is a religion is being untrue to or violating its "essence": The original "essence" peculiar to every religion, its normative origin or canon (its "standard"), is a general criterion for religion by which each can be measured.

5. The Authentic or Canonical: General Religious Criterion

Given religious attitudes and developments that have gone wrong, given religious decadence and deficiencies in its own back yard Christian theology in particular has always brought the *criterion* of the origins or canon into play. This is not because the older is necessarily the better. The old is no better a priori than the new. But because the *original* or *canonical* from the beginning was the normative factor: primitive Christianity, the primal testimony of the Bible; Christ the author and original of Christian faith. Christians measure themselves against their origins, but they are often so measured by non-Christians: "You invoke the Bible and Christ—and you act like this?!" The Bible, particularly the New Testament, serves Christianity as a *canon,* as a normative standard.

And isn't the Torah the normative factor for Jews, as the Qur'an and the figure of Muhammad (as the embodiment of the Islamic way) is for Muslims, and the teaching (*dharma*) and figure of the Buddha is for Buddhists?

But what does it mean, then, in the search for criteria, when, for example, Shaktist Tantrism (for all its striving after salvation) still contradicts, in some essential features, the monastic life that the Buddha said should be aimed at? What about its consumption of alcohol and its sexual practices? To what extent is this Tantrism still (or was it

246 Theology for the Third Millennium

ever) Buddhist? At this point internal Buddhist criticism sets to work: The great majority of Buddhists would likely agree with Christians that sexuality certainly has its own value and place, but precisely for that reason it does not belong in the practice of meditation or worship, especially not in a cultic practice where partners are interchangeable, where religion can no longer be distinguished from sexuality nor sexuality from religion, and the door is flung wide open to a promiscuous misuse of both.

With the criterion of the authentic (original) or canonical (normative), therefore, we have not just a Christian criterion, but a *general religious criterion*, which is applicable, at least in principle, to other religions as well: A religion is measured here by its *normative doctrine or practice* (Torah, New Testament, Qur'an, Vedas), and sometimes too by its normative *figure* (Christ, Muhammad, the Buddha). This criterion of "authenticity" or "canonicity" thus can be applied not just to Christianity, but to all the major religions—*mutatis mutandis*, of course: modified according to each religion, a process that is easier with some religions (Hinduism, say) than with others. It seems to me that this religious criterion, in a time of great social change and rapidly progressing secularization, offers heightened meaning for the basic orientation of the non-Christian religions too. What is "essential," what is "permanent," what is "obligatory," and what is not? The religion's identity is at stake. People in religion are in agreement that the primal religious legacy should not be sold at bargain rates to the modern world; rather, it should be made to bear fruit once more in that world. And so reflection on the original (authentic) or normative (canonical) has given unusually strong impulses to reform movements (which keep breaking out in all great religions): Religious re-formation as thinking one's way back to the original form *and* at the same time re-novation as renewal for the future.

How often has it not been until the criterion of authenticity or canonicity was applied that the *primal and peculiar features* of a religion could be clearly seen. This convincingly answers the question of what—in theory and practice—true Christianity is and is not, and the same for true Judaism, true Islam, Buddhism, and finally even true Hinduism. To be sure, this feedback from the origin or canon—event, person, or scripture—has a quite different meaning in the historically oriented religions, but it is also by no means unknown in the mystically oriented religions.

To give only a brief hint:

(1) *True Hindu religion* is in principle only the religion that is based on the revealed scriptures of the Vedic seers. As dissimilar as the religions and their gods, especially in India, can be, and as great as the tolerance of the Hindus is too, because Buddhism (like Jainism) rejects the Vedas it cannot be the true religion for Hindus. And *it* is rejected (as, still more, Indian Islam is rejected). A similar statement could be made about the canon of the monotheistic religions of India such as Vishnuism or Shivaism.

(2) *True Buddhism* can only be the religion that takes its refuge in the Buddha, who set the "wheel of teaching" in motion, and in the "teaching," the "dharma," and thus in the "community," the "sangha." As great as the differences may be between Theravāda Buddhism and Mahāyāna Buddhism, and as numerous as the different Buddhist "sects" may be, religions that reject the Buddha, the *dharma*, and the *sangha* (the community of monks) are not accepted as the true way.

(3) *True Islam*, finally, is only the religion that can be based on the Qur'an revealed to Muhammad. As momentous for religion and politics as the differences, say, between Shiites and Sunnites were and are, both lean on the Qur'an, for whom it is God's word. Whoever departs from it, stands outside the true religion and falls victim to "excommunication." Similar things can be said—despite all its dogmatic tolerance and the different interpretations of the Law—about *Judaism*.

(4) Far more unequivocally than with the mystical Asian religions, obviously, we can with the historical religions, particularly *Christianity*, answer the question of what true religion is in terms of their *origin*. And with that—we are going on the inward spiral for a second time—the general religious criterion of truth has been concretized in a *specifically Christian* criterion of truth, to which there may be a corresponding specifically Jewish, Islamic, Hindu, or Buddhist criterion.

6. On the Specifically
Christian Criterion

What have we achieved so far? According to the *general ethical criterion* a religion is true and good to the extant that it is *humane,* does not oppress and destroy humanity, but protects and advances it.

According to the *general religious criterion* a religion is true and good if and insofar as it remains true to its own *origin* or *canon:* its authentic "essence," its normative scripture or figure, which it continually invokes.

According to the *specifically Christian criterion* a religion is true and good if and insofar as it allows us to perceive the spirit of Jesus Christ in its theory and practice. I apply this theory *directly* only to Christianity, in posing the self-critical question whether and to what degree the Christian religion is at all Christian. *Indirectly*—and without arrogance—the same criterion can certainly also be applied to the other religions: for critical clarification of the question whether and to what degree one also finds in other religions (especially Judaism and Islam) something that we would label as Christian.

If we wish to come to a solution concerning the central question of the true religion, we absolutely must *distinguish between an inner and an outer perspective.* One can see Christianity, like every other religion, entirely *from the outside,* as a "neutral observer," as a student of religion, as a non-Christian or an ex-Christian—without any special obligation to the Christian message, tradition, or community. Christianity then fits into its place among the world religions and must satisfy the general ethical and religious criteria for truth. In this perspective there are *many true* religions.

But this reflection "from the outside" (as a sort of "foreign policy") does not exclude the *internal* perspective (as a sort of "domestic policy"). And for the individual it is completely honorable and serious to integrate both perspectives. Think about it: This inner-outer relationship holds not only for religion. An international lawyer too, when he compares, as an expert, various national constitutions with one another or tries to reach an accord on a given critical point in international negotiations, sees his national constitution (and his state), as it were, "from the outside." "From the inside," however, he sees the same constitution (and his state), when he feels obliged as a loyal citizen among other citizens of the state precisely to this constitution (and no other) and conscientiously stands by it. In this sense nobody can simply be a one-dimensional person. Reality is more complex than this.

If now as a Christian (and as a theologian) I look upon Christianity *from within*—as every non-Christian does with his or her own religion—if I then speak as a follower of this religion, this message, this tradition or community, then Christianity is for me, as every other religion is to its adherents, more than a system to which I can draw near in a purely intellectual sense. Then Christianity is, like every religion (in contrast to every philosophy), at once a message of salvation and a way to it. I am met here not only by a philosophical-theological chain of arguments that demand my consideration, but by a religious challenge and, in the case of Christianity, a prophetic message that demands that I take an altogether personal position, that I "follow." Only in this way is this religion rightly understood at all. If then, from this point on in my remarks I speak in the language of the religious profession of faith, then this is not because out of fear of "final consequences" I am falling back again on my religion, but because I am working from the assumption that no can can grasp a religion in its depths unless he or she has affirmed it from within, with ultimate existential seriousness. Only when *a* religion has become *my* religion, does the conversation about truth take on exciting depth. What is at stake here for me, then, is truth, *my faith,* just as Judaism and Islam for the Jew and the Muslim, Hinduism and Buddhism for the Hindu and the Buddhist, is at stake—is *his* religion, *his* faith, and so *the* truth. In my religion and in the other religions as well, the issue is not a general, but an existential truth: *"tua res agitur."* In this sense there is for me—as for all other believers—only *one true religion.*

That means that in the search for the true religion no one may simply abstract from his own life history and experience. There is no such thing as a theologian nor a student of religion, neither a religious nor a political authority, that stands so far above *all* religions as to be able to judge it "objectively," from above. Anyone who thinks he can stand in a "neutral" position above all traditions, will get nothing done in any of them. And whoever refuses (to borrow an image from Raymondo Panikkar), while looking out of *his* window to take in the *whole* picture, to speak with the others who are looking out of *their* windows; whoever thinks he can float above everything and judge it, has obviously lost his footing. He will easily melt his waxen wings, as Icarus once did, in the sun of truth.

Thus I profess my faith in my historically conditioned standpoint; This one religion is *for me the true religion* for whose truth I can cite good reasons, that may possibly convince others. For me Christianity is the path that I take, the religion in which I believe I have found the truth for my living and dying. Still at the same time it is true that the *other* religions (which for hundred of millions of persons are the *true* religion) are for that reason still *in no ways untrue, religions,* are by no means simply untruth. Not only do they have a great deal of truth in common with Christianity. They also each have their own truth, which we do not have already have ("anonymously" or "implicitly"). Now it must be left to the Jewish, Muslim, Hindu, or Buddhist theologian (philosopher) to explain exactly why he is a Jew, Muslim, Hindu, or Buddhist. The Christian theologian for his part must at least be able as a matter of principle to name the specific Christian criterion and to try to answer the question of what concretely distinguishes Christians from non-Christians, what should distinguish them, what makes Christians Christians.

Why then am *I* a Christian? It would be worth a separate essay to present, in a new context of comparative religion, the reasons I have for not being a Hindu or Buddhist, nor a Jew or a Muslim, but a Christian. Let me just suggest the bare essentials here: I am a Christian because I—as a consequence of the Jewish, and in anticipation of the Islamic, faith in God—trustingly and altogether practically commit myself to the fact that the God of Abraham, Isaac (Ishmael), and Jacob has not only acted in the history of Israel (Ishmael) and spoken through its prophets, but that he has made himself known in an incomparable and, for us, decisive way in the life and work, suffering and dying of *Jesus of Nazareth.* The very first generation of his disciples was convinced that despite his death of shame on the gallows of the cross Jesus did not remain in death, but was taken up into God's eternal life. He stands now for God himself ("on the right hand of God") as God's definitive envoy, as his Messiah or Christ, as his word made flesh, as his image and likeness, as (to us an ancient royal title of Israel) his son. Thus, in brief, I am a Christian because and to the degree that I believe in this Christ and—though of course the times have changed—I try practically to emulate him (along with millions of others, each in his own way), and I take him as the guide for my path in life. Hence, in accordance with the words of the Gospel of John, he is for us, *the* way, *the* truth, and *the* life.

But this also means, speaking self-critically to Christians, that Christians *do not believe in Christianity.* As a religion, with its dogmatics, its liturgy, and discipline, like every other religion a highly ambivalent historical phenomenon. Karl Barth has quite rightly stressed this. It is therefore untenable to define Christianity as the "absolute religion," in the way Hegel thought he could do this. As a religion Christianity appears in world history just as relative as all other religions.

No, the only absolute in world history is the Absolute itself. For Jews, Christians, and Muslims, of course, this one Absolute is not ambiguous and vague, wordless, without a voice. It has spoken through the prophets. For believing Christians it is also not faceless, without a countenance. No, it became manifest in the relativity of the man Jesus of Nazareth. For believers—and only for them—He *is* the Word and Image, He is the Way, for others, He is at least the invitation to enter upon this way. That is why Christians do not *believe* in Christianity but *in the one God,* who after sending man prophets and enlightened messengers sent this person, Jesus, as *his Christ,* his anointed envoy. Jesus Christ is for Christians the *deciding regulative factor.*

And insofar as concrete Christianity testifies to this one God and his Christ, it can—in a derivative and limited sense—be called for believers themselves *the true* religion, whatever Karl Barth may say. But insofar as concrete Christianity continually deviated from this one God and his Christ, from this, its deciding regulative factor, it was also continually *untrue* religion. It also needed, even *after* Christ, the *prophetic corrective,* the prophets in the Church and—we see this today ever more clearly—the prophets and enlightened ones outside the Church as well, among whom the prophet Muhammad and the Buddha should no doubt be included *par excellence.*

Once again, the decision for the one God, who is not only the God of the philosophers and the learned (the God of the Greeks) and the God of Abraham, Isaac, and Jacob (the God of the Jews), but finally and ultimately the God of Jesus Christ (the God of the Christians), represents a *faith-decision* at its deepest level. This is a rational act of trust: This faith-decision is by no means purely subjective and arbitrary, but is altogether *rationally responsible.* I have presented elsewhere what can be said in detail for making this decision to be a Christian—in comparison with Judaism, Islam, Hinduism, and Buddhism. As Christians we cannot—unless we simply wish to issue dogmatic postulates—avoid the trouble of justifying in a substantial, empirical manner the significance of Jesus Christ. Referring to a dogmatically affirmed doctrine of the Trinity and Divine Sonship is of little help here. Nowadays we must be able to show concretely in a new way that and why we are Christians—even in critical comparison with other great religious figures—in terms of this figure and his message, his way of life, and his destiny. And, to do this, scholarly research on religion is indispensable. What is needed is not the separation of theology and religious studies (as with Karl Barth), but not their identification either (which de facto reduces theology to the study of religion or vice versa), but their critical cooperation.

I would like to have at least called attention here to one aspect, but a thoroughly central aspect, of Jesus of Nazareth, that shows us something in a striking fashion: For Christian faith the *specifically Christian* criterion coincides not only with the *general religious* criterion of the origins, but finally with the *general ethical* criterion of the human element. The spiral endures. For what is the purpose—as a consequence of the proclaiming of the Kingdom and Will of God—aimed at in the Sermon on the Mount and all of Jesus' behavior? Nothing more or less than a new, *true humanity:* the Sabbath, the commandments for the sake of man, and not the other way around.

This new true humanity means a *more radical way of being human,* which is manifested in *the fellowship of solidarity* even with one's opponent. From the perspective of Jesus, the real, true person, this more radical humanity of the Sermon on the Mount—now seen against a completely different world horizon—would have to be put into practice as a fellowship of solidarity with the men and women in the *other religions* as well. A fellowship of solidarity, therefore,

— that not only renounces religious wars, persecution, and Inquisitions, and practices religious tolerance, but that also in relations with the other religions replaces collective egoism (ecclesiocentrism) with philanthropy, the solidarity of love;

— that, for this reason, instead of adding up the debts of history owed by the religions, practices forgiveness and dares to make a new beginning;

— that does not simply abolish the religious institutions and constitutions (which often separate people), but relativizes them for the good of humanity;

— that instead of an open or concealed power struggle between the religious-political systems strives for successive reconciliation. No, there should be no unified religion for the whole world, but peace among the religions as a prerequisite for peace among the nations.

This means that the more humane (in the spirit of the Sermon on the Mount) Christianity is, the more Christian it is; and the more Christian it is, the more it appears to the outside as a true religion. And with that the three criteria of truth should now be developed, and we can summarize the crucial points in a concluding section:

7. On the Way to Ever Greater Truth

By now it ought to have become clear: If we wish to answer the question of what is good for the individual—not only pragmatically or positivistically, but fundamentally; not only abstractly-philosophically, but concretely-existentially, and not only psychologically-pedagogically, but in an unconditionally binding and universally valid way, then we cannot get around religion—or put in its place quasi-religion. But conversely every religion will have to let itself be measured by the general ethical criterion of the human element and for that reason will not be able, given modern conditions, to dispense with the findings of psychology, pedagogy, philosophy, and jurisprudence. This is no vicious circle here, but, as so often, a dialectical interrelationship:

(1) *True humanity is the prerequisite for true religion.* This means that the human element (respect for human dignity and basic values) is a minimal demand leveled at every religion: At least humanity (the minimal criterion) must be given, where one wishes to translate genuine religious feeling into reality.

(2) *True religion is the perfecting of true humanity.* This means that religion (as the expression of an all-encompassing meaning, of highest values, of unconditioned obligation) is an optimal prerequisite for the realization of the human element. It is precisely religion (a maximum criterion) that must be present where people wish to real-

ize the values of humanity on the basis of an unconditional and universal obligation.

What, then, is the true religion? I have tried to give a differentiated answer to this complex question with the greatest possible conceptual clarity and theoretical exactness, with the help of three dissimilar and yet dialectically interwoven criteria—the general ethical, the general religious, and the specifically Christian, as well as the two dimensions, the external and the internal. My answer also includes the answer to the question Is there true religion? In summary we can say

— Seen *from the outside,* from the standpoint of religious studies, there are *different true religions:* religions that for all their ambivalence correspond, at least in principle, to the ethical and religious criteria we have set up: various ways of salvation to the one goal, ways that in part intersect and that can in any event reciprocally benefit each other.

— Seen *from the inside,* from the standpoint of the believing Christian oriented to the New Testament, there is for me *the true religion, which for me, since I cannot possibly take all paths at the same time, is the path that I try to take:* Christianity, insofar as it bears witnesses to the one true God in Jesus.

— This (for me, for us Christians) one true religion in no way excludes the truth in *other religions,* but lets them have a positive validity. The other religions are not simply untrue, but neither are they unconditionally true, but *conditionally* ("with reservations" or whatever) *true religions,* which, so far as they do not contradict the Christian message on decisive points, can by all means complete, correct, and enrich the Christian religion.

From these long and complex remarks it should have become clear that a maximum theological openness to the other religions forces one to suspend neither his faith conviction nor the question of truth. We should struggle—in "fraternal emulation" (Vatican II)—over the truth. But one final limitation, which affects all religions, has to be made. There are not just the two "horizontal" dimensions (external-internal), but also a third dimension (a "vertical" one, so to speak): *For me* as a believer, *for us* as a community of faith, Christianity, *so far* as it attests to God in Christ, is certainly the *true* religion. But no religion has the *whole* truth, only *God alone* has the *whole* truth—Lessing was right about that. Only God *himself*—as we have always mentioned—*is the* truth.

And for that reason one final point here: Christians cannot claim to comprehend him, the incomprehensible One, to have grasped him, the unsearchable One. Even in Christian faith, according to Paul, we recognize the truth itself, which is God, only as in a mirror, in puzzling outlines, fragmentarily, in certain aspects, always dependent upon our quite specific standpoint and place in time. Yes, Christianity too is *"in via,"* on the way: *Ecclesia peregrinans, homines viatores.* And we are not on the way alone, but with millions upon millions of other human beings from every possible religion and denomination, who are going their own way, but with whom the longer we travel together the more we will be in a *process of communication,* where one should not dispute about Mine and Yours, my truth/ your truth; but rather where one should be endlessly ready to learn, should make one's own the truth of the others and ungrudgingly communicate one's own truth.

But whither, some will ask, *will all this lead?* History is open toward the future, and open-ended too is interreligious dialogue, which—unlike interdenominational dialogue—has only just begun. What the future of the Christian religion, which is for me the true one, will bring, we do not know. Nor do we know what the future will bring to the other, non-Christian religions. Who knows what the Christology, the Qur'anology, or the Buddhology, like the Church, the *Umma,* the *Sangha,* of the year 2087, will look like?

As far as the future goes, only one thing is certain: At the end both of human life and the course of the world Buddhism and Hinduism will no longer be there, nor will Islam nor Judaism. Indeed, in the end Christianity will not be there either. In the end no religion will be left standing, but the one Inexpressible, to whom all religions are oriented, whom Christians will only then completely recognize—when the imperfect gives way before the perfect—even as they themselves are recognized: *the* truth face to face. And in the end there will no longer be standing between the religions a figure that separates them, no more prophet or enlightened one, not Muhammad and not the Buddha. Indeed even Christ Jesus, whom Christians believe in, will no longer stand here as a figure of separation. But he, to whom, Paul says, all powers (including death) are subjected, "subjects himself, then, to God" so that *God himself (ho theos)*—or however he may be called in the East—may truly be not just in all things but *"everything to everyone"* (1 Cor 15:28).

D.

KARL BARTH AND THE POSTMODERN PARADIGM

Let me begin on a personal note: I cannot, and will not, speak of Karl Barth as I would of any great theologian or philosopher of the past, Hegel, for example, Schleiermacher, Kierkegaard, or Harnack. I cannot, and will not, pretend to a lofty objectivity and neutrality, least of all in the case of Barth. Talking about him means for me, now as ever, talking about a person and theologian who has remained alive, who was combative—and pious precisely because of this: a man whom I met in a crucial phase of my life and to whom I am indebted for basic insights into theology (not that I ever became an uncritical Barthian). I have no intention of providing an academic (in the bad sense) abstract of our common history, nor of course will I deny the fact that I disagreed with him then, as I do now. In this retrospective I should like to follow a difficult *via media* between sympathy and distance, as I try to convey something of the vitality of this theologian and his theology, as I have seen it not only in Barth's work but in a great many encounters and conversations.

Any young Swiss Catholic from a traditionally Catholic family, region, and canton, growing up, in the years after World War II, far more interested in the daily papers than in academic theology (not to mention *Church Dogmatics,* if he had heard of Karl Barth's opus), could not help knowing one thing: This Protestant professor of theology at Basel had an unusually bad press, and not just in the newspapers of the Catholic camp. To be sure, his name was never missing whenever we Swiss *Gymnasium* students counted up the internationally important names of our Swiss contemporaries. Karl Barth figured in the list along with Emil Brunner, Carl Gustav Jung, Arthur Honegger, Le Corbusier, and so on. No doubt he *was* a great man, this theologian, who with as much bravery as shown—unfortunately—by scarcely any of the bishops, publically defied Nazism and, along with the Synod of Barmen, inspired and helped organize the resistance by the Confessional Church. Barth's "Swiss voice" for Germany's better self—even after his expulsion from his professorship at Bonn in 1935 for refusal to take the official loyalty oath to Hitler—offered guidance and encouragement to great numbers of Christians in the darkest of times.

But now, after the Second World War, now wasn't he, the dyed-in-the-wool socialist and fighter for peace, showing exactly the same inexorably critical attitude toward the red dictatorship of Stalin as toward the brown dictatorship of Adolf Hitler? In 1946 as a visiting professor at Bonn, hadn't he urgently warned a certain Dr. Konrad Adenauer in a private conversation against founding a party based on a "Christian-Democratic" world view? Hadn't he even conferred in Berlin with the SED's (United Socialist Party of Germany) top men, Pieck, Grotewohl, and Ulbricht? Hadn't he taken two trips to communist Hungary (ceremoniously received by the Hungarian State President, only a short time before Cardinal Mindszenty went on trial for high treason)? Hadn't he kept up many contacts with communistic Czechoslovakia as well? Didn't this theologian now stand side by side with his friends Martin Niemöller and Gustav Heinemann, doing battle against a supposed political-ecclesiastical restoration and the rearming of West Germany, which was aimed, however, only at containing communism? Wasn't he arguing for an extremely dangerous "third way between East and West" (he himself practiced it through visits to Eastern Europe), which had gotten him involved in a big public controversy with one of the leading Swiss politicians, Markus Feldmann? Really, this theologian did *not* have a good press, and not just because of the political positions he took.

1. Theological Confrontation

In addition, Catholic journalism had its own particular reasons for bearing a grudge against this Protestant: Although as early as 1920 he had hung a reproduction of Matthias Grünewald's Crucifixion from the Isenheimer altar over his writing desk, Barth had spoken out as a Calvinist reformer opposed to religious images, decisively (and successfully) attacking the use of new stained glass windows in the restored cathedral of Basel. He had also publicly committed himself with the same decisiveness (though this time without success) against the newly discovered medieval frescoes in the same cathedral.

Now, in 1948, Karl Barth had been invited by his friend and coreligionist, the great Dutch churchman Willem Visser 't Hooft, the guiding spirit of the ecumenical movement, to take part in the first *World Assembly of Churches* in Amsterdam. This was to lead to the founding of the World Council of Churches, with Visser 't Hooft as Secretary General. Prior to this Barth had scarcely participated in the ecumenical movement. But here in Amsterdam he learned—above all through conversations with Michael Ramsey, the Archbishop of Canterbury, and the Orthodox theologian Georges Florovski—that in scholarly theology there had to be room alongside "dogmatics" and "symbolics" for something like "ecumenics." "Disagreements within the agreement" and "agreements within the disagreements" was the motto; that is, to seek for differences of opinion *within* consensus and make possible forms of consensus *within* differences of opinion among understanding theologians of the various churches, so as to come a step closer to unity. But Rome—the pope—had refused to attend this assembly, as had the Orthodox Church of Moscow. And Barth's reaction? It was typical of him: in a combination of Protestant freedom and Swiss impudence he proposed simply to pass on to the business of the day. But one must hear him in his original words, to understand just what sort of man he was, how he thought and argued:

> May this freedom (for the one Lord Jesus Christ, *despite* these separate Eucharists) also mean, then, for us, that the sign or the outrage over the refusal we have received from the churches of *Rome* and *Moscow* will take up the least possible room in the negotiations of our first section. Why

shouldn't we simply see in this refusal God's powerful hand raised over us? Perhaps he is using it to give us a sign, by which he aims to take away any crazy notion we might have of building a tower here, whose top would reach the heavens. Perhaps he is using it to show us how wretchedly our light has glimmered till now, that it evidently has not yet even managed to shed its glow into these other purportedly Christian regions. Perhaps he is using it to guard us from conversation partners with whom we could not be a community even in an imperfect sense because they, though for different reasons, are unwilling to make just this move, away from every sort of ecclesiasticism to Jesus Christ, without which Christians of various kinds and sources cannot even speak with one another and cannot listen to one another, much less come together. And he is perhaps using it precisely to put us in a very *good* position, by the fact that *Rome* and *Moscow*, of all places, seem to be agreed in wanting to have nothing to do with us. I suggest that we now seek to praise and thank God for just this, that it pleases Him to block our plans as clearly as He has done![1]

Was Karl Barth an anti-Catholic agitator? That's how it looked to superficial observers. The polemic waged by published Catholic opinions opposing the obviously anti-Catholic Barth—this was after all the heyday of the last pre-conciliar pope, Pius XII—was surpassed only by the Catholic outrage over Hochhuth's dramatic exposé *The Deputy*, which at the time led to street demonstrations in front of the City Theater in Basel.

But Karl Barth's critique of Catholicism had theologically deeper and historically longer roots. For he taught during the five important years of his second professorship (after Göttingen), from 1925 to 1930, in "Münster, that nest of clerics and Anabaptists":

There Catholic dogmatic theology was represented by the neo-Thomist Franz Diekamp, whom Barth often quoted later on;

There he worked intensively on Anselm of Canterbury and Thomas Aquinas;

There—in a novel gesture—he invited the Catholic theologian Erich Przywara, S.J., to come to a seminar discussion and personal conversations, where the unusually learned and clever Przywara developed his ideas—in the tradition of Augustine, Aquinas, and Scheler

—on "God in us and God above us," on an ontologically given similarity—that is, an *analogy of being,*—between God and humanity.

In so doing, of course, Przywara only confirmed Karl Barth in his conviction that Catholic theology and the Catholic Church had indeed kept more of the substance of Christianity than neo-Protestantism, but that they were guilty of the same fundamental mistake: They had usurped God's revelation, they wanted to dispose of grace; in a word—and this was, after all, the original concern of "dialectical theology"—they could not allow God to be God and man to be man any more. To that extent, then, "Roman Catholicism" is a "question put to the Protestant church," as Barth entitled his controversial theological lecture of 1928, because in the mirror of Catholic mistakes the same problems became recognizable within the Protestant context. Abruptly confronting Catholicism Barth makes the case for a Protestantism that must concentrate most strictly on its evangelical concerns. The world is the world, and man is man; but God is God, and reconciliation is in Jesus Christ alone.

As early as the 1920s and 1930s Karl Adam of Tübingen and Erik Peterson of Bonn, and then, along with Erich Przywara, Gottlieb Söhngen in particular had been the first to engage in discussions with the early Barth (the author of *The Epistle to the Romans* and subsequent writings). Around 1940, when the German voices had to fall silent, Catholic theologians were heard from French-speaking countries: the Jesuits Louis Malevez, Henri Bouillard, and the Dominican Jerome Hamer (not to forget the Dutchman Johannes C. Groot). But the majority of these works made little reference to the Barth of the monumental *Church Dogmatics,* which had only been taking shape since 1940: after the *Prologomena* (vol. I, bks. 1–2) in the years 1932–39 Barth did not publish his *Doctrine of God* (vol. II, bks. 1–2), and then in the years 1945 to 1951 his *Doctrine of Creation* (vol. IV, bks. 1–4); the *Doctrine of Reconciliation,* begun in 1953, like his *Doctrine of Redemption* and *Eschatology* (vol. IV, bks. 1–4), was destined to remain unfinished. In the final analysis there was likewise no profit gained from the correspondence that Barth had after Amsterdam with the French Jesuit Jean Daniélou—one of the chief representatives in France of the *"nouvelle théologie,"* which was suspected of heresy. Speaking of Rome's refusal to attend the Amsterdam meeting, Barth brusquely explained to Daniélou, "It was too much to ask us at the same time both to take seriously your absolute claim of superiority *and* despite that to long for your presence."

2. *Catholic Attempts at Understanding*

The first really crucial figure on the Catholic side was another theologian, Hans Urs von Balthasar. At once a student of Przywara and Henri de Lubac, since 1940 von Balthasar (from Lucerne) had been residing, like Barth, in Basel. Von Balthasar had left the Jesuits because he felt a calling, together with his spiritual friend, Adrienne von Speyr, to found a "lay order." Von Balthasar would ultimately write the masterful book that made it possible for Catholic theology to break through to an *inner understanding of Barthian theology: Karl Barth: A Presentation and Interpretation of His Theology* (Cologne, 1951). Looking back from the perspective of Barth's mature work, von Balthasar tried to distinguish between a "period of dialectics" in the early Barth *(The Epistle to the Romans,* 1919 and 1922), and a "turn toward analogy" *(An Outline of Christian Dogmatics,* 1927), which had finally been extended by Barth to the "plenitude of analogy" (from vol. II of *Church Dogmatics).*

Von Balthasar called attention to the artful structure and intellectual-linguistic power of Barthian theology, that can be compared only to Schleiermacher's. He showed how in a radical scheme of Christological foundations creation and covenant become interwoven, how this leads to a new understanding of man as God's partner, to a novel doctrine of sin and reconciliation. . . . The Catholic von Balthasar was fascinated above all by Barth's reinterpretation of predestination, which "sublates" the Augustinian-Calvinistic dualism (a part of humanity is preselected for bliss, another part for hell) in a Christian universalism that almost reminds us of Origen: in this way the Christ-center is mediated by an all-embracing unity of redemption. This is a Christocentrism that now promised to make possible a new accent on the relationship between faith and knowledge, nature and grace, judgment and redemption—for Protestants and Catholics in equal measure. Yet what could that mean?

In the foreword to the first volume of *Church Dogmatics* (1932) we read the famous-notorious sentences (paying no heed to Przywara): "I regard the *analogy of being* as *the* invention of the Antichrist, and think that *on account of it* one cannot become a Catholic. In saying this, I venture at the same time to rate all other reasons one might have against becoming a Catholic as myopic and trivial." We can understand this polemic against the analogy of being, which "levels" God and man, as purely anti-Christian only if we recognize that it takes a stand on two fronts. To be sure, Barth is protesting here first of all against the sort of *Roman Catholicism* that in the train of Scholasticism and the First Vatican Council, coordinates God and man and thereby sets up an interplay between man and God, nature and grace, reason and faith, philosophy and theology. Just how fateful all this was, Barth thought, could be seen in the Catholic Marian dogmas, and in the Catholic understanding of scripture, tradition, and the infallible magisterium of the Pope. "It is precisely in the doctrine and cult of Mary that we see so graphically the presence of the heresy that makes all the other heresies clear" said Barth; and his critique of the "erring papal church" which, when all is said and done, "declares itself identical to God's revelation" could not have struck with a sharper edge.[2] But all this was involved with what he saw as the disastrous Catholic "flattening out" of God and man under the auspices of a leveling concept of being. Barth felt he had to protest against such thinking in the name of a "totally other" God, in the name of God's godliness.

At the same time, however, Barth was no less strenuous in opposing the sort of *liberal neo-Protestantism* that, following the lead of Schleiermacher, oriented itself completely toward the pious religious person instead of toward God and his revelation. Barth thought it was no accident: On the basis of leveling "natural theology" both Roman Catholicism and liberal neo-Protestantism had made their peace in uncritical accommodation to whatever political systems might be in power: first with the empire and its politics of war; and then again with National Socialism. On account of this coordination of God and man Protestant "German Christians" had seen in Nazism something like a new revelation and in Adolf Hitler a new Luther—linking together Christianity and Germanness—indeed a new Christ. On account of the analogy of being between God and man prominent representatives of two-tier (natural/supernatural) neo-Scholastic theology (such as Karl Adam and Michael Schmaus) found that Nazism was not so bad because it aimed on the natural level for what Christianity achieved on the supernatural level. This showed all the political dangerousness of a "Christian" natural theology. This had to be opposed when the political situation became serious. The Synod of Barmen was the most visible symbol for this.

And yet the ironies of history: The most important theological result of von Balthasar's book was that the whole antithesis between the analogy of being and the analogy of faith, so strongly emphasized by Barth, was shown up as a *false problem*. Whatever may go on in popular Catholic piety, Catholic theology and the Catholic Church are grounded in faith, they cannot and will not usurp the grace of God. Barth had been taken in hand, theologically, by von Balthasar's meticulous distinguishing among the shades of meaning in the term "nature," and the more time passed the more he had to concede this. In the mid-1950s when I, as a young man (worried by these problems, like many Catholic theologians) spoke to Barth about this controversy, he showed he was a man not only of holy wrath, but of winning humor too, when he answered, "In theology you never know: Has he got me, or have I got him?" And with respect to the much-disputed analogy of being, the sole reason one could not become a Catholic, he simply said, "I've buried it." And as a matter of fact—without, of course, ever publicly explaining himself—Barth never used the expression afterwards. But that in no way prevented backwards Catholic theologians (and sometimes Protestant ones too), who would have liked to see the schism in the Church grounded and secured not just with the papacy, the Church, and the sacraments, but, more, with the Holy Spirit, with Jesus Christ, or indeed with God the Father himself in person, from lavishing loving care on the analogy of being as the actual point of discord dividing the Church.

But all this is a regression behind von Balthasar, who besides had written in the following year a boldly liberating little programmatic book for *Razing the Bastions* (1952), which likewise betrays Barth's influence. It was a book that came at the time like a loud, impatient trumpet blast, calling for the Church to drop its defensive posture toward the world—a position that Balthasar, admittedly, seems to have left far behind him. Still, this evolution in the theology and church politics of my compatriot and first editor will not stop me from acknowledging, thirty years later, the fact that without von Balthasar's book on Barth my own work on Barth would not have been possible. I learned from von Balthasar that Catholic and Protestant tradition can be reconciled precisely in the areas where they are most consistently themselves. From him I learned above all that Karl

Barth, *because* he embodied the most thorough and logical development of Protestant theology, also comes closest to Catholic theology.
Totally oriented as he is, in Protestant fashion, to the Christ-center,
for that very reason he has a universal, Catholic scope. He reaches out
and offers the possibility of a new *ecumenical theology.*

Ever since the days of Martin Luther and the Council of Trent,
one of the tenets of faith, an *"articulus stantis et cadentis Ecclesiae"*
(by which the Church stands and falls), and hence a basic obstacle to
understanding between Catholics and Protestants, has always been
the *justification of the sinner* not on the grounds of good deeds but
solely of faith and trust. If we could show that there was a conver-
gence or, *a fortiori,* a consensus here, that would go a long way toward
healing the split in the Church.

My work on Barth aimed at showing just this: that in the doctrine
of justification, seen as a whole, we can recognize a fundamental
agreement between the teaching of Karl Barth and the teaching,
properly understood, of the Catholic Church; and that from this perspective there was no further basis for a schism between Protestants
and Catholics. Sly as he was, Karl Barth wrote carefully in his covering
letter responding to my book: *"If* what you have cited from Sacred
Scripture, both old and new Roman Catholic theology, and then too
from 'Denziger' and hence from the texts of the Council of Trent,
really *is* the teaching of your Church, and can be confirmed as such
(perhaps will be confirmed by the consensus greeting your book),
then I shall no doubt have to hasten, in order to commune with the
genius loci, to the church of Santa Maria Maggiore in Trent. I have
already been there twice; now I shall have to make a third trip, this
time to confess with a contrite heart, 'Patres, peccavi!' "

My book *Justification* (1957) was not placed, as some had hoped
and some had feared, on the Index of Forbidden Books. By 1971 it was
possible for a well-prepared document, released in Malta jointly by a
study commission of the Lutheran World Alliance and the Roman
Catholic Church, to certify that "today a wide-ranging consensus is
emerging on the interpretation of justification. Even Catholic theologians, in treating the issue of justification, stress that God's gift of
salvation for the believer has no human conditions attached to it.
Lutheran theologians emphasize that the process of justification is not

limited to the forgiving of the individual's sins, and they see in it
something more than an outward declaration holding the sinner to be
just. . . . As a foundation of Christian freedom over against legal
conditions for receiving salvation the message of justification must
continually be broached anew as a momentous explanation of the
core of the Gospel."[3] Thus the confirmation from Rome was there
before us. Karl Barth, of course, no longer had the opportunity of
going on pilgrimage to Trent, since he had been dead for three years.

3. Ecumenical Understanding

The message of justification "as a foundation of Christian freedom over against legal conditions for receiving salvation" naturally
has radical consequences. This is true not just for the individual, but
also for the Church, which has meaning only as a community of
believers that keeps being invested anew with the right to live on the
grace, forgiveness, and liberation of God. That is why "the Church is
always to be reformed" *(Ecclesia semper reformanda).*

Barth's intentions, then, were thoroughly programmatic—in the
face of both liberal and Kierkegaardian individualism—when he
changed his original title *Christian Dogmatics* (the false start of 1927)
to *Church Dogmatics.* He did this not only to fight against the facile
use of the word "Christian," but above all—despite the "lamentations
over the general course of my development"—to make it clear that
dogmatics cannot be some sort of absolutely "free discipline," but
"one that is bound to the realm of the Church, where—and where
alone—it is possible and meaningful."[4] Thus long chapters on ecclesiology can be found as early as the *Prologomena* (on the Church's
kerygma, on the Church as audience and as teacher), then in the
Doctrine of Election (the election of Israel and of the Church), and of
course in the three volumes of the *Doctrine of Reconciliation.* There
are all sorts of material here on the gathering, the building up, and the
mission of the Church through the power of God's Spirit, which awak-
ens to faith, vivifies in love, and calls to hope; on the one, holy,
Catholic, and apostolic Church. And all this—although von Balthasar
no longer takes it seriously—represents the evolutionary peak of Protestant tradition and the closest approximation to Catholic tradition: a
Catholic ecclesiology, focused on the Gospel and hence truly ecumenical.

Ecumenical understanding on both sides became difficult only when the talk turned to the *organizational structure* and the practical politics of the Church: to the meaning of the sacraments and especially to the theological understanding and practical exercise of church offices, the priesthood, and episcopacy; above all, of course, to the question of the papacy. Karl Barth was thoroughly fascinated by the enormous possibilities of the papacy, but he was repelled by its concrete form and practice: He used to say, "I cannot hear the voice of the Good Shepherd from this Chair of St. Peter." That was under Pius XII.

Karl Barth was profoundly moved by the pontificate of John XXIII, of epochal importance though it lasted only five years. He was particularly moved by the Second Vatican Council and the *double paradigm change* it introduced—the integration of both the Reformation and the modern paradigms into the Catholic Church and Catholic theology. Barth was the man who had challenged me, as a Catholic theologian trained in the Roman style back then, to speak publicly about something so archetypally Protestant (and therefore suspicious-sounding to Catholic ears) as *"Ecclesia semper reformanda"*: I did this in a lecture at "his" university in January 1959—literally six days before the utterly surprising announcement of the council. Barth had taken a lively interest in the conciliar reform program later sketched out in my book *The Council and Reunion: Renewal as a Call to Unity;* indeed he had even suggested this title. The council then adopted the ostensibly so Protestant principle of the necessity of constant reform *("Ecclesia semper in reformatione")* in its Constitution on the Church and also put it into practice by endorsing many requests, on the one hand, of the Reformers (for greater appreciation of the Bible and preaching, and of the laity too, going so far as introducing the vernacular into the liturgy) and, on the other hand, of the moderns (for freedom of faith, conscience, and religion, for tolerance and ecumenical understanding, for a new attitude toward the Jews, the world religions, and the secular world as a whole). Karl Barth began to marvel at intellectual agitation that had broken out in the Catholic Church, which seemed to contrast with a widespread rigidity in Protestantism. Touched not simply by the human qualities of the conciliar pope, but by the deepest evangelical elements in him,

Barth had no hesitation this time in saying about John XXIII, "Now I can hear the voice of the Good Shepherd."

For all that he did not become a Catholic. He did not in any case believe in converting to other churches, but he held the highest opinion of the constant re-conversion of all churches to Jesus Christ. Anyhow in 1966 the new situation provoked him to travel to Rome. *"Peregrinatio ad limina Apostolorum,"* he called it. It was a pilgrimage to the graves of the Apostles, after he could not accept an invitation to the council for health reasons. In Rome, after conversations with various Roman authorities, he found his positive overall impression of conciliar Catholicism confirmed: "The Church and theology over there have swung into motion to a degree beyond what I had imagined." But Roncalli's successor, Paul VI, impressed him as a respectable, even lovable man, who was, however, somehow to be pitied. When he met Barth, the pope told him how hard it really was, to bear and handle the keys of Peter entrusted to him by the Lord. This was still before Paul VI issued his disastrous encyclical against "artificial" birth control; but the postconciliar dilemmas—which were the upshot of the conciliar compromises—could already be seen in the offing.

We don't know what Karl Barth thought of the two subsequent popes, who—in an expression at once of compromise and perplexity —wished to combine the names of both their very different predecessors, John and Paul. A few months after his visit to Rome—his creative powers having exhausted themselves long before his death—he broke off for good his work on *Church Dogmatics.* He hoped to publish just one remaining lecture fragment, from the fourth, ethical part of the *Doctrine of Reconciliation.* It was to be his last major publication. His great thirteen-volume work remained an unfinished symphony, like the *Summa* of Thomas Aquinas, who had likewise suddenly and mysteriously interrupted work on his magnum opus several months before he died. In his last, unfinished outline of a lecture, Karl Barth wrote that in the Church we always have to listen to the faith of our fathers: " 'God is not the God of the dead, but of the living.' 'They all live unto Him'—from the Apostles to the fathers of yesteryear and yesterday." These were the last lines written by the eighty-two-year-old Barth. The next morning, December 10, 1968, his wife found he had peacefully passed away.

In his last years Karl Barth often thought of himself as "outdated." He used to say, "Now I wish I were young again, as young as you are—then I'd go back onto the barricades." Karl Barth back on the barricades? On the barricades in the seventies and eighties? I have often wondered in the past two decades where and how he would have gone onto the barricades, what he would likely have done, if he had become, not a Barthian, but a real Karl Barth, young all over again. And I should like to offer some reflections on this question, after addressing Barth's shift from confrontation with Catholic theology to attempts at understanding and finally to ecumenical assent to it. From Then to Now, in other words, but not in arbitrary hypothetical speculations about the "what if"; rather in objective inquiry and constructive continuation of Barth's theology: What now?

4. Karl Barth—Initiator of a "Postmodern" Paradigm in Theology

The first question here is the crucial one for every theologian: Where and how is Karl Barth to be incorporated into the history of theology? Is he the monumental (and scarcely read) "Neo-Orthodox," as he is almost universally classified—and dismissed—in America and in the Bultmann school?

Or is he the unsurpassable theological innovator of the century, as the Germans—far beyond the limits of the Barthian school—extol him and thereby block their own path?

My comprehensive, Catholic thesis argues against both the antagonists who would disqualify Barth and the epigones who would glorify him. It maintains that Karl Barth is the *initiator* of—as we would say nowadays—a *"postmodern" paradigm in theology*. This means two things: First, I would like to make it clear to Barth's despisers that Karl Barth really is an initiator, indeed the *main initiator* of a "postmodern" paradigm in theology, which had already begun to set in back then. But, second, I would say to uncritical admirers of Barth that Karl Barth is *only an initiator* and not the perfecter of such a paradigm.

Three points can be easily proved from Barth's writings and from *The Life of Karl Barth*, as Eberhard Busch has exemplarily presented it, "from his letters and autobiographical texts" (Munich, 1976):

At first Barth was a *vigorous supporter of modern theology:* By nature he had a cordial attachment to the bourgeois world (from poetry and music to beer and fraternity life to the army). Early on he felt enthusiasm for Schiller's idealism and Richard Wagner's *Tannhäuser* "Proclamation." As a student of theology, who from his very first semester in the university had become familiar with the historico-critical method, he quickly chose Kant and Schleiermacher as the lodestars of his thought. And so he became the student of the great liberal masters: first of Harnack (in Berlin) and then, more importantly, of Wilhelm Herrmann (in Marburg), a man who managed to combine Kant and Schleiermacher with a pronounced Christocentrism. As an editorial assistant to Martin Rade at the liberal *Christian World* he dealt with the intellectual products of all the notable liberal figures, from Bousset and Gunkel to Troeltsch and Wernle.

But *then* Barth evolved into the *harshest critic of that enlightened-modern paradigm,* which, after a phase of strict Lutheran and Calvinist orthodoxy, took shape as early as the seventeenth century, won general acceptance in the eighteenth, and finally in the nineteenth century reached its classic stage of development with Schleiermacher; and with the liberal theology inspired by him took on its position of leadership. Barth's ten years of experience as the pastor of Safenwil (1911–21), an increasingly industrialized Swiss farming community with every kind of social distress had, even before the First World War, led him to doubt the optimistic bourgeois faith in progress and the conformist spirit of cultural Protestantism. Indeed they led him to become a socialist committed to the cause of the workers. He realized that in the severe plight facing the preacher —empty pews and ineffective confirmation classes—all his scholarly knowledge about the Bible was of little use. And despite his respect for the modern liberal mentality he sensed that historical relativism had increasingly left Christianity drained and empty. But it was the outbreak of World War One in 1914 that, to Barth's mind, plunged the modern paradigm into a radical crisis: On the one hand liberal theology had completely betrayed its modern accommodating nature, when ninety-three German intellectuals, including almost all of Barth's renowned theological masters, with Harnack and Hermann leading the way, signed a public manifesto, identifying themselves with Wilhelm II's war policy and the surprise attack on neutral Belgium. On the other hand, however, European socialism had also failed completely vis-à-vis the war ideology, and in the end everywhere supported the war. Karl Barth's personal theology developed into a "theology of crisis," which in 1918 was dramatically highlighted by the downfall of the German empire and of control of the Protestant church system by the prince, by the Revolution in Russia and the social turmoil in Germany.

In the end Barth became the *chief initiator of a postmodern paradigm in theology* in the following way: In the many-layered crisis of the whole existing order it had become supremely clear to him that Christianity can in no way be reduced to a critically graspable historical phenomenon of the past and a largely moral inner experience of the present. In the face of the epochal collapse of bourgeois society and culture, of its governing institutions, traditions, and authorities, Barth outdid everyone in mobilizing the critical power of faith. And in connection with *The Epistle to the Romans* of 1919 and 1922, together with his friends Emil Brunner, Eduard Thurneysen, Friedrich Gogarten, and Rudolf Bultmann, Barth issued a programmatic call "in between times" (the name of a magazine they put out) for a shift to a "theology of the word," often called "dialectical theology." This meant a move

— away from the historical-psychological self-interpretation of the "religious" person and of theology as a science of history and culture, toward God's own word as attested to in the Bible, toward God's revelation, kingdom, and deeds;

— away from religious discourse on the concept of God, toward proclamation of the Word of God;

— away from religion and religiosity, toward Christian faith;

— away from the religious needs of humanity (the modern "man-God"), toward God, who is the "totally Other," manifest only in Jesus Christ (the "God-man" in the biblical sense).

In the general political, economic, cultural, and spiritual upheaval after the catastrophe of the First World War the theology of Karl Barth—with Barth himself serving as a model for "theological existence"—introduced the paradigm change from the modern-liberal to what we can call in retrospect the "postmodern" paradigm, which at the time was recognizable only in vague outline. To that extent it is Barth—and not Ritschl, Harnack, Hermann, or Troeltsch—

who deserves the title the "Father of the Church in the twentieth century."

In view of the crisis of the modern paradigm Karl Barth demanded and fostered a basically new orientation for theology. Earlier than other theologies, his thought, in its theological critique of ideology, saw through the despotic-destructive forces of modern rationality, relativized the absolutist claims of Enlightenment rationality, and confronted the self-consciousness of the modern subject with its self-deceptions. In short, his theology, earlier than that of others, recognized the "dialectic of the Enlightenment" and carried on an Enlightenment of the Enlightenment. As opposed to the liberal diffusion of the Christian into the universally human and historical, Barth posits a new Christological concentration of salvation in Christ; as opposed to the cultural-Protestant accommodation to social and civic trends, he stresses the political and social challenge of the Gospel. It remains a source of astonishment how Barth early on spoke out decisively against every form of nationalism and imperialism, the pernicious legacy of modernity, taken over and lifted to the level of absurdity by the totalitarian systems; how he spoke out *for* a politics of peace and social justice, for a critical-prophetic attitude on the part of the Church toward all political systems.

Still a fundamental element in all this was a fascinating new theological thrust, which showed its power in 1934 against the quasi-religion of Nazism at the Synod of Barmen. This could be seen in the Synod's lucid confession, conceived by Barth, of Jesus Christ as the "one Word of God," alongside which "other events and forces, figures and truths" had no right to be recognized "as God's revelation." Unlike other theologians, Barth was not blinded by Nazi-Fascist totalitarianism; he did not see it as the necessary tremendous culmination of modern evolution. Instead Barth viewed it rather as the terrifying vestige of a modernity that urgently needed to be transcended, as the "end of modern times," to use Romano Guardini's phrase from after the Second World War.

Thus it is a complete misunderstanding of (at least the young) Barth to label him as neo-orthodox. On the contrary, it seems to me that even today in theology we must *cling firmly to the broad intentions of Karl Barth:* The biblical texts are not mere documents for philological-historical research. They make possible an encounter with the "totally Other." In the human testimony of the Bible we are dealing with *God's* word, which the individual may recognize, realize, and confess. Man is therefore challenged to do more than engage in neutral observation and interpretation. He is called upon for penance, conversion, and *faith*, which always remains a risk. At stake here are man's salvation and perdition. And the task of the Church is uncompromisingly to bring this Word of God to society through the human words of her preaching. The Church's preaching, like church dogma, have to be wholly concentrated on *Jesus Christ*, in whom, for believers, God himself—and not just an exemplary "good person"—has spoken and acted. Jesus Christ is the decisive criterion for all discourse about God and man.

So far so good—more than good. Still the question must ultimately be posed to this theology as well: *How* are these broad theological intentions to be realized in a new age? Is Barth's *Church Dogmatics*, which as theology sought not to be revered but to be read and further developed, already the theology we need in the postmodern paradigm? It seems to me that a clear counterpoint has to be set forth here—and to do that we must return once more to the beginning of Barthian theology, to the early 1920s.

5. Karl Barth—Not the Perfector of the Postmodern Paradigm in Theology

In order to assemble the most essential ingredients for his lectures, the former pastor of Safenwil and now Professor of Reformed Theology at Göttingen (happily he had been made a Doctor of Theology, *honoris causa*, by the University of Münster) fell back on the legacy of the Reformation (Calvin and the Heidelberg Catechism). But that was not enough. Whether it was chance or fate, in 1924 after his first two years of teaching the newly minted professor stumbled upon a dusty, long out-of-print book that in any event became part of his destiny. It was *The Dogmatics of the Evangelical-Reformed Church* by Heinrich Heppe, from the year 1861; and it offered him the answers of *old reformed orthodoxy* on all dogmatic issues between heaven, earth, and hell. Thus there occurred in Barth's first lecture on dogmatic theology a *shift backwards* that was certainly not uncritical, but, with regard to the spectrum of dogmas often controverted in modern times, from the Trinity to the Virgin Birth to Christ's descent into hell and ascension into heaven, quite remarkable. Barth turned back not only to old Protestant orthodoxy, but also—where, in the final analysis, did this school draw its wisdom from?—to medieval scholasticism and the ancient writings of the Fathers of the Church. As for the other leaders of "dialectical theology," they were not unanimous in going along with Barth's shift. Rather they followed after, shaking their heads. The problem, of course, was not the falling back on patristic, medieval, and reformed tradition in itself, but the way Barth did this: by simply ignoring, often even defaming important findings of modern exegesis, history, and theology.

Naturally that did not mean that Barth became some sort of orthodox Calvinist or Lutheran sectarian, much less a medieval scholastic. His own theological approach and his specific theological epistemology were too original for that. After his *Outline of Dogmatics*, which he did not continue, he further radicalized that epistemology. The key work in this process was his book on Anselm of Canterbury, *Fides quaerens intellectum* (Munich, 1931). What does Anselm's *"credo ut intelligam"* (I believe that I may understand) mean for Barth? From the very beginning, he says, we must leap into the heart of the matter. We must not wish to understand first (the historical, philosophical, anthropological, and psychological presuppositions of belief) so as to believe later. Rather, it is just the other way around: first believe, in order to understand faith in the subsequent exploring of its "possibilities."

Faith is defined as the knowledge and affirmation of the word of Christ, which is, however—and here the problems start—very quickly identified with the Church's creed, with the confession of faith as it has evolved historically over a long period of time. This was now Barth's approach, based on Anselm: Presuming *that* it is true: God exists, is one essence in three persons, became man, is now reflected on only *insofar as* all that is true. Thus *Church Dogmatics* (with the stress on *Church*), which was published after the *Outline of Dogmatics,* now becomes the *Reflection on the Creed,* as *already recited* and *affirmed.* And so hardly anyone will be surprised to find a two-hundred-page treatment of the Trinity, elaborated not from the New Testament but from church teaching of the fourth century, in so early a text as the "Pro-legomena" (what has to be said, not "before," but "first of all") to the *Dogmatics.* If Barth does not quite ground this treatment in his ingeniously extended conceptual dialectic, at least he tries to make it comprehensible. Thus his fundamental thesis on revelation now has a thoroughly trinitarian ring to it: ("God's Word is God himself in his revelation. For God reveals himself as the Lord, and according to Scripture this implies for the concept of revelation that God himself is the revealer, the revelation, and the being-revealed in both indestructible unity and indestructible difference")—or, in biblical terms, Father, Son, and Spirit.[5]

This procedure can be clarified by a comparison: Barth's radicalized theology of the Word, which is completely self-centered, so to speak, bears structural resemblances—for all the obvious differences in substance—to Hegel's philosophy of Mind (Barth always had a "certain weakness" for Hegel). That philosophy likewise circulates within itself and, moving forward in a three-beat rhythm, presupposes the totality of truth, calls for a similar leap into the heart of the matter, and brings us face to face with a similar alternative.

— *Either, Hegel* would say, one rises above everything empirical and abstract to truly concrete speculative thinking, and then as one "thinks things over" the truth of Mind dawns on one of itself—*or* one does not rise to this speculative height, and then one is simply not a real philosopher.

— *Either, Barth* would say, one submits—untroubled by all the historical, philosophical, anthropological, and psychological difficulties—to God's Word, as it is attested in Scripture and proclaimed by the Church, and believes, then, at that point, as one "thinks things over" the truth of revelation will dawn on one of itself—*or* one just does not believe, and then one is simply not a real Christian.

And for the Christian—Barth says now in *Church Dogmatics,* in his sharpest, but *exclusive,* Christological focus—for the Christian Jesus Christ is the one incarnate Word of God, the *one,* the *only* light of life, alongside which there are and can be *no* other lights, no other words of God, no revelations.

6. Creation-Revelation: The Permanent Challenge of "Natural Theology"

Many theologians trained in Barth's work see no problems here. They are, after all, part of an in-group. For my part I cannot conceal the fact that I have, and from the beginning have had, difficulties with Barth's position from the standpoint of the great *Catholic tradition* (which on this point has also remained largely the same as the Reformation's). No, Barth's theology is too important; we cannot evade an objective confrontation with it. We cannot limit ourselves to a purely immanent paraphrase of Barth, however useful that might be in making Barth's theology come alive for the current generation of theologians (which is basically the purpose of a volume in the series *Objections*, entitled *Karl Barth: The Troublemaker?* [Munich, 1986], with contributions from Dieter Schellong, Friedrich-Wilhelm Marquardt, Michael Weinrich, and Peter Eicher). But we can never be content with a mere internal correction of a conventional picture of Barth, while otherwise largely agreeing with this theology. To my taste, these objections to Barth's theology should have a sharper edge to them.

Thus we have to ask

— If God's creation is no longer, as the young Barth argued in his early phase, merely a bomb crater made by God's grace, if God's creation can now be taken with complete seriousness in the later Barth and viewed even as God's good work, so that it will be possible to write four volumes of *Church Dogmatics* on the subject; if all that is so, then why shouldn't this have consequences for a true knowledge of God based on creation, a knowledge accessible in principle not only to Christians but to everyone?

— If God, *theologically-objectively* speaking, undoubtedly stands *at the beginning* of all things, why must it be *theologically-methodologically* forbidden to start off with the needs and problems of the modern person, so as to direct our questioning from there to God, where the ontological order and the epistemological order are not, after all, simply identical?

— If the *biblical message* is undoubtedly for Christians the *decisive criterion* of all discourse about God, why then should all discourse about God be dependent on the Bible?

And, finally, if the *negative statements* in the Bible about the error, darkness, lying, and sins of the non-Christian world are taken seriously as a challenge to conversion, then why should we conceal, repress, or obscure the fact that the God of the Bible—and the New Testament witnesses to this likewise—is the God of all men and women, and as such is near to all of them, so that non-Christians too (a point attested to as early as the Letter to the Romans, and emphatically confirmed by the Acts of the Apostles) can know the true God?

In response to such questions Karl Barth referred even back then to the third book—in preparation at the time—of his *Doctrine of Reconciliation, Jesus, the Light of the World.* And theologians have paid all too little attention to the fact that in this last, self-contained volume of *Church Dogmatics* (1959) the old Karl Barth—exactly forty years have passed since his *Epistle to the Romans* and exactly twenty-five years since the Synod of Barmen—does return to his harshly exclusive thesis: Jesus Christ "is the *one,* the *only* light of life." But then, having repeated it, he goes on—with many precautions and without making, like Augustine, public "retractions"—to concede that in the final analysis there are, in fact, *"other lights"* alongside the one light of Jesus Christ ("tail lights," as it were, of the one light), that there *are* "other true words" alongside the one Word.[6] Obviously a new evaluation of the knowledge of God from the world of creation and from "natural theology" is emerging in Barth's late theology, a new evaluation too of philosophy and human experience as a whole. Indeed we find, in an indirect, concealed fashion, a new evaluation of the world religions, which Barth had earlier lumped together—even the grace and faith religions of Indian Bhakti and Japanese Amida Buddhism (vol. I, bk. 2, 372–79)—and simply dismissed as forms of unbelief, or, worse yet, of idolatry and works righteousness.

All this means that in the end *Church Dogmatics*—which after the completion of the paradigm change from modernity to postmodernity reached back *behind* modernity (back past the modern critique to Protestant orthodoxy, scholasticism, and the Fathers of the Church) and had involuntarily led to a kind of neo-orthodoxy—in the end this so cogently constructed dogmatic world had been, at least in principle, exploded (though most of the Barthians had failed to notice this). What Dietrich Bonhoeffer had once criticized from his Nazi prison cell as "revelation positivism" had had the bottom knocked out of it.

This much should be clear from the foregoing: As early as the beginning of the 1920s, after fully revising the *Epistle to the Romans* and then once again in the beginning of the 1930s, after repudiating and later entirely re-editing the first volume of *Church Dogmatics*, Karl Barth had declared that he could and would say the same things he had before. But he could no longer say things the way he once had. I am convinced that if this Barth could once again go up on the barricades as a young man, he would say, just as he had back then, "What recourse did I have except to start all over again and once more say the same thing, but the same thing once more in a totally different way?"[7] And so perhaps he would do what Tillich in the last lecture before his death pointed to as a great desideratum: He would try to elaborate a *Christian theology in the context of the world's religions and regions.*

Toward the end of his life, stressing now the humanity of God rather than simply his divinity, Karl Barth had become reconciled with his old comrade-in-arms *Emil Brunner*. Barth had quite needlessly broken with Brunner, simply because the latter thought he had to speak of a "point of contact" in human beings for God's grace. ("No" was the title of Barth's piece written against Brunner in 1934.) The question one asks oneself here is certainly not an idle one: Mightn't this same Karl Barth perhaps have wound up also being reconciled with his great antagonist, Rudolf Bultmann? (Barth did make a programmatic effort to understand him, "Rudolf Bultmann: An Attempt at Understanding Him" (1953), but it proved a thorough failure.) Mightn't there have been a reconciliation, then, with the Bultmann who affirmed Barth's basic theological intentions (the divinity of God, God's Word, *kerygma*, and human faith), but was not prepared simply to abandon the key concerns of liberal theology, and for that reason absolutely insisted on the historico-critical method in exegesis and the necessity of demythologization and an interpretation of Scripture oriented to human understanding?

7. Criticism of "Theological Exegesis": The Permanent Challenge of Rudolf Bultmann

Nowadays there can be no question of deserting Barth for Bultmann. Replacing Barth with Bultmann is equally wide of the mark: Both great Protestant theologians must be taken, in their fashion, as seriously as possible; both have their strengths and their weaknesses. And Karl Barth had clearly seen *Bultmann's weakness* ever since the day back in Göttingen in 1925, when Bultmann had read to him from Martin Heidegger's Marburg lectures, which Bultmann had heard and taken down. Now, he thought, theology had to turn in an *existential direction* and strive for an understanding of the Gospel documented in the New Testament, just as it would try to understand any other great human achievement. Barth's criticism was not directed against the notion that Scripture had to be interpreted in terms of human existence; he did that too in his way. Rather the point was that Bultmann, fettered to the early Heidegger, had committed himself to an *existential reductionism:* He dimmed the brightness of the cosmos, nature, the environment, in favor of human existence. He reduced concrete world history to human historicity, and the authentic future to human futurity. He neglected concrete society and the political dimension in his theology of Being-in-the-world.

Conversely, Bultmann early on caught sight of and noted *Barth's weaknesses:* Barth liked to withdraw from hermeneutical discussions, so he could continue working "as thetically as possible." After his shift to Protestant orthodoxy and Anselm in 1930, Barth went so far as to cancel an already promised lecture to the "old Marburgers" on the burning problem of "natural theology." This greatly angered and annoyed his friend Bultmann. And thus Barth aborted the long-planned discussion of their differences, which had by that time increased. Barth was forever more emphatically maintaining that he could do "theological exegesis," without actually denying the historico-critical variety, but also without really paying any heed to it. Barth also largely ignored the critical history of dogma in favor of the principle of tradition that de facto bound the Christian for all time to the Hellenistic conceptualization of the relationship between Father, Son, and Spirit—although, when he wanted to be, he was capable of making conceptual corrections in classical Trinitarian doctrine (e.g., substituting "mode of being" for "person"). Finally, contrary to his intentions, in his *Church Dogmatics* Barth had enlisted the aid of church tradition to carry out a *restorational restructuring* of *premodern* dogmatics that over broad stretches was lacking in exegetical support. This sort of approach to dogma, with its ties to a "bygone world picture" and its want of relevance to contemporary experience, could hardly succeed in "making the Christian message so comprehensible to people today that they become aware of the fact that *'tua res agitur'* (this concerns *you!*)."[8]

As a matter of fact, in the face of the challenge of modern exegesis and the history of dogma, Karl Barth (like the Swiss army in the Second World War) had withdrawn into the Alpine citadel of the sixteenth and seventeenth (or the fourth and fifth) centuries. In this defensive strategy he was prepared, for the sake of God's freedom and independence from all human experience, to surrender the most fruitful parts of the country. And what would happen today? I believe that if Barth, by some miracle made young again, wished to complete in postmodern style the theology to which he gave a postmodern inauguration, then Karl Barth would not be Karl Barth if he did not begin again from the beginning and, starting out from the recovered center, he did not try to advance in an altogether new way, with better strategic-hermeneutic cover.

In other words—and to drop all the military metaphors: He would once again "begin all over" in a far more radical manner and "say the same thing altogether differently." He would take as his point of departure the historico-critically established biblical data— not only on Purgatory, Marian and papal dogmas, for which he sharply criticized the Catholics, but also on original sin, hell and the devil, even on Christology and the Trinity. In other words, he would try to work out a *historico-critically responsible dogmatics based on a historico-critically validated exegesis.* That task would allow him to translate the original Christian message (in keeping with Bultmann's demands, but without Bultmann's existentialist narrowness) into the newly dawned future, so that it once again might be understood as God's liberating word. He would speak of God in relation to human beings, of an "theanthropology" even, which the old Barth had in view, though in his youth he had denounced anthropology as the secret of modern theology blabbed by Feuerbach. It seems to me of the greatest importance and urgency that in this process the "historical Jesus" (without whom, as Ernst Käsemann says, the "Christ of dogma" turns into a myth that can be manipulated any way one wants) should be allowed to come into play, once again in a way totally different from that of Barth *and* Bultmann: for example, with regard to the true liberation of humanity in individual life, in society, and in the Church. No, there is no going back: neither to Schleiermacher nor to Luther, neither to Thomas Aquinas nor to Athanasius. Rather, together with Athanasius and Aquinas, Luther and Schleiermacher—with Barthian intrepidity and decisiveness, concentration and consistency—forward!

8. A Critical-sympathetic Rereading of Barth Against the Background of Postmodernity

"We lack," Barth once critically observed, "the consciousness of our own relativity."[9] And with reference to his own work he could say, "I understand . . . *Church Dogmatics* not as the conclusion but as the opening of a new common discussion."[10] This new common discussion would have to take place nowadays under changed theological and social conditions in a *critical-sympathetic rereading* of *Church Dogmatics.* Such a rereading against the background of postmodernity, for all the criticism it voiced, would have to take a constructive approach in bringing the grand themes and enormous richness of this theology into the contemporary scene, and in dealing freshly with them in the context of the world's religions and regions. Indeed, what an overflowing wealth this theology has in its teaching on God, creation, and reconciliation, which as time went on would work increasingly at being not Reformed or Lutheran but ecumenical theology. What systematic power and profundity in the altogether autonomous and original penetration of central theological *topoi* such as the dialectic of God's qualities, the connection between creation and covenant, time and eternity, Israel and the Church, Christology and anthropology, concretely extended all the way into an ethics of freedom before God, in community, for life, in limitation. . . . This was radical liberation theology before all the theologies of liberation.

And, at the same time, with all its superabundant complexity, with all its uncontrollable profusion of material (9,185 pages in

Church Dogmatics alone), this theology never lost its center. What Karl Barth said about the "great free objectivity" of Wolfgang Amadeus Mozart, the musician he loved the most, he could say about himself. His portraits of Mozart, both in *Church Dogmatics* (vol. III, bk. 3, pp. 337–8) and in his short piece on Mozart from 1956, are something like thumbnail sketches of his own theology. What he heard in this music was the chord he wished to evoke in his theology. Mozart's music, he said was, "in a quite unusual sense free from all exaggerations, from all logical breaks and oppositions. The sun shines, but it does not blind, consume, or burn. Heaven arches over the earth, but it does not weigh down upon it, it does not crush or swallow it up. And so the earth is and remains the earth, but without having to assert itself in a titanic revolt against heaven. Thus darkness, chaos, death, and hell show themselves, but not for a moment are they allowed to prevail. Mozart plays his music, aware of everything, from within a mysterious center; and so he knows and defends the boundaries right and left, up and down. He maintains proportions. . . . There is no light here that does not also know the darkness, no joy that does not also contain suffering, but conversely too, no terror, no rage, no lament that does not have peace standing by, whether close up or far off. Thus there is no laughter without tears, but also no tears without laughter."[11]

Barth's theology too emerges from this mysterious center, which was for him God himself, who in Jesus Christ has graciously turned toward the human race. And because this God who became visible in the crucified and risen Jesus was the center, this theology too can defend the boundaries, can let God be God and man be man. This theology also knows about the dark, the evil, the negative, the futile things of this world, and yet at the same time it is written out of a grand trust that the good and compassionate God will himself have the last word. In fact the demonic and tragic features of the world do not break through in Karl Barth's theology either, which like the music of Mozart stops short of the extreme limit. It is familiar with the "wise confrontation and mixture of the elements," which assures that every No continues to be borne by a great Yes. Anyone who hears this music, anyone who listens to this theology, "may feel himself to be the prisoner of death and the tremendously alive person that all of us are, understood and even called to freedom."

Notes

DIRECTION: ON THE WAY TO "POSTMODERNITY"

1. Cf. Franz Schulze, *Mies van der Rohe: A Critical Biography* (Chicago-London, 1985), p. 299.

2. Cf. H. U. Gumbrecht, Article on "Modern," in *Geschichtliche Grundbegriffe. Historisches Lexikon zur politisch-sozialen Sprache in Deutschland*, vol. IV (Stuttgart, 1978), pp. 93–131.

3. Cf. R. Koselleck, article on "Progress" in, *Geschichtliche Grundbegriffe*, vol. II (Stuttgart, 1975), pp. 351–423.

4. A. Huyssen, K. R. Scherpe, eds., *Postmoderne. Zeichen eines kulturellen Wandels* (Hamburg, 1986).

5. J.-F. Lyotard, *La condition postmoderne* (Paris, 1979); German translation, *Das postmoderne Wissen. Ein Bericht* (Graz-Vienna, 1986), p. 13.

6. J. Habermas, *Die neue Unübersichtlichkeit* (Frankfurt, 1985).

7. J. Ratzinger, V. Messori, *Rapporto sulla Fede* (Milan, 1985); German translation, *Zur Lage des Glaubens* (Munich, 1985).

8. Cf. H. Küng, *Freud und die Zukunft der Religion.* Piper Series, vol. 709 (Munich, 1987).

9. Cf. Albrecht Wellmer, *Zur Dialektik von Moderne und Postmoderne* (Frankfurt, 1985).

10. Cf. Hans Küng, *Existiert Gott? Antwort auf die Gottesfrage der Neuzeit* (Munich, 1978), chapter C.

11. N. Luhmann, "Society, Meaning, Religion—Based on Self-Reference," in *Sociological Analysis*, vol. 46 (1985), pp. 5–20. All of the first issue of *Sociological Analysis* is devoted to the subject of "Religion and Ultimate Paradox: A Symposium on Aspects of the Sociology of Niklas Luhmann."

12. D. Bell, *The Cultural Contradictions of Capitalism* (New York, 1976).

13. M. Horkheimer, *Die Sehnsucht nach dem ganz Anderen. Ein Interview mit Kommentar von H. Gumnior* (Hamburg, 1970).

14. E. Lévinas, *De Dieu qui vient à l'idée* (Paris, 1982); German translation, *Wenn Gott ins Denken einfällt. Diskurse über die Betroffenheit von Transzendenz* (Freiburg/Munich, 1985), p. 107.

15. Cf. W. Oelmüller, ed., *Wiederkehr von Religion? Perspektiven, Argumente, Fragen* (Paderborn, 1984); P. Koslowski, ed., *Die religiöse Dimension der Gesellschaft. Religionen und ihre Theorien* (Tübingen, 1985).

16. Cf. K. Gabriel, "Zur Sozialreform des neuzeitlichen Katholizismus," in *Orientierung* 15, 31 July 1986. On this subject see K. Gabriel, F. X. Kauffmann, eds., *Zur Soziologie des Katholizismus* (Mainz, 1980).

17. Cf. N. Greinacher, H. Küng, eds., *Katholische Kirche—wohin?* (Munich, 1986).

A. I. ECUMENICAL THEOLOGY CAUGHT
   IN THE CROSS FIRE

1. On Carafa and Pole cf. (no reference made to Erasmus, however) J. Fischer, *Die Reformideen der Kardinäle Gian Pietro Carafa (1476–1559) and Reginald Pole (1500–1558)* (Dissertation, Paris, 1957).

2. F. H. Reusch, *Der Index der verbotenen Bücher,* vol. 1 (Bonn, 1883), p. 347.

3. A. Flitner, *Erasmus im Urteil seiner Nachwelt* (Tübingen, 1952).

4. H. A. Obermann, "Luthers Reformatorische Ontdekkingen," in *Martin Luther. Feestelijke Herdenking van zijn Vijhonderste Geboortedag* (Amsterdam, 1983), pp. 11–34; quotation from p. 31.

5. E. Iserloh, article on Erasmus in *Lexikon für Theologie und Kirche,* vol. 3 (Freiburg, 1959), pp. 955–57.

6. E. Iserloh, ed., *Katholische Theologen der Reformationszeit,* vols. 1 and 2 (Münster/Vienna, 1984–85).

7. S. Zweig, *Triumph und Tragik des Erasmus von Rotterdam* (Vienna, 1938).

8. C. Augustijn, *Erasmus von Rotterdam. Leben-Werk-Wirkung* (Munich, 1986).

9. Ibid., p. 27.

10. R. H. Bainton, *Erasmus of Christendom* (New York, 1969).

11. Augustijn, loc. cit., pp. 44–45.

12. Ibid., p. 46.

13. J. Lindeboom, *Erasmus* (Wiesbaden, 1956).

14. Erasmus, *Opera omnia,* Leiden edition, vol. V, 140c.

15. Erasmus, *Opera omnia,* Amsterdam edition, vol. IV–3, pp. 753–56, 768–71.

16. A. Renaudet, *Études Erasmiennes (1521–1529)* (Paris, 1939); L. Bouyer, *Autour d'Érasme. Études sur le christianisme des humanistes catholiques* (Paris, 1955).

17. Erasmus, *Opus epistolarum,* Allen edition, vol. III, pp. 785, 786.

18. Ibid., p. 518.

19. Various traditions; cited in Flitner, loc. cit., p. 50.

20. Erasmus, *Opera omnia,* Leiden edition, vol. X, p. 1258A; Welzig-Lesowsky edition, vol. IV, p. 248.

21. Erasmus, *Opera omnia,* Amsterdam edition, vol. IX–1, p. 210.

22. F. Nietzsche, *Werke,* vol. 1, ed. Karl Schlechta (Munich, 1954), p. 467.

23. F. Heer, *Die Dritte Kraft. Der europäische Humanismus zwischen den Fronten* (Frankfurt, 1959), p. 7.

24. Augustijn, loc. cit., p. 175.

25. Erasmus, Letter to Johannes Lang of 17 October 1518, *Opus epistolarum,* Allen edition, vol. III, p. 872.

26. W. Kaegi, "Die Heimat des Erasmus," in *Neue Zürcher Zeitung* of 26 October 1969.
27. Erasmus, *Opus epistolarum*, Allen edition, vol. V, p. 1, note 9.
28. Cf. E. Ringel, A. Kirchmayr, *Religionsverlust durch religiöse Erziehung* (Vienna, 1985).
29. Erasmus, *Opera omnia*, Leiden edition, vol. X, p. 1258A; Welzig-Lesowsky edition, vol IV, p. 248.

A. II. THE BIBLE AND CHURCH TRADITION

1. H. Denziger, *Enchiridion symbolorum, definitionum et declarationum de rebus fidei et morum* (Barcelona-Freiburg-Rome, 1960), p. 1501.
2. Denziger, loc. cit., p. 1501.
3. Ibid., p. 3006.
4. The remarks newly conceived here had already been given a foundation in the following publications of mine: *Justification. Die Lehre Karl Barths und eine katholische Besinnung* (Einsiedeln, 1975, 4th ed., 1964), chapter 20; new edition, Munich, 1986; *Unfehlbar? Eine Anfrage* (Zurich-Einsiedeln-Cologne, 1970), chapters IV, IX, and X; *Fehlbar? Eine Bilanz* (Zurich-Einsiedeln-Cologne, 1973), part e, VI. All documentation is in these books.

A. III. SCHISM BECAUSE OF THE BIBLE?

1. Cf. H. Küng, "Der Frühkatholizismus im Neuen Testament als kontroverse-theologisches Problem," in *Theologische Quartalschrift* 142 (1962), pp. 385–424.
2. E. Käsemann, *Begründet der neutestamentliche Kanon die Einheit der Kirche? Exegetische Versuche und Besinnungen* I (1960), pp. 214–23.
3. Ibid., p. 214; p. 216.
4. Ibid., p. 215: "Putting it schematically, Mark shows with his many miracle stories the secret epiphany of the one who receives his full glory at Easter, Matthew shows us the bringer of the Messianic Torah, John shows the *'Christus praesens,'* while Luke historicizes and describes salvation history as an evolutionary process, and so writes for the first time a so-called life of Jesus."
5. Ibid.
6. Ibid., pp. 215–16: "Matthew, for example, takes offence at the drastic way with which Mk 5:27 ff. told the healing of the woman with the hemorrhage. The idea that the garments of the miracle worker communicate divine power, which leaps forth and is capable of healing, is a vulgar Hellenistic notion that appears in exactly this way in the account of Peter's healing shadow and Paul's miraculous handkerchief (Acts 5:15; 19:12) and later shapes the cult of relics. Matthew corrects this crudely magical view by making the cure take place no longer through the touching of the garment as such, but through Jesus' word of power. He reduces in general the broad depiction of the miracle stories in Mark, which reveal a novelistic joy in narrative, and where even motifs of profane narrative technique are sounded, in the strongest way, in order to place a stronger emphasis on the mysterious grandeur of Jesus."
7. Ibid., p. 218.

Notes

8. Ibid., p. 216.

9. Ibid.: "As surely as we may say that the great mass of this tradition does not yield the historical Jesus to us, so all the most perfected methods of historical science allow us at this point only a more or less correct probable judgment, as can be recognized from the many extremely disparate presentations of the life and message of Jesus and from the splendid history by Albert Schweitzer of the research on the life of Jesus."

10. Ibid., p. 217.

11. Ibid., p. 218.

12. Ibid.

13. Ibid.

14. Ibid., pp. 219–21: For example, in non-Gospel writings, the opposition between Paul's and James's teaching on justification, the judgment on the Pauline apostolate in Acts and in Galatians, the eschatology of John and Revelation, etc.

15. Ibid. As an example Käsemann cites, among others, the fact that "the word of Jesus in Mk 2:27 about the Sabbath's being made for man is limited by the addition in verse 28 that the Son of Man is Lord of the Sabbath. The community could approve something in its Master that it dared not claim for itself. Its limiting addendum shows that it was frightened by the freedom it had been given, and took refuge back in a Christianized Judaism. Conversely, with its polemic against Pharisaism as hypocrisy—think only of Mt 23—it flattened out Jesus' attack on Pharisaism, which in truth is aimed at the striving for self-righteousness and thus pointed at every kind of performance-piety and, in fact, every individual. Whenever the Pharisees are made out to be hypocrites through and through, Jesus' criticism still applies to immorality, but the way is opened wide to Christian performance-piety, which had barred Jesus' attack on real Pharisaism."

16. Ibid., p. 221.

17. Ibid.

18. Ibid., p. 223.

19. Cf. E. Käsemann, "Zum Thema der Nichtobjektivierbarkeit," in *Exegetische Versuche und Besinnungen* I (Göttingen, 1960), pp. 223–36, especially 229–32.

20. Cf. also W. G. Kümmel, "Notwendigkeit und Grenze des neutestamentalichen Kanons," *Zeitschrift für Theologie und Kirche* 47 (1950), pp. 311–12: "The actual limit of the canon thus runs right through the canon, and only where this state of affairs is really known and acknowledged can the appeal by Catholic or sectarian doctrines to specific *individual passages* be countered with really valid arguments."; H. Braun, "Hebt die heutige neutestamentlich-exegetische Forschung den Kanon auf?" *Fuldaer Hefte* 12 (1960), p. 23: "Exegesis that pays attention to the message paralyzes the dross and makes restriction of the canon dubious, as far as individual passages go. Thus it does not say Yes to the canon as a whole, not Yes because it is the canon. It takes the canon critically, but while applying the core criterion that derives from the New Testament itself. And therefore it clings to the canon, as far as its center, the basic phenomenon of the New Testament, is concerned. It has this, of course, only *in*

the canon, later not at all, and even in the canon not in any pure or unalloyed fashion."

21. Käsemann, "Zum Thema der Nichtobjectivierbarkeit," loc. cit., p. 232. Cf. both the essays by E. Käsemann, "Zum Verständnis von Römer 3:24–26," ibid., I, 96–100; and "Gottes Gerechtigkeit bei Paulus," in *Zeitschrift für Theologie und Kirche* 58 (1961), pp. 367–78. This latter essay, a brief lecture at the Oxford Congress on "The New Testament Today," delivered on 14 September 1961, comes extraordinarily close to a deepened Catholic understanding of the justification of the sinner.

22. Let me just note in passing that Käsemann has taken cognizance of the more recent Catholic exegesis. Cf. E. Käsemann, "Neutestamentliche Fragen von heute," in *Zeitschrift für Theologie und Kirche* 54 (1957) 2: "Justice obliges us to admit that modern Catholic exegesis, at least in Germany and its near environs, has likewise reached a level that in general no longer lags behind Protestant work, and not seldom even surpasses it in carefulness. This fact shows that the historico-critical method has basically become common knowledge. It no longer characterizes a theological camp of exegesis, but serves as the de facto divider between scholarship and speculation or primitiveness. The converging of the different fronts is perhaps the characteristic feature of our epoch."

23. E. Käsemann, *Begründet der neutestamentliche Kanon die Einheit der Kirche?* loc. cit., p. 223.

24. H. Diem, *Theologie als kirchliche Wissenschaft,* vol. II: *Dogmatik. Ihr Weg zwischen Historismus und Existentialismus* (Munich, 1955, 2nd ed. 1957), pp. 196–208.

25. Ibid., pp. 197–98.

26. Ibid., pp. 198–99: "With this doctrine of Scripture, however, the Protestant Church has above all *undermined* its actual foundation, namely *preaching:* The proclamation of Scripture as a witnessing and passing on of testimony in the concrete act of preaching turned into an academic explication and demonstration of the Bible's statements as truths and facts. Beyond that *faith* too had to change in its relationship to Scripture: One no longer believed *on the basis of the Scripture that was preached,* in the salvific significance of the event attested to, but one had to believe primarily in an act of faith, as *fides quae creditur, in the divinity of Scripture* and all the predicates of Scripture that resulted from that or were thought to be necessary for it."

27. Ibid., p. 199.

28. Ibid., p. 202.

29. Ibid., pp. 203–4; on Diem's concept of "kerygmatic history," according to which in the community's preaching the history of *Jesus Christ proclaiming himself as a history that has happened and is continually happening afresh* is proclaimed, and precisely in this way the proclaimed *justificatio impii per fidem sola* takes place, cf. especially ibid., pp. 102–31.

30. Ibid., p. 204.

31. Ibid., pp. 204–5.

32. Cf. ibid., pp. 128–29.

33. Ibid., p. 205.

34. Ibid., p. 206.

35. Cf. H. Schlier, article on *hairesis* in the *Theologisches Wörterbuch Zum Neuen Testament* (Stuttgart, 1933, 2nd ed., 1957) I, p. 182: This term, which is a priori suspect in Christianity "owes its existence, therefore, not first of all to the development of an orthodox creed, but the basis for the formation of the Christian concept of *hairesis* lies in the *new situation that was created through the appearance of the Christian ekklesia*. *Ekklesia* and *hairesis* are essential opposites. The former will not bear the latter, and the latter excludes the former. This can be read as early as Gal 5:20, where *hairesis* is reckoned among the *erga tes sarkos* along with *eris, echthrai, zelos, thumoi, eritheiai, and dichostasiai*. *Hairesis* in this context does not yet have a technical sense, no more than it does anywhere else, on the whole, in the New Testament. In 1 Cor 11:18–19 the impossibility of *hairesis* within Christianity appears still more often. In mentioning the cultic gathering in which the community comes together as *ekklesia*, Paul refers back to the *skhismata* of 1 Cor 1:10–11. *Skhismata* are the splits in the community caused by personally motivated disputes. Paul believes some of the reports that he has learned about divisions in the community. He believes them because even *(kai) hairseis en humin* have to be, so that those who tested and approved (can) be made apparent. Regardless of whether Paul is using an apocryphal saying of Jesus (cf. Jus Dial 35, 3; Didask 1118, 35) or not, it is for him an eschatological-dogmatic maxim (cf. Mk 13:5–6 par; Acts 20:29–30; 2 Pet 2:1; 1 Jn 2:19), and *hairesis* is understood as an eschatological quantity. *Hairesis* here is clearly set off against *skhismata* and constitutes a heightening of it. But the heightening consists in the fact that the *haireseis* affect the foundation of the Church, its teaching (2 Pet 2:1) and indeed in such a basic way that a newly formed community comes into existence alongside the *ekklesia*."

36. Diem, loc. cit., pp. 203–4.

37. Ibid., p. 204.

38. Diem explains this in connection with G. Eichholz by the example of Paul's doctrine of justification and James's: ibid., pp. 206–8.

39. Ibid., p. 205.

40. Ibid., p. 206.

41. K. H. Schelkle, *Die Petrusbriefe (Herders Theologischer Kommentar zum Neuen Testament* XIII, 2 (Freiburg-Basel-Vienna, 1961), p. 245.

42. The Tübingen Old Testament scholar H. Haag says out loud what many people whisper: "With the greatest alarm groups of *exegetes* notice that the freedom granted to Catholic biblical scholarship by the encyclical *Divino afflante spiritu* seems to be in danger again. Again it happens, as it did only too often in the past fifty years, that on account of a statement or an idea that is looked on in Rome as erroneous or quite often only as inopportune, an exegete is removed from office or prohibited from writing or speaking about his subject. And this without his having gotten a hearing on the matter or his being informed where he has erred." ("Was erwarted Sie vom Konzil?" in *Wort und Wahrheit* 10 [1961], p. 600.)

43. Cf. the discussion of the problems in H. Küng, *Strukuren der Kirche* (Freiburg-Basel-Vienna, 1962), pp. 161–95.

44. K. H. Schelkle, loc. cit., p. 245.

45. E. Käsemann, ed., *Das Neue Testament als Kanon* (Göttingen, 1970).

46. Ibid., general discussion on pp. 371–78; quotation on p. 374.
47. Ibid., p. 374.
48. Ibid.

A. IV. DOGMA VERSUS THE BIBLE?

1. J. Blank, "Exegesis als theologische Basiswissenschaft," in *Theologische Quartalschrift* 159 (1979), pp. 2–23.
2. Denziger, loc. cit., 1601.
3. J. Auer, *Kleine Katholische Dogmatik*, vol. VI (Regensburg, 1971), pp. 84–85.
4. O. Semmelroth, *Die Kirche als Ursakrament* (Frankfurt am Main, 1953, 2nd ed. 1955), p. 40.
5. K. Rahner, *Kirche und Sakramente* (Freiburg im Breisgau, 1960), p. 38.
6. Presented in detail in H. Küng, *Die Kirche* (Freiburg im Breisgau, 1967), chapter E II.
7. A. Grillmeier and H. Bacht, eds., *Das Konzil von Chalcedon. Geschichte und Gegenwart*, vol. I–III (Würzburg, 1951–54), vol. III, pp. 3–49 (K. Rahner).
8. Ibid., vol. I, pp. 5–202 (Grillmeier).

B. I. HOW DOES ONE DO CHRISTIAN THEOLOGY?

1. Cf. E. Schillebeeckx, *Jesus, het verhaal van een levende* (Bloemendaal, 1975), German translation, *Jesus. Die Geschichte von einem Lebendem* (Freiburg im Breisgau, 1975); *Gerechtigheid en liefde. Genade en bevrijding* (Bloemendaal, 1977), German translation, *Christus und die Christen. Die Geschichte einer neuen Lebenspraxis* (Freiburg im Breisgau, 1977).
2. H. Küng, "Auf dem Weg zu einem neuen Grundkonsens in der katholischen Theologie?" in *Theologische Quartalschrift* 159 (1979), pp. 272–85.

B. II. PARADIGM CHANGE IN THEOLOGY AND SCIENCE

1. Thomas S. Kuhn, *The Structure of Scientific Revolutions* (Chicago, 1962).
2. Cf. H. Küng, D. Tracy, *Theologie—wohin? Auf einem Weg zu einem neuen Paradigma* (Zurich, Gütersloh, 1984), pp. 37–75.
3. Cf. Thomas S. Kuhn, "Die Entstehung des Neuen," in L. Krüger, ed., *Studien zur Struktur der Wissenschaftsgeschichte* (Frankfurt, 1978), pp. 392–93.
4. I. Lakatos, A. Musgrave, *Criticism and the Growth of Knowledge* (London, 1970).
5. G. Cutting, *Paradigms and Revolutions: Appraisals and Applications of Thomas Kuhn's Philosophy of Science* (Notre Dame–London, 1980); for our problem of the applicability of Kuhn's analysis to historiography and theology the articles by D. Hollinger and I. Barbour are especially important.
6. Stephen Toulmin, *Human Understanding: The Collective Use and Evaluation of Concepts* (Princeton, 1972).

7. Cf. the volume mentioned in note 2, H. Küng, D. Tracy, *Theologie—wohin?* (Zurich-Gütersloh, 1984).

8. M. Planck, *Wissenschaftliche Selbstbiographie* (Leipzig, 1948), p. 42.

9. C. G. Jung, *Psychology and Religion* (Studienausgabe Olten, 1971), p. 143.

B. III. A NEW BASIC MODEL OF THEOLOGY?

1. Draft papers for the symposium are published in H. Küng, D. Tracy, *Theologie—wohin?* (Zurich-Gütersloh, 1984); papers presented at the symposium itself are found in H. Küng, D. Tracy, eds., *Das neue Paradigma von Theologie. Strukturen und Dimensionen* (Zurich-Gütersloh, 1986), see especially pp. 205–16.

B. IV. THEOLOGY ON THE WAY TO A NEW PARADIGM

1. Cf. J. B. Bauer, ed., *Entwürfe der Theologie* (Graz, 1985), pp. 181–207.

C. I. ON PARADIGM CHANGE IN THE WORLD RELIGIONS

1. Rome has taken a stand against modernity with all the available means of ideology, politics, and the Inquisition—ultimately without success. On the Index of Forbidden (to Catholics) Books stood a large percentage of the representative minds of European modernity: alongside countless theologians and critics of the Church there were the founders of modern science, Copernicus and Galileo, and the fathers of modern philosophy: Descartes and Pascal, Bayle, Malebranche and Spinoza, as well as the British empiricists Hobbes, Locke, and Hume—but Kant too, and naturally Rousseau and Voltaire, later Cousin, John Stuart Mill, Comte, together with the great historians Gibbon, Condorcet, Ranke, Taine, and Gregorovius. They were joined by Diderot and D'Alembert with their *Encyclopédie* and the *Larousse Dictionary,* by the expert on national and international law, Hugo Grotius, by Pufendorf and Montesquieu, finally by an elite group of modern literary figures: Heine and Lenau, Hugo, Lamartine, Dumas *père et fils,* Balzac, Flaubert, Zola, d'Annunzio, and Leopardi, and in our century the philosophers Bergson, Croce, Gentile, Unamuno, Sartre, and Simone de Beauvoir, plus Malaparte, Gide, and Kazantzakis.

Needless to say, the authorities of the Roman Inquisition had long since failed to keep up with it all. Cardinal Merry del Val, a Grand Inquisitor and gray eminence of the antimodernist campaign under Pius X, complains in a circular letter, which was reprinted in the official 1948 edition of the Index, "Even though the Apostolic See applies every effort to do away with writings, their number has still grown so great that it is impossible to list them all," in *Index Romanus. Verzeichnis sämtlicher auf dem römischen Index stehenden deutschsprachigen Bücher, desgleichen alle wichtige fremdsprachigen Bücher seit dem Jahre 1750. Zusammengestellt auf Grund der neuesten vatikanischen Ausgabe sowie mit ausführlicher Einleitung versehen von Professor Dr. Albert Sleumer.* 11th enlarged edition (Osnabrück, 1956), quotation from p. 135. One is surprised only how this same Roman Inquisition—now under cardinal Joseph Ratzinger—after such a *"chronique scandaleuse,"* still thinks it can impose its medieval paradigm, in the face of all the findings and results from the Reformation and the modern period, in the midst of the transition to postmodernity, with the old methods.

C. II. IS THERE ONE TRUE RELIGION?

1. For a full treatment of the issues here the reader is referred to H. Küng, J. van Ess, H. Bechert, *Christianity and the World Religions: Paths to Dialogue with Islam, Hinduism, and Buddhism* (New York, 1986).
2. Cf. H. Küng, "Was ist die wahre Religion? Versuch einer ökumenischen Kriteriologie," in *Gottes Zukunft—Zukunft der Welt. Festschrift für Jürgen Moltmann zum 60. Geburtstag* (Munich, 1986), pp. 536–58.
3. Denziger, loc. cit., p. 1351.
4. Ibid., pp. 1295 and 1379.

D. KARL BARTH AND THE POSTMODERN PARADIGM

1. Karl Barth, *Evangelische Theologie* 8 (1948/49), "Die Unordnung der Welt und Gottes Heilsplan," pp. 181–88; quotation from p. 185.
2. ———, *Kirchliche Dogmatik*, vol. I, bk. 2 (Basel, 1932–59), p. 157; pp. 606–52.
3. *Herder-Korrespondenz* 25, 1971, p. 539.
4. Barth, loc. cit., vol. I, bk. 1, Foreword.
5. Barth, *Letters, 1961–68*, p. 357.
6. Barth, loc. cit., vol. I, bk. 1, p. 311.
7. Ibid., vol. IV, bk. 3, pp. 40–188.
8. Cf. R. Bultmann to Barth, 11–15 November 1952, in *Correspondence 1922–1966*, ed. B. Jaspert (Zurich, 1971), p. 170.
9. *Die Woche*, 1963, no. 4.
10. *The Christian Century*, 1963, no. 1, p. 7ff.
11. *Mozart*, p. 38; pp. 43–45.

Dates and Places
of Original Publication

"Direction": Unpublished.

A.I: Unpublished.

A.II: Unpublished.

A.III: First published in *Theologische Quartalschrift* 142 (1962), pp. 385–424.

A.IV: First published in *Theologische Quartalschrift* 159 (1979), pp. 24–36.

B.I: First published in *Theologische Quartalschrift* 159 (1979), pp. 272–85.

B.II: First published in H. Küng, D. Tracy, *Theologie—Wohin? Auf dem Weg zu einem neuen Paradigma* (Zurich: Benziger Verlag; Gütersloh: Gütersloher Verlagshaus Gerd Mohn, 1984), pp. 37–75.

B.III: First published in H. Küng, D. Tracy, *Das neue Paradigma von Theologie. Strukturen und Dimensionen* (Zurich: Benziger Verlag; Gütersloh: Gütersloher Verlagshaus Gerd Mond, 1986), pp. 205–16.

B.IV: First published in J. B. Bauer, ed., *Entwürfe der Theologie* (Graz: Styria Verlag, 1985), pp. 181–207.

C.I: Unpublished.

C.II: First published in *Gottes Zukunft—Zukunft der Welt. Festschrift für Jürgen Moltmann zum 60. Geburtstag* (Munich: Chr. Kaiser Verlag, 1986), pp. 536–58.

Index of Names

Abelard, Peter, 124
Abraham, 250, 251
Adam, Karl, 263, 265
Adenauer, Konrad, 260
Adorno, Theodor, 9
Aleander, Hieronymus, 38
Alexander VI, 16
Anastasius (pope), 160
Anselm of Canterbury, 124, 276, 281
Apel, Karl Otto, 133
Aquinas, Thomas. *See* Thomas Aquinas
Aristotle, 135, 142
Athanasius, 58, 98, 124, 140
Auer, Alfons, 19
Auer, J., 88
Augustijn, Cornelis, 20, 36, 39
Augustine, 52, 98, 124, 133, 136, 140–41, 145, 147, 150, 151, 155, 157, 158, 160, 213, 231
    Christian paradigm built by, 183
    macromodel of, 146

Bainton, Roland H., 20
Balthasar, Hans Urs von, 105, 264, 266
Barth, Karl, xv, 48, 64, 126, 157, 162, 198, 251, 252, 257–84
    author's attitude to theology of, 188–91
    author's relationship with, 259, 266
    death of, 270
    faith and reason in theology of, 202–3, 276–77
    later backward movement by, 275–76
    postmodern paradigm and, 271–77
Basil, 140
Baudelaire, Charles, 3
Baum, Gregory, 170, 174–76
Baur, Ferdinand, 124
Bayle, Pierre, 163
Bell, Daniel, 8
Bellarmine, Robert, 48, 232
Bernstein, Richard, 133
Berquin (translator of Erasmus), 32
Bérulle, Pierre de, 157
Blank, Josef, 85, 96, 170, 177, 193
Bloch, Ernst, 8, 127
Boff, Leonardo, 170, 173, 174, 176
Bonaventure, 124
Bonhoeffer, Dietrich, 162, 191, 280
Born, Max, 148

Index of Subjects

ABOUT THE AUTHOR

Hans Küng is one of the world's most respected and controversial theologians and philosophers. Currently, he is a professor of Dogmatic and Ecumenical Theology and director of the Institute for Ecumenical Research at the University of Tubingen, West Germany. The author of *Christianity and the World Religions, Does God Exist?, On Being a Christian,* and others, Küng is also the co-editor of various periodicals and a recipient of several honorary doctorates.

Printed in the United States
by Baker & Taylor Publisher Services